Equity
ALTERNATIVES

Restricted Stock, Performance Awards,
Phantom Stock, SARs, and More

16th Edition

Equity

ALTERNATIVES

Restricted Stock, Performance Awards,
Phantom Stock, SARs, and More

16th Edition

Joseph S. Adams
Barbara Baksa
Daniel D. Coleman
Daniel Janich
Blair Jones
Scott Rodrick
Corey Rosen
Martin Staubus
Robin Struve
Dan Walter

The National Center for Employee Ownership
Oakland, California

This publication is designed to provide accurate and authoritative information regarding the subject matter covered. It is sold with the understanding that the publisher is not engaged in rendering legal, accounting, or other professional services. If legal advice or other expert assistance is required, the services of a competent professional should be sought.

Legal, accounting, and other rules affecting business often change. Before making decisions based on the information you find here or in any publication from any publisher, you should ascertain what changes might have occurred and what changes might be forthcoming. The NCEO's website (including the members-only area) and newsletter for members provide regular updates on these changes. If you have any questions or concerns about a particular issue, check with your professional advisor or, if you are an NCEO member, call or email us.

Equity Alternatives: Restricted Stock, Performance Awards, Phantom Stock, SARs, and More, 16th Edition
Edited by Scott Rodrick. Indexed by Achaessa James.
Book design by Scott Rodrick.

ISBN: 978-1-938220-67-8

Originally published as *Beyond Stock Options* in July 2003. Second edition January 2004. Third edition February 2005. Fourth edition January 2006. Fifth edition January 2007. Sixth edition February 2008. Seventh edition February 2009. Eighth edition February 2010. Ninth edition February 2011. Tenth edition, titled *Equity Alternatives: Restricted Stock, Performance Awards, Phantom Stock, SARs, and More*, published in February 2012. Eleventh edition February 2013. Twelfth edition February 2014. Thirteenth edition March 2015. Fourteenth edition February 2016. Fifteenth edition February 2017. Sixteenth edition March 2019.

The National Center for Employee Ownership
1629 Telegraph Ave., Suite 200
Oakland, CA 94612
(510) 208-1300
www.nceo.org

Contents

Using the Model Plan Documents   279

Index   283

About the Authors   295

About the NCEO   299

Plan Documents on the CD:

Omnibus Incentive Plan
  Joseph S. Adams

Phantom Stock Grant Notice and Agreement
  Joseph S. Adams

Stock Appreciation Rights Award (Cash-Settled)
  Robin Struve

Stock Appreciation Rights Award (Stock-Settled)
  Robin Struve

Restricted Stock Award and Agreement
  Joseph S. Adams

Restricted Stock Unit Grant Notice and Agreement
  Joseph S. Adams

Performance Unit Award and Agreement
  Joseph S. Adams

Introduction

Corey Rosen

Employee ownership has become commonplace in the U.S. economy and, increasingly, worldwide. We at the NCEO now estimate that at least 25% of the U.S. workforce owns stock in its employer through an employee stock ownership plan (ESOP), stock option plan, 401(k) plan, or stock purchase plan. Employee ownership can be found in companies of all sizes and in all lines of business. From the two-person startup to the 2.3 million employees of Wal-Mart, employee ownership has become just part of the business fabric.

This growth is not surprising in light of consistent research showing that companies that share ownership broadly with employees consistently outperform those who do not, especially if they combine ownership with a highly participative management style that shares both corporate financial information and the right to make decisions concerning work-level issues. It is also consistent with a changing economy in which speed, innovation, and information are essential business resources. For companies to succeed, they need to engage their employees in a daily effort to come up with better products and services, more efficient processes, improved quality control and customer service, and more creative ways to reach new markets. The more people who can be thinking and acting along these lines—thinking and acting like owners—the more successful a company will be. Even the employers who most famously succeed at this still see more opportunity; as Bill Hewlett famously noted, there is no telling what Hewlett-Packard could have done if it had only known what its employees knew. And this from a company leader who was considered the model of getting employees engaged in creative enterprise.

At the same time, the growth of employee ownership builds a momentum of its own. As more employees get ownership, more employees ask for and expect it. Sharing ownership becomes a prerequisite for attracting and retaining quality people.

For many companies, the route to employee ownership will be through a formal employee ownership plan such as an ESOP, 401(k) plan, stock option, or employee stock purchase plan (ESPPs—a regulated stock purchase plan with specific tax benefits). But for others, these plans, because of cost, regulatory requirements, corporate considerations, or other issues will not be the best fit. Or, some companies may have one or more of these plans but want to supplement them for certain employees with another kind of plan. For these companies, phantom stock, stock appreciation rights, direct stock purchase plans, performance awards, or restricted stock may work better. This book is written for these companies.

There are a number of situations that might call for one or more of these plans:

- The company's owners want to share the economic value of equity but not equity itself.

- The company cannot offer conventional kinds of ownership plans because of corporate restrictions, as would be the case, for instance, with a limited liability corporation, partnership, or sole proprietorship.

- The company already has a conventional ownership plan, such as an ESOP, but wants to provide additional equity incentives, perhaps without providing stock itself, to selected employees.

- The company's leadership has considered other plans but found their rules too restrictive or implementation costs too high.

- The company is a division of another company, but it can create a measurement of its equity value and wants employees to have a share in that even though there is no actual stock.

- The company is not a for-profit stock corporation—it is a nonprofit or government entity that nonetheless can create some kind of measurement that mimics equity growth that it would like to use as a basis to create an employee bonus.

This book provides an overview of the design, implementation, accounting, valuation, tax, and legal issues for the plans it covers, and also provides sample plans. It is not, however, a comprehensive manual. None of these plans should be set up without the detailed advice of qualified legal and financial counsel. Sharing equity is a major step that should be considered thoroughly and carefully.

Note to the 16th Edition

In the 16th edition, chapters 2, 3, 4, 6, and 7 have been revised and updated (as of late 2018) where needed. Chapter 5 was replaced by a new chapter on the same subject.

CHAPTER ONE

Basic Issues in Plan Design

Corey Rosen

Contents

For many companies, the idea of sharing equity growth with employees is appealing. Often these companies will turn to a formal employee ownership plan such as an ESOP (employee stock ownership plan), 401(k) plan, or tax-qualified employee stock purchase plan. But many company owners or corporate boards may be put off by the complexity, costs, or regulations that govern these plans, or by the legal and practical issues for their company in having employees own actual shares. Historically, many of these companies turned instead to stock options. Options became common currency in the 1990s, covering about 10 million employees. Their (then) favorable accounting treatment, steadily rising stock prices, and the fact that "everyone else" was doing it seemed to make them the equity vehicle of choice. Moreover, accounting rules at the time did not require that the company record any compensation cost for the grant of options. That favorable accounting treatment ended in 2005 (2006 for private companies), meaning that options were now on a level accounting playing field with other forms of individual equity awards. At the same time, investors and the press started looking at options granted to key executives more skeptically. Options reward volatility more than any other corporate factor (it's better to have an option on a stock that can reach great highs, even if it also can reach deep lows, because you can exercise at the highs and ignore the lows). That may have induced some top executives to take excessive risks.

Options also seemed more appealing in markets that kept going up. Options reward employees for the increase in share prices, but when share prices are more stable or go down, they have much less or no value. Even in up markets, many more mature companies may find that their share price growth slows. Research also shows that even in most strong markets, in any given year, a very higher percentage of companies, and often a majority, see a decline in stock price rather than a gain. The reason is simple math. Stocks can only go down to zero, but have no limit on the upside. A stock market average includes some very big winners who may grow by more than 100%, but no one loses more than 100%. So average gains will almost always exceed median gains. This means that stock options are often out of the money, at least over the short term.

While options still make sense for many companies and remain the most common form of individual equity grant, there are other equity alternatives worth considering, either to replace options and/or other ownership plans or to supplement them by providing a different kind of equity reward, either just to certain people or to everyone.

This book is designed to discuss alternative approaches. It focuses on five types of plans: phantom stock, stock appreciation rights (SARs), restricted stock, direct stock purchase plans, and performance awards. Each of these plans is briefly defined below.

1.1 Types of Plans

1.1.1 Phantom Stock

A reward paid to an individual for the value of a defined number of shares. The award is not actually made in shares but in a promise to pay the employee the value of the shares at some point in the future. The award is usually paid in cash, but could be paid in shares. For instance, a company might provide that an employee will have the right to an amount of money equal to a certain number of shares after a specified number of years of employment, but would not actually get the shares. Phantom stock is not a legal term but rather a commonly used way of describing these kinds of awards.

1.1.2 Stock Appreciation Rights (SARs)

A stock appreciation right (SAR) provides the right to the monetary equivalent of the increase in the value of a specified number of shares over a specified period of time. As with phantom stock, this is normally paid out in cash, but it could be paid in shares (this is usually called a "stock-settled stock appreciation right").

1.1.3 Restricted Stock

Any shares whose sale or acquisition is subject to restrictions is called restricted stock. In employee ownership plans, this typically would mean that an employee would be given shares or the right to buy shares (perhaps at a discount), but could not take possession of them until some time later when certain requirements have been met (or, to put it differently, restrictions have been lifted), such as working for a certain number of years or the company reaching a certain size. While the restrictions are in place, the employee could, if the plan allows it, still be eligible for any dividends paid on the shares and could be allowed to vote them as well. If the employee does not fulfill the terms of restrictions, the shares are forfeited. Some plans allow the restrictions to lapse gradually (for instance, an employee could buy 30% of the stock when the shares are 30% vested); others provide the restrictions lapse all at once.

1.1.4 Restricted Stock Units

A restricted stock unit (RSU) is equivalent to a phantom stock plan paid out in cash or shares. Employees are given a restricted right to receive the payout at some future date or subject to some performance condition. They cannot make a Section 83(b) election (a potentially favorable tax decision) on an RSU as they can on restricted stock. The accounting, tax, and securities laws issues for RSUs are identical to those for stock-settled phantom stock.

1.1.5 Direct Stock Purchase Plans

In a direct stock purchase plan, employees can purchase shares with their own funds, either at market price or a discount. In some cases, employers provide below-market or non-recourse loans to help employees purchase the shares. Employees then hold the shares as individuals with the same rights as other holders of the same class of securities.

1.1.6 Performance Awards

While most of the book focuses on these equity or equity-like plans, a separate chapter looks at performance awards, defined here as essentially profit or gain sharing plans that are designed to pay out (in cash or stock) for performance over a few to several years, rather than annually. These plans provide an alternative to rewarding performance based on the long-term improvement in share price, substituting instead a measure such as improvement in EBITDA, sales, quality, or any other measure deemed critical. Some companies may want to combine equity-based and performance awards. When the awards are made in the form of shares (usually granted as restricted stock or restricted stock units), they are generally called performance shares.

1.2 Basic Issues in Choosing a Plan

One of the great advantages of the plans we are discussing in this book is their flexibility. But that flexibility is also their greatest challenge. Because they can be designed in so many ways, many decisions need to be made about such issues as who gets how much, vesting rules, liquidity concerns, restrictions on selling shares (when awards are settled in shares), eligibility, rights to interim distributions of earnings, and rights to participate in corporate governance (if any). In this chapter, we discuss some of the considerations in deciding on these plan rules. Before turning to these details, however, we need to discuss why a company would choose one plan or another in the first place.

Because all the details about these plans can become complicated, it is helpful to map out their basic dimensions. In deciding how to provide equity or equity-like awards to employees, companies need to think about three sets of issues:

- Will the award be paid in stock or cash?
- Will the employee get the value of the shares, only the increase in the value of the shares, or an award based on something other than share value?
- Will the employee have to pay anything for the stock?

Table 1-1 provides a quick visual overview of the plans described in this book by showing what kind of plan results from the decisions made on the above issues. In many cases, we have found that corporate boards or owners have very fixed views about issues such as whether employees should be required to pay something for an equity award or whether they want employees to be able actually to own shares. By

Table 1-1. Choosing an Individual Equity or Equity Equivalent Award Plan

Type of plan	Employee pays for all or part of award	Employee does not pay for all or part of award	Award normally paid in cash	Award paid in stock	Award based on share value	Award based on increase in share value	Award based on profit or other non-equity measure
Phantom stock settled in cash	No	Yes	Yes	No	Yes	No	No
Phantom stock settled in shares (RSUs)	No	Yes	No	Yes	Yes	No	No
Direct stock purchase	Yes	No	No	Yes	Yes	No	No
Stock appreciation right (SAR)[a]	Yes	No	Normally	Sometimes	No	Yes	No
Stock-settled stock appreciation right	No	Yes	No	Yes	No	Yes	No
Restricted stock[b]	Rarely	Usually	No	Yes	Yes	No	No
Performance award[c]	No	Yes	Yes	No	No	No	Yes

a. While SARs are normally paid out in cash, they occasionally are paid out in the form of shares.

b. With restricted stock, the employee may or may not pay for the award on grant.

c. Performance awards may pay out in cash or shares.

looking first at these core issues, you can focus specifically on the kind of plan that will work best for you.

1.3 Corporate Organizational Form Issues

Companies using these plans can be organized in any of the standard corporate forms. C corporations and S corporations issue shares, and their plans would be based on actual stock or its value. Limited liability companies (LLCs) and partnerships have membership interests, not shares. They can issue the equivalent of these kinds of awards, but the terms used for them differ and, in some cases, there are different tax considerations. The NCEO has a separate publication, *Equity Compensation in Limited Liability Corporations*, that covers these issues in detail, so this chapter focuses just on S or C corporations. In the NCEO's experience, partnerships, although they can issue equity to employees, very rarely do so.[1]

C corporations have few restrictions on the kinds of shares they can issue and the number of shareholders they can have. S corporations are more limited. First, S corporations can only have 100 shareholders. Employee holders of restricted stock can be considered owners for this purpose unless (1) the stock is "substantially unvested" ("sub-

---

1. For LLCs and partnerships, there cannot be restricted stock or direct stock purchases because there is no stock. However, an employee can have a right to a capital interest in the company through a restricted capital interest award (the right to a capital interest that is subject to certain restrictions lapsing), a profits interest (largely analogous to a stock option), or their synthetic equivalents, often called a membership unit right (analogous to phantom stock) or a membership unit appreciation right (analogous to an SAR). If these rights can convert to an actual membership interest, however, it is important to consult with your attorney over how the income of the employee will be taxed. If the employee is not considered a limited partner in the entity, then the employee could be considered self-employed and have to pay the entire payroll tax obligation of his or her salary, rather than just half. LLCs and partnerships can offer the equivalents of phantom stock or SARs without these issues if, as is usually the case, the awards are paid in only in cash. In that case, the employee is not really an owner but is just getting a bonus based on an equity measurement. Similarly, if employees do end up with actual membership interests, companies need to be very clear about just what their rights will be with respect to being a partner in the firm.

stantially" is a confusing word here; it just means that the shares can still be forfeited), and (2) the employee has not made a Section 83(b) election for the shares (a Section 83(b) election allows the employee to pay capital gains tax on any increase between the fair market value of the stock on the grant date and the sale price, in return for paying ordinary income tax on the value of the shares awarded, minus any consideration the employee paid for them, at the time the award is granted). Second, S corporations can only have one class of stock, although the same class can have different voting rights for different shares. This means that if some shares have benefits other shares do not, they are not allowed. Stock appreciation rights, phantom stock, and restricted stock granted to employees as compensation for services are not considered to be separate classes of stock, provided they are not transferable (i.e., holders cannot transfer them to others) or are subject to buy-sell or redemption agreements that are structured so as to circumvent the one-class-of-stock rule. Buy-sell agreements or redemption agreements that provide for repurchase at book value, appraised value, or a formula value established by the board of directors that can be shown to have a reasonable basis all are considered not to violate the one-class-of-stock rule.

Paying distributions on restricted stock that is not vested is not required under the regulations governing the one-class-of-stock rule for S corporations, but once the shares are actually fully owned by employees, they would have to receive the same economic benefits other shareholders do. Companies can, however, pay distributions before vesting, as would be common with restricted stock. They would be paid pro-rata to distributions on other shares, but normally they would be paid as a bonus and taxed as compensation rather than as a distribution of earnings. A potential problem can come up if holders of restricted stock (or phantom stock or SARs that are paid out in the form of stock) actually take full ownership of the shares in S corporations that have previously taxed but undistributed earnings (this is called the "accumulated adjustment account"). If amounts from this account are distributed to owners, the employees who exercised their rights now are entitled to a pro-rata share of the distributions, *even though the other owners have already paid taxes on them.* So it is usually advisable to pay out the earnings prior to employees taking ownership of the shares.

Finally, keep in mind that certain professional corporations (medical practices and law firms, most notably, and also accounting firms, subject to some flexibility in some states) are prohibited by state laws from being owned by anyone who is not a member of that corporation. Synthetic equity, such as a stock appreciation rights, would not be a problem.

1.3.1 Divisions of Companies

Sometimes a company might want employees of a division or other business unit to have an equity interest just in the value of that operation. Of course, these operations do not have their own shares, but they may nonetheless have a very specific way of measuring their own performance. For instance, a division may have its own income statement or even its own balance sheet (or can construct one), as might be the case in a division that makes or provides a service that it sells, either to the parent, the market, or both. Even if the division could not be conceptualized as an independent for-profit entity, it may still have measurements of contribution to the parent corporation. For instance, it might track its "equity" growth in terms of a multiple of the margins on the products or services it provides to the parent, or create a stock value equivalency measure based on what the parent would have to pay for these services or products on the marketplace. To the extent the division beats what the market can provide, this could be considered "profit"; a multiple of the profit can be applied consistent with what the multiple would be for similar companies, and an equity value is thus created. Establishing these formulas, of course, takes expert advice and the input and acquiescence of the parent.

1.4 Picking a Plan

A separate chapter of this book looks in some detail at why a company might not want one of these plans, focusing particularly on a comparison of these plans to ESOPs and 401(k) plans. While these more formal plans have many advantages, companies may choose a phantom stock plan or other alternative plan for a number of good reasons. In all of the plans below, a major advantage is flexibility in deciding who gets how much under with what rules. That is not repeated here as an advantage in the description of specific pros and cons of each plan, however.

One general consideration in picking a plan is tax treatment. Stock option plans require employees to exercise an award by purchasing shares. That purchase is in after-tax dollars. If the option is a nonqualified award, there is additional tax on the spread on the option at exercise. Restricted stock grants are either taxable at grant or when the restrictions lapse. Any further increase in share price after taxes are paid is taxed as a capital gain on sale. Phantom stock plans, stock appreciation rights, and performance awards are generally taxable when paid. If employees incur a current tax obligation on an award before being able to realize value for it, they may view the award more as punishment than reward.

1.4.1 Phantom Stock Plans and Stock Appreciation Rights Settled in Cash

For phantom stock plans and stock appreciation rights (SARs) plans, the most common arguments are:

- Owners may be concerned about employees owning actual shares. In some cases, this may be for fear of losing control, although, in fact, other kinds of stock plans can usually handle the control issue with little or no difficulty. Actual ownership can also require dividend payments to be made. In S corporations, if employees own shares they will have a tax obligation on corporate profits, and having too many owners could cause a violation of the 100-shareholder rule.

- Closely held company owners may be concerned that there is no foreseeable market for actual shares given to employees. It may be simpler in these cases just to give employees cash rather than to buy shares back from them or try to find other buyers. Such sales may also raise securities law compliance issues. Even the issuance of shares can trigger securities law compliance issues, although it is usually a fairly simple process to obtain an exemption from these rules.

But there are also arguments against phantom plans and SARs:

- They provide no significant tax benefits to employers or employees, especially relative to such tax-qualified employee ownership plans as ESOPs, 401(k) plans, and incentive stock options.

- They may be difficult to communicate to employees who are skeptical about whether the plans will really deliver value. Whereas stock comes with specific contractual and general corporate law rights, and carries the same value as shares of the same class held by other owners of the company, phantom stock or SARs are based only on a contractual agreement to pay out based on management's determination of what the company is worth.

The arguments for phantom stock and SARs are presented together here because these plans generally have the same pros and cons. Stock appreciation rights, however, provide value only if the stock price rises. On the one hand, this can be a positive in that employees benefit only if corporate stock performance improves; on the other hand, phantom stock allows employees to get some reward if the company's own performance improves but its stock price or equity value, because of broader market factors, does not.

Also note that phantom stock awards are subject to the requirements of the deferred compensation rules under Section 409A of the Internal Revenue Code (described in more detail below). Restricted stock that does contain a deferral feature as part of the grant, incentive stock options, stock appreciation rights, and non-discounted nonqualified stock options all are exempt from these rules. Closely held companies, however, must follow specific valuation guidelines to assure that SARs and options are priced at fair market value.

1.4.2 Stock-Settled Stock Appreciation Rights and Restricted Stock Units

Stock-settled stock appreciation rights (SSARs) are stock appreciation rights paid in shares, and restricted stock units (RSUs) are equivalent to phantom stock paid in shares.

SSARs and particularly RSUs have become more popular in recent years, particularly since the 2006 change in accounting rules ended the favored treatment for options relative to other equity plans. The economic benefit to employees is equivalent to a nonqualified option that is exercised at vesting, but SSARs are less dilutive than options because the company issues only enough shares to equal the difference between the price of the stock at the award date and the price at vesting, usually net of taxes (a company will usually deduct the shares needed to satisfy payment of ordinary income tax). In addition, employees get actual shares, which may encourage them to remain shareholders. By contrast, options count as issued shares when calculating dilution at the time the options are granted, which by definition is a much higher number.

Unlike restricted stock that does not have a deferral feature, RSUs are subject to deferred compensation tax rules. RSUs delay any dilution until the shares are paid, but at that point, they are as dilutive as the issuance of any other face-value stock award. Unlike restricted stock, they rarely pay dividends or carry other stock rights until the shares are paid out (these rights would have to be assigned in some way other than attaching them to actual shares, however).

From a tax standpoint, both of these kinds of awards are deductible to the company when paid out, but taxed to the employee as ordinary income. Both types of plans could also encourage employees to hold on to shares if they are paid out in shares net of taxes, an approach that also minimizes dilution.

1.4.3 Direct Stock Purchase Plans

Direct stock purchase plans also have their pros and cons. Among the arguments for these plans are the following:

- If employees own shares as individuals, as opposed to through some kind of trust or similar arrangement, they may feel more like real owners, although there is no research showing this one way or another.

- If employees have to buy shares, they are making more of a real commitment to the company.

- The purchase of shares infuses new capital into the company.

- Ownership is held only by people interested enough to make a financial sacrifice.

On the other hand:

- If employees have to buy shares, how many will be able to do so? Will ownership end up being distributed mostly to higher-paid people? While this may be the company's objective, it will mean the company will be unlikely to be able to develop an ownership culture in which most or all employees will think and act like owners. Some owners think just making stock available to people is enough to accomplish this purpose, even if they do not buy it, but there is little reason to believe this is the case.

- If a company asks employees to buy shares, will they feel pressured to purchase them even when they are not in a financial position to take that risk? Will they resent what they may perceive as subtle—or not so subtle—pressure? Will they rush to sell shares at the first opportunity to minimize their financial risk?

- Will employees who own shares directly be able to sell them when they like, thus reducing the incidence of employee ownership in a company? If they cannot sell when they like, will this make them less interested in owning shares?

- If there are stock registration or other legal forms and procedures to comply with, will the costs of compliance justify the amount of investment employees make?

- Direct stock purchases must be made with after-tax employee dollars; other plans can arrange for more favorable terms.

1.4.4 Restricted Stock

Restricted stock plans have a number of advantages:

- They provide some kind of service or performance target for employees to achieve before actually receiving shares or having the right to buy them. For instance, a seniority target can help assure that people don't "take the money and run" before making a contribution to the company. A profit or growth target can be a useful way to focus the attention of employees as a group on an objective.

- They can carry dividend or voting rights, if the company chooses.
- Unlike stock options or stock appreciation rights, restricted stock retains some value for employees even if the price goes down.
- Employees can receive capital gains treatment on all or part of the gain on the shares, provided they make a Section 83(b) election, as described in the chapter on restricted stock.

There are, of course, disadvantages as well:

- The restrictions may make ownership seem like an unlikely benefit. If an employee purchases shares, especially at the market price, but then cannot actually take possession of them until certain events occur, buying the shares may not seem very attractive.
- Restricted stock has no value unless there is a market for the shares at some point. Employees must believe this is a real possibility, not just a corporate intention.
- The company cannot take a tax deduction for the value of the gain employees eventually realize if employees have made a Section 83(b) election to have the gain taxed as a capital gain.
- Relative to other plans, restricted stock is a more complicated approach and can involve significant financial risks for employees if they choose to make a Section 83(b) election to obtain capital gains treatment on any increase in share value they eventually realize.

1.4.5 Performance Awards

Performance awards have several advantages:

- They can be settled in cash or stock.
- They are directly linked to performance targets.
- They are infinitely flexible in design.
- When settled in cash, they can more specifically link what an employee does to a desired result than do stock awards because part

of the value of shares is created by things beyond the employee's control.

Among the disadvantages are:

- Awards settled in cash do not provide an ownership stake.
- Determining accurate and acceptable measures of performance can be tricky.
- Focusing employee effort on one or more goals, such as sales, quality, or profit, may lead the employee not to focus on other important objectives.
- Individually based awards may discourage teamwork.

1.5 Deciding on Key Plan Features

The sections below explore a variety of issues that affect all kinds of employee ownership plans. Subsequent chapters look at specific issues that affect stock option plans, stock purchase plans, profit-sharing type plans, and phantom plans.

1.5.1 How Much of Your Company's Equity or Equity Value Will You Share?

The first question you must ask is how much stock will be available for employees or, if you have a phantom stock plan or SAR plan, how much equity value you will share. It may seem at first blush that if you are not actually giving up stock, then you are not really giving people equity value, but rather just a bonus based on equity performance. In fact, however, if you pay people out based on equity value, you are giving up an important part of ownership. The value of a company is, in most companies, a function of the present value of future cash flows or earnings. If you pay people based on equity value or appreciation, your future stock value is being reduced in exactly the same way as if you gave them shares or stock options (the realized value of an option to an employee is the same as SARs on an equivalent number of shares). So whatever kind of plan you have, if it is based on equity in any way, you should think of it in terms of sharing ownership or its equivalent.

Deciding how much ownership to share is obviously an essential, if difficult, first step in setting up a plan.

Generally, companies approach this issue in one of two ways. The most common is to determine in advance some percentage of total shares or equity value that the existing owners are comfortable in sharing. Unless employees pay fair market value for the stock in a direct share purchase plan, sharing ownership or equity value dilutes the economic value of the ownership already held by dividing the claims on the company's assets into more pieces. If employees have to purchase shares at a fair market value, however, this economic effect is offset by the infusion of cash, so all owners end up having a smaller share of a larger company. Any ownership plan that allows employees to vote their shares or their share equivalents (such as phantom stock), however, dilutes control rights.

Owners' tolerance for stock or equity value dilution will depend in part on what they see as the alternatives. For instance, assume that owners are willing to share 10% of the stock or equity value of their company. What if this turns out to provide an insufficient incentive to attract, retain, and motivate those employees targeted by the plan? What else can be done? Will more current cash be needed to reward people, either with straight pay or bonuses? If more cash is spent, how will that affect future share price? Would it be better to share more of the company's future growth through some form of ownership than to deplete current cash that can be used to help the company grow?

Other factors come into play as well, however. In companies listed on stock exchanges, there are often informal norms about how much dilution is acceptable, as well as formal rules requiring shareholder approval for dilution. For any particular company, the range of acceptable dilution will vary with industry norms, company performance, the makeup of shareholders (some institutional shareholders, for instance, are more opposed to dilution than others), and the distribution of ownership rights to employees (generally, shareholders are more tolerant of broadly distributed ownership rights than concentration of ownership rights among a few key people). Going beyond what shareholders or the broader market of potential stock buyers find acceptable may be a signal to investors that the company wastes too much of its assets on excessive compensation.

Companies now can partially address this issue by paying in phantom stock or SARs (settled in cash or shares). These plans had been subject to very unfavorable accounting rules in that they required a current charge to earnings, whereas options did not (this changed with the new accounting rules effective in 2006). As a result, public companies especially tended to use these plans on a very limited basis (closely held companies tend to be less concerned with dilution). Shareholders may not look kindly, however, on what they perceive as attempts to disguise stock ownership by providing it in an equivalent form. Public companies need to evaluate their total equity compensation package and be prepared to justify that to their investors.

In closely held companies, owners may have plans or obligations to provide family members, partners, or investors with a specific percentage of the company, either for control or economic reasons. Or, in many cases, they may have a conviction that they cannot share more than a certain percentage of total ownership rights. In some closely held companies, there are venture capital investors who may place strict limits on how much equity value can be shared, in whatever form. They may also have *minimum* guidelines from these investors for how much ownership they want key employees, or even all employees, to have, either by corporate contribution or by employee purchase. Companies with significant debt may also want to check whether there are any loan covenants that would make it difficult or impossible to pay out employees for their equity awards during the term of the loan.

The most common approach to this problem is to set a fixed ceiling on how much ownership or equity value can be shared, such as 10% of the shares at any time or 5% of the equity value of the company (earned in shares or in cash) in any two-year period. Deciding in advance on a fixed percentage, however, is probably the least rational way to make a decision on this issue. First, companies that are growing often make the error of setting aside a certain percentage of stock ownership or equity value for employees and giving out most or even all of these shares to whoever is there early on. As the company grows, it then has only a small and shrinking pool of stock ownership or equity value to make available to new employees. The result is that a two-class system emerges of owners and those owning little or nothing, even among people doing the same jobs.

Another problem with the fixed percentage approach is that even if employment remains fairly stable, the job market can change. While departing employees may surrender their shares to the company to give out to new employees, the new employees may now expect more stock ownership or equity value than the company can make available. Similarly, company philosophy can change, calling for a greater emphasis on equity awards.

Finally, 10%, or any percentage, of one company is not the same as 10% of some other company. Giving employees 10% of a startup without a product or profits is a very different matter than 10% of an established, profitable corporation. Very few employees actually care what percentage of a company they own, individually or (even less) collectively. They care about what it is worth. Deciding on how much to share should be a function of what is needed to attract, retain, and motivate people over time, including the possibility of growth, while at the same time not scaring off investors or existing shareholders.

Some companies take a slightly modified approach, saying they want to provide people at various positions a percentage of equity based on what surveys say people in those positions in similar companies get. This is even more problematic. First, the surveys are subject to multiple biases (many are of client companies of the survey firm and may reflect that survey firm's advice, for instance). Second, it just replicates the percentage of the company problem on an individual scale. People care about value, not abstract percentages.

There are three good alternative approaches to the percentage-of-equity approach. The first provides an initial percentage of stock ownership or equity value for employees that is below what the company expects to need in the long run. An upper parameter is also set, but set high enough to leave enough for expected contingencies. For example, the company's board of directors may agree that in no case should employee ownership (whether in actual shares or the rights to the value of shares) exceed 25% of the company's total equity value. The employee ownership plan might start by providing half of this for employee plans currently, providing additional reserves as the company grows. If market conditions or a change in company philosophy demands more, the company can reconsider its positions and ask existing owners to authorize more stock ownership or equity value as needed. This ad hoc approach is simple and flexible, but shareholders often come to resent repeated requests for further dilution, seeing it perhaps as a sign of management incompetence or employee greed.

One solution to this is that within the fixed limit for additional share or equity award issues, a company might create some automatic devices for issuing stock ownership or equity value that will not require periodic shareholder approval. For instance, in the example here, shareholders might agree that not more than 25% of the stock ownership or equity value can be given out at any time. As long as the company stays under that number, however, it might be authorized to issue enough additional stock ownership or equity value each year so that any equity awards that are cashed in are used to provide opportunities for other employees. Or the formula might be adapted so that the total amount of stock ownership or equity value available will increase with employment, sales, profits, or some other measure up to a limit, with additional awards issued as needed to supplement those that are cashed in.

A second approach would be to base the amount of stock ownership or equity value given out on employee compensation or job responsibilities. Owners can be told at the outset that they should expect the amount of stock ownership or equity value available to increase as the total number and composition of the work force changes. If owners can agree that the formulas used to provide stock ownership or equity value to employees make sense for the current work force, they might agree that the same guidelines would make sense for a future work force. If the employment composition changes more dramatically than anticipated when a calculation was made about how much dilution this formula would cause—because of growth or hiring more higher paid or specialized people—this would normally be a sign of company success and, hopefully, share value growth, so owners may be persuaded to share some of the unexpectedly good performance. There may be some employees, however, whose regular compensation is intentionally set below market with the understanding that they will receive additional equity awards. That may be especially true of certain key people in younger companies seeking to conserve cash, so the compensation approach will need modifying in these cases.

A third approach is to base the total pool of stock ownership or equity value available on corporate performance. Owners would agree in advance that if certain performance targets are exceeded during a given period (such as each year), employees would get a percentage of the resulting increment in the form of additional equity rewards. It may be possible to calculate how much an increase in value going over a target creates by using standard valuation formulas, but the calculation can also be a simpler one, such as 15% of the additional profit over a target will be used to provide more shares. The pool is divided among participants based on whatever formula is being used to allocate them. It makes sense to test possible outcomes in advance to see whether they comport with how much the company thinks is appropriate. Because the owners dilute their position only if employees help create more value for that position, they should be more willing to share than if some automatic formula gives out awards regardless of performance. It also gives employees a more specific reason to focus on performance targets. In talking with companies, this is the option we at the NCEO have found owners usually adopt when they think about the alternatives. The dynamic design of the plan adapts to a company's growth and allows employees to gain more than they might under more static approaches. On the other hand, the equity grants are not just an entitlement—employees can only get more if they help the company make more. While this approach is often the most sensible for companies, we have also found that most advisors, who often have only set up a few plans, tend to suggest a fixed percentage, arguably the least rational approach.

1.5.2 Liquidity

An equity sharing plan has no value if the shares that are awarded cannot be sold or the promised cash payments for phantom stock or SARs cannot be made. Generally, this is not a problem in companies listed on stock exchanges, but this is true only if there is an active market for the shares and the employee receives a class of shares that can be sold. If employees get non-voting shares, for instance, these shares might not be among those traded and may have little if any value. Securities rules may also restrict the ability of key employees to sell their shares, at least for certain periods of time.

If employees need to exercise awards before a liquidity event is near (a design that can be avoided by conditioning vesting on liquidity), they may have to come up with after-tax money to exercise the award (for options) and/or pay tax on the spread at exercise or vesting, depending on the kind of award. The result can seem more like punishment ("I am out of pocket a lot of money for an uncertain, far-off future") than reward.

Liquidity is a more serious issue for closely held companies. By definition, there is no ready market for shares of these companies. In the case of restricted stock, directly purchased shares, performance awards paid out in shares, or the unusual case of phantom stock or SARs paid out in shares, liquidity can be provided in these cases in a number of ways:

- *Share repurchase by company:* The company can agree to repurchase the shares from employees at stated intervals (every so many years, every time share value exceeds a certain amount, when the employee leaves the company, when the company has more than a certain amount of cash on hand, or some other rule). Companies can modify this in a variety of ways. If shares are held a certain number of years, for instance, employees may be paid full value, but if an employee leaves before then, the company might only pay the employee back what the employee paid for the shares, perhaps with interest. Or the company might agree to a reduced price buy-back feature but allow the employee to sell the shares elsewhere for full price. Note, of course, that money used to buy back shares is a non-productive expense providing the company with no new investments it can use to make more money. On the other hand, either of the two methods below risk that employees will not get paid or, almost as bad, believe that they may not be paid.

  If the company does buy the shares, it should consider an employee stock ownership plan (ESOP). As explained in the final chapter of this book, an ESOP can provide a way to buy out owners with tax-deductible corporate dollars. If the owners bought their shares at full price in a direct share purchase program, and have held them for at least three years before the sale, they can also defer taxes on the gain by reinvesting the proceeds in the securities of domestic corporations not receiving more than 25% of their income from passive investments. This benefit applies only if the company is a C corporation, however.

If a company does not use an ESOP to buy back shares, it must use after-tax dollars to make the purchases. Note this applies only to actual purchases of shares. Cash-settled nonqualified options, phantom stock, and SARs all generate a tax deduction for the company equal to the amount of ordinary income declared by the employee.

- *Internal market:* The company can try to set up an internal market for employees to buy and sell from one another. This can supplement other approaches or be the entire approach (which will probably mean some employees will not be able to sell their shares for longer than they want). In the past, securities rules imposed onerous requirements on such markets, making them impractical for most companies. The SEC, in a ruling on an internal market at a company called TEOCO (The Employee Owned Company, then a small but now a large software provider), provided guidelines for how companies can do this in a cost-effective manner. Short of a formal market, of course, employees may informally be allowed to buy and sell from one another. These approaches only work, of course, if there are active buyers and sellers.

- *Liquidity only on the occurrence of certain events:* The company can allow liquidity only on certain events occurring—for example, the shares may be sold only if someone else buys the company, the company goes public, or a major investor is brought in. In the interim, the company might agree to buy shares from employees at a fixed lower price if they did not want to wait. Not allowing liquidity unless one of these events occurs, however, may be risky if employees do not believe that the event is likely in the reasonable future. This is especially true with respect to IPOs. Although thousands of companies believe they are good IPO candidates, over the last 10 years, only an average of about 225 companies have gone public per year, a number of them spin-offs of large companies.

- *Outside investors:* Some entrepreneurial companies may be able to attract investors who will purchase some of the shares held by employees, although many investors would prefer that their stock purchases be used to help the company grow. In recent years, as the number of companies going and staying public has declined sharply, many more companies are staying private by having multiple rounds of equity investments.

- *Secondary markets:* Secondary markets such as NASDAQ Private Market and SharesPost provide markets for certain investors to buy shares in private companies, often shares resulting from employee equity awards. While this market has grown, only a small number of companies likely to do a substantial IPO or sale are likely to attract buyers for their shares.

If the awards are made in cash rather than shares, the company has to arrange for funds to be available. One approach is to set up a corporate sinking fund. Companies simply can set aside cash to be used to pay off their obligations under employee awards. These accumulated earnings, however, could be subject to an excess accumulated earnings tax. The law provides that earnings accumulated in excess of reasonable business needs are subject to the highest marginal tax rates. Virtually any corporation can accumulate up to $250,000 ($150,000 for service-type corporations) without this tax applying, but amounts above this could be taxable. Many advisors argue that accumulating earnings for the purpose of paying out employee awards such as phantom stock or SARs, however, is a legitimate business purpose. It is advisable to discuss this matter with counsel before creating a reserve fund.

If a company does establish a fund to pay for employee awards, the fund would most likely be a "rabbi trust" or "secular trust." A rabbi trust holds funds that must be paid to employees at the time the plan states they can get paid for their equity awards. This may be when they exercise an award or could be after some required post-exercise holding period. While the funds are being held, the employer cannot use them to fund ongoing business needs. However, if there are creditor claims against the company, the fund can be used to satisfy them if other funds are not available. The advantage of a rabbi trust is that the fact that the availability of the funds is contingent means employees will not be taxed on the employee's pro-rata portion of the earnings or contributions to the trust.

By contrast, a secular trust actually sets aside money for the employee and is not subject to claims of corporate creditors. As a result, the employee is taxed on contributions to the trust and earnings of the trust as they occur. The employer, however, can take a tax deduction for contributions to the trust when they are made, while in a rabbi trust the company only gets a deduction when the funds are paid out. Secular trusts also provide more certainty to employees that they will actually get paid for their equity interests than do the more contingent rabbi trusts.

In practice, most deferred compensation plans, whether based on equity or other measures, use rabbi trusts. Taxing employees currently on a benefit they will receive later (or may not receive at all if they do not vest in the award or forfeit the award subject to some condition in the plan) may be a significant demotivator.

There is, of course, a more basic problem with accumulating earnings this way, namely that they are not being used to help the business grow. An alternative would be to plan to borrow money as the need arises. The argument here is that rates of return on invested capital in corporate operations should, almost by definition, normally exceed rates of return on debt. The risk is that the company will be unable or unwilling to borrow the funds needed when they are needed. Telling employees their awards will be funded this way will also not generate a lot of confidence.

As with actual stock ownership, it is possible to write the plan so that the award of phantom stock or the exercise of SARs is available only if there is a liquidity event, such as going public or a sale to a third party. Similarly, companies could restrict the sale of shares acquired under any of the plans described in this book until a liquidity event occurs. Because employees do not have the same legal claim with these awards that they would have if they actually owned shares, however, companies need to write into their governing contracts with employees that liquidity will occur on these events. Employers then need to commit to negotiate with buyers to make sure they agree to pay for these awards. Remember, because employees do not own stock, the buyer is not legally obligated to honor the award; it is, after all, a contractual agreement between the selling employer and the employee, not the buying employer and employee. If the company goes public, then investment bankers must be agreeable to having the company provide liquidity on or soon after the IPO, and this information will have to be disclosed in a prospectus. These elements of uncertainty can make employees more skeptical about the potential value of the awards.

Finally, if employees do actually end up with shares, companies should consider whether they want to have a "right of first refusal." This allows companies to require an employee to sell shares back to the company, rather than to another buyer, provided the company matches the competing offer within a specific reasonable period of time. If such a right is created, companies should have employees sign an agreement granting this right when the equity award is made.

Liquidity options are explored in depth in the NCEO's book *Staying Private: Liquidity Options for Entrepreneurial Companies.*[2]

1.5.3 Deferred Compensation Rules Under Section 409A

In the American Jobs Creation Act of 2004, a complex change was made to the treatment of deferred compensation by the addition of Section 409A to the Internal Revenue Code. Employees can now defer the receipt of a vested (and thus taxable) deferred compensation award, such as one of the equity awards described here, by making an election. So, for instance, an employee might elect to defer receipt of a phantom stock payout for some years after it vests, paying tax only at the time the award is actually paid out. This approach has been used by (and generally only offered to) executives. Under Section 409A, employees will be able to elect to defer only if several conditions are met:

1. The employee dies, becomes disabled, there is a change in control, there is an unforeseen emergency (as rigorously defined in the law), or there is a fixed date or schedule specified by the plan.

2. Elections for deferral must be made not later than the close of the preceding taxable year in which the award would vest or, if made in the first year of the award, within 30 days after the employee first becomes eligible for an award. If the employee is a key employee (as defined by statute) of a public company, receipt of the benefit must be not earlier than six months after separation.

3. If the award is performance-based, the election must come not later than six months before the end of the performance period.

---

2. Aziz El-Tahch et al., *Staying Private: Liquidity Options for Entrepreneurial Companies* (Oakland, CA: NCEO, 2014) (see www.nceo.org/r/staying-private).

4. There can be no acceleration of benefits once a deferral election has been made.

5. Any subsequent elections for an award must be at least twelve months after the prior election and must defer receipt for at least five years in the future.

Section 409A does not apply to qualified benefit plans, such as ESOPs or 401(k) plans, as well as sick leave, death benefits, and similar arrangements. Existing rules for incentive stock options or employee stock purchase plans (ESPPs) qualifying under Section 423 of the Internal Revenue Code are not changed by this law. If the employee is granted an option on stock at not less than the fair market value, normal deferral features of such plans are not covered. The effective date of the rules initially was set at January 1, 2005, but it was changed in regulations to January 1, 2009. Plans and awards in place before January 1, 2009, however, are subject to transition rules that are beyond the scope of this discussion.

The IRS's regulations under Section 409A clarify that stock appreciation rights, including stock-settled stock appreciation rights, can be used in both closely held and public companies, provided the rights are granted and awarded based on a fair market value. Restricted stock that does not contain a deferral feature as part of the grant is also exempt from the requirements. Phantom stock, restricted stock units, and performance awards, however, are covered by the rules.

For closely held companies, one critical consideration is that the rules require a reasonable method of determining fair market value for any kind of option or stock appreciation right. Companies with an appraisal for an employee stock ownership plan (ESOP) can use that price; other companies can follow the rules for ESOP appraisals. These require an independent, outside appraisal performed at least annually by a qualified appraiser using standard methods of business appraisal (that is, determining what a willing buyer would pay a willing seller, generally determined by an analysis of comparable transactions, capitalization of earnings or cash flow, net asset value, and other considerations). Startup companies in their first 10 years can use a somewhat simpler method. Formula appraisals can be used only under certain limited circumstances, including that the same price be used consistently for corporate transactions and that the formula be based on reasonable assumptions.

1.5.4 Who Will Be Eligible?

Deciding who is eligible depends on the company's goals and the kind of plan it operates. For instance, if the company is simply allowing employees to buy shares, it may want to base eligibility rules on how many shareholders it is willing to have, how it can structure an offer to avoid costly securities law requirements, or which employees it believes can legitimately take the risk. The tax and financial planning complexities of restricted stock and direct stock purchase plans generally make them more appealing as key-person plans. Phantom stock and SARs, by contrast, can more easily be used as broad-based plans. Performance awards, which can function much like a bonus, can be made to anyone, as well as to teams or groups.

Corporate goals for the plan raise even more important questions. For instance, the company may just want to provide an incentive for exceptional performance. By definition, then, only some employees will get stock awards in any one year. If the company is trying to establish a culture in which most or all employees think and act like owners, however, such restrictive practices may create a few winners and lots of losers. A 2007 *BusinessWeek* poll found that 90% of employees believe they are in the top 10% of company performers, so ranking people by performance will automatically leave a lot of people unhappy. Even if everyone is eligible for an award, but in practice only a few people actually get one, there will inevitably be resentment and concern about favoritism. Another common corporate goal with an equity award plan is to attract and retain specific talented employees. In most cases, these plans will then only be made available to a few people, although a company may offer a different plan more broadly.

1.5.5 Arguments for Broad-Based Ownership Rights

Many readers of this book will have purchased it to help figure out how to attract, retain, and motivate key people. While this is a legitimate goal, it is also worthwhile to consider expanding ownership more broadly. In the last 20 years, broad-based employee ownership has become a mainstay of American business and, increasingly, of multinational companies as well. About 25 to 30 million U.S. employees now participate in one kind of broad-based plan or another (or about 25% of the non-governmental work force), primarily ESOPs, stock options, ESPPs, and 401(k) plans with employer stock as an investment alternative. Employers of all sizes, industries, and regions are participating in this trend.

While tax incentives account for some of this growth, most of it is a result of a growing belief that broad-based employee ownership helps companies perform better. More and more, companies are relying on their employees to share ideas and information about how to move the company forward. Employees at all levels have more responsibility, often working in teams to make an increasing number of decisions. Ownership, it turns out, is a very effective reward for employees who are making the effort to improve the corporate bottom line. Research from a variety of academic studies shows that companies that set up broad-based employee ownership plans grow 2% to 3% per year faster in employment, sales, and productivity than would have been expected otherwise. When broad ownership is combined with a high involvement work style, companies perform even better still. Looking specifically at stock options, in the largest study ever done Yael V. Hochberg of the Kellogg School of Management at Northwestern University and Laura Lindsey at the W. P. Carey School of Business at Arizona State University found that companies that granted options broadly to their employees showed a significant improvement in industry-adjusted return on assets (ROA), while companies that granted options more narrowly showed a decline in performance. The study, "Incentives, Targeting and Firm Performance: An Analysis of Non-Executive Stock Options," appeared in the November 2010 (vol. 23, no. 11) issue of the *Review of Financial Studies*. The study looked at 1500 companies over a 17-year period.

For instance, in 2002 we at the NCEO profiled DPR Construction in Redwood City, CA, for our newsletter. DPR made all non-union and some union employees (about half its work force) eligible for phantom stock awards. Actual awards, however, were based on merit (it uses the same approach today). Founders Peter Nosler, Doug Woods, and Ron Davidowski felt strongly that an informal, egalitarian environment would encourage creativity and enthusiasm that would translate into more efficient planning and procedures as well as a happier and more productive work force. As a result, DPR had no titles, no private offices, no hierarchy, and plenty of camaraderie. The company also experienced phenomenal growth, from the proverbial "three men and a dog" to a privately held company of over 2,500 employees with 18 offices and revenues of over $1.2 billion. It has continued its plan and growth.

As many as 90% of the eligible staff members received grants during a year, from which they might reasonably expect, after fully vesting, an annual bonus equivalent to about 20% of their ordinary compensation. A five-year vesting schedule allowed the employees to secure 20% of their total grant for each full year of employment. The holders of phantom stock did not receive any payment on a particular grant, however, until the entire five years elapsed or they left the company (in which case they were paid on a pro-rata basis for the percentage of time completed). Moreover, most eligible employees received additional grants, thereby achieving a "rolling" equity interest. While DPR became very large company, it started its phantom plan when it just had a handful of employees. One of the most appealing things about phantom plans and similar approaches, in fact, is that they can fit companies of any size.

Many companies will choose instead some kind of gainsharing (a system of awards for employees, as individuals or groups, in which employees get a specified percentage of gains resulting from meeting preset performance targets) or profit-sharing mechanism to reward non-management employees; many others will provide no incentive pay. The research on these issues strongly suggests, however, that broad ownership is the most effective way to create a more innovative and productive corporate environment.

1.5.6 Key Issues in Thinking About Eligibility

Once a decision is made about how broadly the coverage of the plan should be, employers need to consider several other issues, as described below.

1. *Tenure:* At the simplest level, companies can require that people can get awards only after they have worked a minimum amount of time, often one year. This assures at least some commitment on the part of the employee to the company.

2. *Full-Time/Part-Time:* In the past, it was unusual to provide equity incentives to part-time employees. Innovators like Starbucks, however, have provided awards to everyone (in Starbucks' case, stock options), arguing that many of their part-time people would (or if properly rewarded could) be long-term employees. Changes in both the work force and the nature of some jobs have made part-time workers more an integral and, in some cases, stable part of a company's total employment. Given the high cost of training and recruitment, providing an incentive for part-time people to stay makes sense for them. In making this decision, companies need to consider how important enough it is to retain part-time people, or whether these employees are more seasonal and short-term and thus very unlikely to stay with the company more than a short time under any circumstances.

3. *Merit:* One of the most common ways to define eligibility is some assessment of merit. This can be done in a variety of ways. Company or unit managers may be given the authority to decide who will get a stock award that year. There may be specific criteria established that measure employee performance (such as employee review ratings, personal sales or production goals, not missing days of work, or some other measure). Merit might also be defined at a team or group level so that if that unit meets certain performance targets, everyone will get an award. Merit is often seen as political, however. Studies show that about 70% of employees think they are in the top 10% of performers, so merit approaches can create the perception of a lot of losers.

4. *Position:* Many companies provide awards only to people above a certain position. This may just be managers or it could go much further down, such as technicians, assistant store managers, production supervisors, etc. Companies need to consider, however, that such an approach may make it very difficult to establish a culture of ownership that affects the entire company.

5. *On-Hire or Promotion:* For some companies, awards are granted to people only when they are hired or promoted. This can create something of a lottery effect, however, because the awards could have very different value depending on when the employees joined

or were promoted. A company could end up with employees doing the same job with very different amounts of equity.

6. *Avoiding ERISA Requirements:* The "Employee Retirement Income Security Act" (ERISA) governs retirement plans such as ESOPs, pension plans, 401(k) plans, and profit sharing plans. Plans that fall under its control must follow specific guidelines for eligibility, allocations, distributions, and other matters of plan operation. They must also file periodic reports and, for plans with over 100 participants, have annual plan audits. Phantom stock, SAR, and restricted stock plans can all fall under ERISA if they are designed to benefit more than just key employees (this issue is discussed more in the chapter in this book on phantom stock and SARs) *and* they are designed to pay out benefits on retirement or, some advisors say, after long periods of employment even before termination. Restricting coverage requirements is thus one way to avoid being subject to ERISA, but plans can avoid these rules by following the approach of DPR and paying out awards on a periodic basis.

1.5.7 How Much Will Each Person Get?

The same criteria that might be used for eligibility might also be used for determining how much ownership people will get (tenure, promotion, position, and merit). Awards can also be made equally or based on hours worked or, as is common in qualified employee ownership plans such as ESOPs, according to relative pay. Each of these approaches, of course, has very different consequences for the kind of ownership culture the company is creating. The issue of allocation also applies primarily to stock award programs, not programs where employees buy shares.

A formula that indicates that people will get equity awards in proportion to relative pay (someone with 1% of pay would get 1% of the total stock award) sends a message the awards are simply part of the overall compensation system. If people regard current salary, benefit, and bonus systems as fair, they will probably view the equity award allocation formula as fair as well. Companies can also combine the relative pay approach with another formula, such as tenure or equal allocation, or can cap the amount of pay that is eligible.

A formula that indicates awards will be allocated on the basis of hours worked, on the other hand, says that ownership is more a basic right in the company and that everyone's contribution is valued equally. This can be helpful in creating a culture of common ownership, but may also cause some resentment, and perhaps recruitment and retention problems as well, among higher-paid people.

A third formula provides awards based on promotion or a merit assessment. The message here is meritocracy. If employees believe that the system for judging merit or giving out promotions is fair, this may work well; if not, they may see ownership as just another way to enrich the undeserving. These approaches also send a message that all employees are not thought deserving of ownership, something that could make it harder to create an ownership culture. Some companies address this issue by creating merit award systems in which everyone is expected to earn ownership at some time in their tenure—or not stay with the company.

A fourth approach is seniority. This obviously encourages people to stay with the company, but may mean that only the very long-tenured people will see much benefit. It may also be discouraging to hard-working younger employees who may see the years required to get much stock as daunting or unrealistic.

Finally, the amount allocated may be based on the position held. Of all the formulas, this is the least likely to help create an ownership culture because it reinforces the notions of hierarchy that an effective ownership culture seeks to undermine. On the other hand, this approach may be appealing as a strategy to help attract and retain keep people.

Of course, these formulas can be combined in a variety of ways. A point system may give so many points for pay, so many for merit, etc. A multiple system approach may award some shares based on merit, some on tenure, and some on position.

1.5.8 Holding Periods and Forfeiture Rules

Where plans make awards in shares, a common concern of executives is that employees will not hold on to their shares long after they are awarded them or buy them. These executives believe that unless employees hold the shares, they won't ever think of themselves as owners.

This may not be as obviously true as it seems, however. If employees are being awarded shares or even some equity equivalent on a periodic basis, they have an ongoing interest in the future share value of the company. The ability to cash in their shares periodically may be a very attractive plan feature. It also allows employees to avoid excessive risk from a concentration of their assets in company stock.

If companies do want employees to hold on to their shares, however, they can either require a minimum holding period (which may cause some resentment if share prices are volatile or fall) or provide incentives to hold shares, such as awarding bonus shares or options if the shares are held beyond a certain point. That way, employees are themselves making the investment decision. Of course, in many closely held companies, the issue of whether people hold their shares after their award may be moot because the company has no plans for providing any immediate cash value for them.

An important consideration in phantom, RSU, and SAR plans for setting requirements on holding periods after the award or exercise is whether employees will have to pay tax at the exercise of the award. The doctrine of constructive receipt states that an employee is taxable on a benefit once the employee has the right to control the timing of its payment. So if the plan structure says that employees have the right to the value of their SAR, RSU, or phantom stock once vested but can defer it to a later point, they would be taxable at the time this right becomes effective. The employee could defer the taxation by agreeing before earning the award (prior to its vesting) to defer its actual receipt until a later point, but this is much less practical under the new deferred compensation rules, which require the employee to specify in advance the date to which it will be delayed. Alternatively, if the employee has to pay something to get the award after it is exercised, that could also defer taxation. The issue of the taxation of the equity awards described in this chapter is discussed in detail in subsequent chapters of this book. The point here is that in designing these plans, companies must consider carefully how plan design can effect employee taxation.

On the flip side of the rules for holding shares is the requirement that employees disgorge the gains made on some or all of any equity award, share or cash-based, if they are fired for cause or go to work for a competitor. In the stock option arena, "claw-back" arrangements for CEOs and other top executives are required by the Dodd-Frank Act where there has been a restatement of earnings. Claw-backs for other conditions the company might specify, most commonly going to work for a competitor, are possible, but can be difficult to enforce. Many states (most notably California) have very strict limitations on noncompete agreements that make most of them unenforceable. Forfeiting benefits on termination for cause, while it may be spelled out clearly in an employment agreement and/or equity award contract, can lead to lawsuits if the amounts involved are significant. Employees have sued employers over these provisions, for instance, claiming that they were fired only to prevent them from realizing significant gains. On the other hand, employers are understandably concerned about enriching employees who, in their view, have damaged the company. Finally, aside from legal concerns, "claw-back" agreements other than those legally mandated may raise employee doubts about the awards when they are granted.

1.5.9 Vesting

Most employee ownership plans have some kind of vesting provisions. Vesting is the term used to describe the amount of time an employee must work for the company after getting an equity award (or, in some cases, buying shares) before actually having a right to them. Vesting can either be all-at-once (after five years, for instance, someone has the right to 100% of the award) or gradual (an employee might get a right to 20% of the awards for every year worked, for instance). When plans are first set up, some companies give partial or full credit for prior years worked, while others start everyone from the date the plan is started.

Vesting obviously encourages employees to stay with the company. The trick is to find a schedule that retains good people without making them think that the chance of vesting is so remote that the stock awards are irrelevant. Careful attention to company turnover patterns is also essential. If the company has very high, and unavoidable, turnover in the first three years, it might want to not start vesting till the third year. If turnover is very low anyway, faster vesting can be an attractive benefit that has few negative consequences for the company. Giving credit for prior service will be well received by employees, but can increase plan costs and raise the risk that some people may get their benefit and leave. Not giving credit for prior service, however, may cause serious resentment among senior employees.

In any event, the analysis for all these issues should be combined with an assessment of who the company really wants to end up owning shares, as vesting schedules can preclude whole classes of people this way.

1.5.10 Voting and Control

Perhaps the most contentious issue about employee ownership is whether employees will have the right to vote their shares or other ownership rights and/or have other representation rights in company management. To some people, the notion that employees can really be owners without voting or control rights seems absurd; it's one of the basic rights of ownership. Others note that there are different kinds of ownership, and that ownership rights are largely a function of what people have contributed to get them. Owners who have made an investment of capital, time, and/or risk, they say, deserve control rights in a way that employees who get actual ownership or ownership equivalency rights as a benefit of employment do not.

Our research at the NCEO indicates that this is a less important issue than it seems. Employees generally do not care intensely about whether they can vote for members of the board or other typical corporate voting issues and usually have only mild interest in being represented on the company's governing bodies. When employees do have control rights, they tend to exercise them very conservatively, and their board representatives tend to act very responsibly. They almost never use their power to throw out management. Where employees buy shares or make concessions to get them, their attitude would certainly be different. In a direct stock purchase plan, for instance, employees would most likely argue that they should have the same rights as any other shareholder.

1.5.11 Dividends

Dividends can be paid on shares that have been delivered to employees. In fact, dividends are often paid on unvested restricted stock.

Under the deferred compensation rules of Internal Revenue Code Section 409A, the right to receive accrued dividends upon the exercise of a stock option, stock appreciation right (SAR), or restricted stock unit is tantamount to a discount from the grant date fair market value. However, arrangements for dividend-like payments that are separate from the award ("dividend equivalent rights") are acceptable under the regulations under Section 409A. For those arrangements, the date at which the dividend equivalents will be paid must be determined in advance to avoid the payment itself being taxed as deferred compensation.

When a dividend equivalent right is paid, the amount is taxed as ordinary income. The company must withhold taxes and is eligible for a corresponding tax deduction.

Because restricted stock usually pays out when it vests, it is not treated as deferred compensation under Section 409A, and as a result recipients can be, and usually are, paid dividends on unvested shares.

- *Stock options:* Typically there are no dividends or dividend equivalents on unexercised awards. Once options are exercised, the holder receives dividends like any other shareholder as long as he or she holds the stock.

- *Restricted stock:* They typically carry dividend rights even before vesting. Dividends paid on unvested awards for which no Section 83(b) election has been filed are taxed as ordinary income. The company must withhold taxes on these, and it can take a corresponding tax deduction. Dividends paid on awards for which a Section 83(b) election has been made are taxed as dividend income. In that case, no withholding is required, and the company is not eligible for a tax deduction on the dividend payment.

- *SARs:* Dividend equivalent rights can be offered only as separate arrangements not tied to the exercise of the SAR, even if the employee has control over the SAR's exercise date.

- *Phantom stock/RSUs:* There are no dividends; there may be dividend equivalent rights.

1.6 Making the Plan Effective

Designing the plan well is only the first part of the battle. An effective employee ownership plan requires an ownership culture. The first step in creating this culture is good communications. On the most basic level, employees need to understand how the plan works. In most companies, this means providing material that outlines legal rights and responsibilities. Employees sign off on documents acknowledging they have received and read these materials. These "rules of the game," however, are no more effective as communication tools than, say, the rules for a board game are effective means to get people to know how to play. How many of you read the rule book first? So in addition to these legal documents, companies need to provide plain-English explanations, hold employee meetings, and, if needed, meet with employees one-to-one to explain how the plan operates. On an ongoing basis, updates on company activities, changes in the plan, corporate performance, equity value growth, and other key ownership issues need to be provided. Larger companies often create an employee committee charged with the task of finding effective ways to keep this communication going.

While a strong communications program is a good start, research is very clear that economic performance will not significantly improve just because people have a financial incentive, even if they are really tuned in to how it works. Part of this is because of the so-called "1/n" problem. Scratch up just about any economist and ask about employee ownership, and he or she will tell you about this dilemma. It's the argument that if an incentive is provided to a group of people to achieve a collective aim (such as improving the stock price), the value of that incentive to any individual employee will diminish directly in proportion to the number of employees. It assumes employees will look at all the other people they work with and say "look, I'm just one of 10, or 50, or 1,000, or 100,000." The bigger the n, the less they are motivated by the reward.

It seems like a very compelling argument. Why should I put in a lot of extra physical or mental effort when my efforts alone really won't affect the stock price in any meaningful way? Moreover, I can always rely on the efforts of other people to get the stock price up, so I can be a "free rider." People who make the 1/n argument say that it is better to design incentive systems that apply to smaller groups of people and that provide rewards for specific things that they do.

The argument seems persuasive if one assumes people act (1) only for their own narrow economic self-interest and (2) they believe that their self-interest is not furthered by cooperative behavior. But ownership is a more complicated motivation than an "if I do this, I'll get that" calculation. In an effective employee ownership or equity sharing program, people's behavior changes not so much because they perceive that there is an incentive to do x or y, but because the company has changed its organizational approach so that certain kinds of cooperative behaviors are now structured into the work place. In return for people living up to higher expectations, they get ownership as a reward.

When people identify with an organization, they see its success as their own. In this sense, as the organization grows (and "n" usually becomes larger), each individual feels more successful. To get to that point, organizations need to show that they value each employee. Employee ideas are sought out in active and ongoing ways. Employees have opportunities to implement projects they and their colleagues create, provided they can make a good case for them. There are opportunities for individual growth and learning. And the company makes an effort to respect the needs of the individuals as people with lives outside their jobs. This kind of loyalty to employees usually engenders a return loyalty to and identification with the organization.

But motivation itself is not enough. Just getting people to work harder or more carefully at the same things is less valuable than getting people to think about how things can be done better. That requires what organizational development experts now call "high-involvement management." The studies on employee ownership and corporate performance could not be clearer on this point. It is the combination of employee ownership and a highly participative management style that distinguishes successful employee ownership companies from less successful ones. For instance, the NCEO found that companies that combine ownership and employee participation in work-level decisions grow 8% to 11% per year faster than they would have been expected to grow without this combination. Subsequent academic studies in New York and Washington confirmed both the direction and magnitude of these findings. A U.S. General Accounting Office study of ESOPs found that productivity growth rates jumped 52% when ownership and participation were combined. Neither ownership nor participation, on their own, make much difference.

Employee involvement can take many forms. Employee task forces, ad hoc and permanent, can be established to solve problems. In larger companies, permanent teams might be set up in discrete work areas, such as warehousing, customer service, marketing, and production. In smaller companies, periodic staff meetings might serve this purpose. Employees can be given greater authority over their own jobs as well.

Aside from getting employees more involved in decisions, companies need to give them the kind of business information they need to make decisions intelligently. At Springfield ReManufacturing in Springfield, MO, for instance, employee owners are taught to read detailed financial and production data. Meeting in workgroups, they go over the numbers then figure out ways to improve them. The company has grown from 119 employees in 1983 to over 1,200 in 2013, while its stock price has gone from 10 cents to over $240. It also is important to share not just financial information with employees, but also "critical" numbers that look at measures of their own work processes. These measurements help employees assess the effectiveness of their efforts and create a kind of "game" environment that is motivating on its own.

1.7 Conclusion

Sharing the rewards of equity has repeatedly been shown to have the potential to improve corporate performance in a variety of ways, especially when shared broadly and in combination with the creation of an "ownership culture." Even when only shared with specific employees, however, it can still help companies attract and retain critical talent. As this chapter has made clear, however, sharing equity cannot be just a "back of the envelope" exercise. It requires careful deliberation about the form equity sharing should take, plan structure, legal and tax issues, and corporate culture. The input of qualified advisors is essential. Just as there is much to gain, there is also much to lose. Disgruntled employees who believe they have not received what they were promised not only will be demotivated themselves but also can poison the atmosphere for other employees. In the worst case, they can sue over the plan. Most lawsuits in this field are generated from just a few kinds of disputes:

- Improper valuations of the stock.
- Failure (or perceived failure) to live up to the terms of the plan.
- Promises made (or perceived) that were not delivered.
- Employees who are terminated prior to their equity interest vesting who claim their terminations were to prevent them from getting an award.

Companies can never fully insulate themselves against these potential problems. Careful plan design, clear and thorough communication with employees, and a willingness to operate the plan in a way that is genuinely fair to all parties can avoid most problems, however. There are few, if any, attributes of a business more important than ownership. Sharing it deserves the most thoughtful consideration.

CHAPTER TWO

Phantom Stock and Stock Appreciation Rights

Joseph S. Adams

Contents

The vast majority of public companies and many private companies reward their key employees with equity-based awards. Many companies make these awards to employees below the key employee level as well. The simple explanation for including equity grants as part of an employee's compensation package is to provide the employee with the incentive to improve the company's financial performance and increase shareholder value.

This objective is straightforward, but the selection of the appropriate equity-based incentive program to achieve the objective is much more complicated. Equity grants come in many forms, such as stock options, stock grants (i.e., "restricted stock" or restricted stock units [RSUs], which may be subject to service-based and/or performance-based restrictions), stock appreciation rights (SARs), and phantom stock.

In addition to choosing the right equity compensation *vehicle,* choosing the right program *design* is equally important. For example:

- Will the employee vest in the grants based on (1) the passage of time, (2) achievement of performance goals, or (3) a combination of the foregoing? (Performance-based awards are increasingly common and preferred by shareholder advocacy groups.)

- Will payments be made while the recipients are employed, or will they be deferred to termination or retirement? (Awards that defer payment for at least some period of time are also becoming increasingly common and are also preferred by shareholder advocacy groups.)

- Which employees should receive the equity-based grants and in what amount? One overarching objective for any company that implements an equity-based program is to *increase* overall shareholder value, not to *dilute* it.

Fundamentally, equity-based programs may be separated into two types of awards:

1. *Appreciation-only awards:* Awards that provide the employee with appreciation, if any, in the value of the underlying stock after the award

date. A classic example is the grant of stock options with an exercise price equal to the fair market value of the underlying stock on the date of grant. If the value of the underlying stock fails to appreciate before the expiration of the option, the employee receives no benefit but is not harmed because no investment was required. SAR grants are similar to stock options, except that the employee generally has no obligation to pay an exercise price, and the award is generally settled in cash (but may also be settled in shares of stock).

2. *Full-value awards:* Awards that provide the employee with the under-lying value of the stock on the award date, as adjusted for positive or negative changes in value following the award date. Restricted stock grants and RSUs are basic examples of this type of award. Phantom stock awards are similar to restricted stock and RSU awards except that the phantom stock award is generally settled in cash rather than shares of stock.

Whether to use appreciation-only awards (such as stock options or SARs) or full-value awards (such as restricted stock/RSUs or phantom stock) depends on whether the company's objective is employee retention or providing a performance incentive. Although it may be an overgen-eralization, programs that provide the employee with the underlying value of the stock (e.g., restricted stock/RSUs or phantom stock) have a stronger retention element, whereas appreciation right programs (e.g., stock options or SARs) are designed to motivate employees to improve financial performance and grow shareholder value. Many companies grant a combination of full-value awards and appreciation-only awards or use performance-based full-value awards in an attempt to accomplish both goals. For example, under an approach increasingly referred to as the "portfolio" approach, employees may receive a combination of stock options, traditional time-based restricted stock, and performance-based cash or equity awards.

As noted above, with each of these two broad types of awards, there is a follow-up question as to whether the award should be settled in cash or in shares.

- In general, public companies are more likely to make actual stock awards, either in the form of a stock option or in the form of a (restricted) stock grant, because (1) their stock is already widely held and the value can be more easily determined, and (2) *significantly* better accounting treatment applies to equity awards that settle in shares rather than cash.

- In contrast, private company owners may prefer not to provide their employees with actual stock awards (for instance, if they want to retain ownership of the actual shares of the company to family members); however they may still be interested in providing employees with an incentive to increase shareholder value with equity-based grants. In that case, a cash-settled SAR or phantom stock award might be more appropriate.

The focus of this chapter is "phantom" equity awards: SARs and phantom stock awards. The chapter will define SARs and phantom stock awards, and distinguish them from each other and from other forms of equity-based grants, such as stock options and stock grants. It will discuss the reasons for implementing a SAR or phantom stock program and the plan design issues that should be addressed. The income tax, securities law, and ERISA consequences of making SAR or phantom stock awards will be discussed in detail because those issues are critically important to the understanding and success of the program. Accounting issues are separately addressed in this book's chapter on accounting.

Practitioners sometimes use the terms "phantom stock," "phantom award," "phantom share plan," "phantom share unit," "phantom stock option," and "SAR" interchangeably to describe an incentive compensation program similar to either a stock option or restricted stock. In this chapter, we will use the term "SAR" to refer to a phantom award that provides a benefit equal only to the *appreciation* (if any) in the underlying stock. The term "phantom stock" award or grant will denote an award similar to restricted stock/RSUs that provides the *full value* of the underlying stock as adjusted for changes in value after the award date.

2.1 Distinguishing SARs and Phantom Stock

A SAR is a right to be paid an amount equal to the difference between (1) the value of the employer's underlying stock on the date of grant, and

(2) the value of the employer's underlying stock on the date of exercise. SARs reward the participant only for the appreciation in the underlying stock value. In contrast, participants in a phantom stock program receive an award of hypothetical shares of company stock and are entitled to payment at a specified date for the full value of the underlying shares at that time, including any positive or negative changes in the value of the shares occurring after the date of grant.

Generally, SARs and phantom stock awards are designed to provide for a cash payment of the benefit rather than payment in the form of shares of company stock. However, as discussed later in this chapter, a SAR may be designed to provide for payment in the form of company shares (a "stock-settled SAR").

2.1.1 Stock Appreciation Rights (SARs)

A SAR is a variation of a stock option. Like a stock option, a SAR provides the grantee with the appreciation, if any, in the value of the underlying stock from the date of grant to the date of exercise. A SAR program has traditionally included the following features:

- Participants do not make a capital investment in the company but instead have a contractual right to receive a future payment from the company, pending satisfaction of the terms and conditions of the program.

- Participants generally have the right to "exercise" and realize the value of their SARs at their election (once vesting has occurred) or upon the occurrence of specified payout events, which can include any or all of the following: a specified date in the future, termination of employment, a change in control, or a public offering.

- Participants are rewarded based only on the excess, if any, of the value of a share of company stock as of a future payout event over the value of a share of company stock as of the date of grant (the "exercise price").

- Participants generally receive a cash payment for their award and do not become shareholders of the company. (However, SAR programs may be designed to provide for payouts in shares of company stock.)

Section 409A of the Internal Revenue Code of 1986, as amended (the "Code")[1] contains deferred compensation tax rules that potentially affect the design of SAR programs. Section 409A provides two general approaches to SARs: (1) the SAR program can be designed to be *exempt from* the requirements of Section 409A, or (2) the SAR program can be designed to *comply with* Section 409A. A SAR program that neither is exempt from nor complies with Section 409A will result in severe tax penalties for participants.

A SAR program can be designed to be exempt from Section 409A, provided the program meets the following requirements:

- The SAR must be granted on what Section 409A calls "service recipient stock" (essentially, common stock of the entity benefiting from the employee's service or a 50%-or-more-owned parent of such entity; special exceptions allow the 50% ownership interest to drop to 20% or more if it is due to legitimate business criteria).

- The SAR must provide for payment not greater than the difference between the fair market value of the underlying common stock on the date of exercise and the fair market value of the underlying common stock on the date of grant. (See section 2.3.3 below for a discussion of the definition of "fair market value" under the final Section 409A regulations.)

- The "exercise price" cannot be less than the fair market value of the company's common stock on the date of grant, and dividend equivalents cannot be accumulated in a manner that decreases the exercise price of the SAR. As discussed in section 2.3.3 of this chapter, ensuring the SARs are granted at fair market value can often be one of the most challenging issues for SARs that are intended to be exempt from 409A. See section 2.3.10 of this chapter for a discussion of dividends.

---

1.   "Section 409A," as referred to here, includes the applicable guidance issued by the IRS for that section. The Section 409A rules are complicated and comprehensive. A complete discussion of Section 409A is beyond the scope of this chapter. However, a brief discussion of the important Section 409A rules that are applicable to SARs and phantom stock is included.

- The number of shares covered by the grant must be fixed at or before the date of grant.

- The SAR cannot provide for a deferral of income beyond the date the SAR is exercised. (This means that when the employee exercises the SAR, the employee must receive a lump-sum cash payment in that taxable year, as opposed to a promise from the employer to pay in installments over several years.)

This chapter refers to a SAR program that meets the above requirements as a "409A-exempt SAR."

If the above requirements are *not* met, then SARs granted or vesting after 2004 must comply with the requirements of Section 409A both in form and in operation.[2] Generally, this means that participants will not be permitted to exercise their SARs freely. Instead, the SAR grant will have to specify the applicable 409A-compliant payment events, which could include one or more of the following:

- a specified payment date;

- separation from service (as defined in Section 409A);

- death;

- disability (as defined in Section 409A); or

- a change in control (as defined in Section 409A, which does *not* include an initial public offering [IPO]).

---

2. SARs that were granted and vested before 2005 are grandfathered—i.e., they remain subject to the old tax rules and are exempt from Section 409A, provided they are not materially modified in any way. Grandfathered SARs can continue to be exercised at the participant's election much the same as the 409A-exempt SARs discussed in this chapter. However, in the event a grandfathered SAR is materially modified in any way, the SAR could automatically become subject to the requirements of Section 409A (and could immediately be in violation of Section 409A if the SAR did not meet the requirements for a 409A-compliant SAR). Accordingly, employers desiring to preserve the grandfathered status of pre-2005 SARs should take care to not inadvertently materially modify those SARs. To avoid an issue about whether SARs may constitute an ERISA retirement plan, many advisers recommend limiting the exercise period for SARs (and stock options) to 10 years; as a result, grandfathered SARs are becoming increasingly rare.

The exercise price and value of the stock underlying a SAR award that complies with the requirements of Section 409A are not required to be valued in accordance with the strict "fair market value" definition that is required for 409A-exempt SARs. Instead, the employer may designate the valuation methodology based on an objective formula (e.g., a multiple of cash flow, EBITDA, operating earnings, net earnings, or book value; or another financial measurement such as a trailing average of the last three years' net earnings) or a good-faith determination by the board of directors. The ability to use an exercise price less than fair market value can be helpful if an employer wants to give a group of employees the benefit of the appreciation of company stock that occurred *before* the date the company granted the SAR. (Note, however, that many equity plan documents prohibit the issuance of SARs and stock options at less than fair market value.) This chapter refers to a SAR program that meets the applicable requirements of Section 409A as a "409A-compliant SAR."

An employer will want to comply with all requirements of Section 409A if its SAR program will not qualify for the exemption because the penalties for failure to comply are extremely onerous. In the event of a failure to comply:

- The employee[3] is taxed on the difference between the exercise price and the value of the stock underlying the SAR in the year of the failure (or the year of vesting, if later) and is subject to a 20% income tax penalty. This tax is payable each year the non-compliant SAR is outstanding (with respect to amounts not previously included in income).

- Interest is also payable, in an amount equal to the underpayment rate plus one percentage point, imposed on the underpayments that would have occurred had the compensation been includible in income for the taxable year when first deferred, or if later, when vested.

---

3. Section 409A applies to nonqualified deferred compensation arrangements involving common-law employees as well as other service providers, such as independent contractors, consultants, and nonemployee directors. When the requirements of Section 409A are addressed in this chapter, the term "employee" or "participant" should be understood to include all types of service providers.

- Note that all "like" arrangements are generally treated as a single arrangement for purposes of these rules. The Internal Revenue Service (IRS) has established nine categories of arrangements:
  - account-based arrangements that provide for nonelective deferrals (i.e., employer-provided amounts);
  - account-based arrangements that provide for employee elective deferrals;
  - non-account-based arrangements;
  - separation pay plans;
  - in-kind benefit or reimbursement plans;
  - split-dollar life insurance arrangements;
  - foreign plans;
  - stock rights (generally including SARs and other forms of equity-based arrangements); and
  - all other types of arrangements not specifically identified above.

  If a failure occurs with respect to an arrangement in *one* of these categories, then *all* other arrangements in that same category are deemed to have failed as well. As a result, the aforementioned penalties would apply to *all* arrangements in that category—even if some or all of those other arrangements comply with Section 409A.

- The penalties for failure to satisfy Section 409A are imposed entirely on the affected employees (although penalties can be assessed on the employer for failure to satisfy applicable reporting and withholding requirements).

If there is a Section 409A failure, the employer must report the deferral amount includible in income on the individual's Form W-2 or Form 1099-MISC (for a nonemployee) for the year in which the failure occurred. Generally, the employer must withhold income tax on the deferral amount in the year of income inclusion, but not later than the date on which the amount is actually or constructively received by the employee. Penalties and interest could be assessed on the individual if the employee fails to include these amounts when he or she files Form 1040 for the applicable year.[4]

---

4. See Notice 2008-115 (as modified by Notice 2010-6) for interim guidance on the applicable reporting and withholding requirements. Also note that the IRS has

In Notice 2008-113 (as modified by Notice 2010-6), the IRS provided various options for correcting certain unintentional failures to comply with Section 409A *in operation*. In Notice 2010-6, the IRS provided similar opportunities to correct failures to comply with Section 409A in form, i.e., *plan document failures*. In addition (and potentially more useful and practical than the formal IRS correction programs), it may be possible to correct 409A violations under the IRS proposed income inclusion regulations with respect to unvested amounts. Depending on the type of failure involved and the timing of correction relative to date of failure, correction may be made under those proposed regulations without any penalty or with reduced penalties.[5] Special reporting requirements apply to employers and employees who intend to take advantage of the relief offered under the two notices (but no such reporting requirements apply to corrections made pursuant to the IRS proposed income inclusion regulations). Note, however, that relief is *not* available under the IRS notices for any exercise of a stock right that otherwise would result in a Section 409A failure.

Table 2-1 briefly summarizes the different design characteristics for 409A-compliant SARs and 409A-exempt SARs.

2.1.2 Phantom Stock

Phantom stock awards are analogous to restricted stock or RSU grants but provide no actual shares to employees. Such awards provide the recipient with the benefit of the full value of the underlying company stock, not just the appreciation in stock value. As a result, such "full value" awards can still reward employees in down markets where the stock price might not increase or might even decrease.

Like a SAR program, a phantom stock program *generally* does not require the participants to make a capital investment in the company.

---

issued proposed regulations addressing the calculation of the amount includible in income under Section 409A in the event of a failure and the calculation of the additional taxes under Section 409A. Once the regulations are finalized and become effective, the final regulations will obsolete Notice 2008-115 with respect to those topics.

5. In 2016, the IRS updated the proposed income inclusion regulations. See 81 F.R. 40569.

Table 2-1. Characteristics of 409A-Compliant SAR vs. a 409A-Exempt SAR

	409A-Compliant SAR	409A-Exempt SAR
Strike price must be no less than fair market value on the date of grant (no formula value)	No	Yes
Participant can receive payments on a vested SAR at any time, at his or her discretionary election to exercise the SAR	No	Yes
Payments may be made over a period of years	Yes (if specified at the outset)	No (payment must be made in a lump sum upon exercise to prevent an impermissible deferral)
Must comply with 409A distribution timing election requirements (including no distribution on an IPO)	Yes	No
Failure to comply with 409A distribution and deferral election requirements in form or operation results in immediate taxation upon vesting and 20% excise tax to the participant	Yes	No
Employer is required to report and withhold income tax, Social Security, and Medicare when payment is made	Yes[a]	Yes

[a] Under Section 409A, any deferral of compensation technically must be reported by the employer in the year of deferral, regardless of whether the amount is then taxable to the employee, although the requirement to report deferrals has not yet gone into effect.

Instead, a participant has a contractual right to receive future payment(s) from the company, subject to satisfaction of the program's terms and conditions.

However, in some circumstances, companies use modified phantom share programs in connection with their executive deferred compensation plans. In such cases, the executive's deferred compensation is deemed "invested" in phantom shares instead of or in addition to other hypothetical investment options such as mutual funds offered under the deferred compensation plan.

The features of a phantom stock award that differ from the features of a SAR award include the following:

- Participants receive an award of units in the form of hypothetical shares of stock, usually with no "exercise price" or required employee investment (except in the case of a deferred compensation plan deemed to be invested in phantom shares).

- Participants have phantom stock units credited to their "accounts"; these accounts most often are bookkeeping entries, as opposed to actual "accounts" custodied with a third party.

- Participants vest in the phantom stock units either over a number of years, or after the company has satisfied certain financial performance metrics, or perhaps after satisfying a combination of time and performance requirements. (If the participant "invested" deferred compensation otherwise payable to him or her in phantom stock units, those units typically are fully vested at the date of grant because the amounts represent compensation that would have otherwise been paid free and clear to the participant absent the deferral.)

- Generally, the participant's phantom stock account will also be credited with any future cash or stock dividend equivalents and any stock splits attributable to the shares although, in some cases, participants are not entitled to dividend equivalents until they vest in the phantom shares.

- Participants are generally entitled to payment at a specified date in the future (e.g., the earliest of a date certain, termination of employment, change of control, or a public offering).

Section 409A generally applies to a phantom stock award granted or vesting after 2004 unless the award pays out shortly after vesting. Specifically, if full payment of an award is made within 2½ months of the end of the employer's fiscal year or the calendar year (whichever is later) in which the award vests, and the arrangement does not require payment on a date or event that could have occurred after the 2½-month period, then the award is exempt from Section 409A as a "short-term deferral."[6] To the extent a phantom stock award is subject to Section 409A (i.e., because it was vested or granted after December 31, 2004, and payments on the units are not considered short-term deferrals), then Section 409A requires phantom stock awards to comply in form and operation with strict distribution and deferral election requirements. For example, the participant's benefit may be paid only upon a permissible distributable event, which includes a specified payment date, separation from service (as defined in Section 409A), death, disability (as defined in Section 409A), and a change of control (as defined in Section 409A, which does *not* include an IPO). Initial deferral elections as well as redeferral elections are subject to specific timing requirements set forth in Section 409A.

---

6. The plan need not affirmatively specify a payment date within the 2½-month period; rather, it must not provide a right to a "deferred payment," meaning one to be made or completed on or after any date or event that may occur after the 2½-month period (Treas. Reg. § 1.409A-1(b)(4)(i)(D)). For example, the final Section 409A regulations provide the example of a bonus awarded on November 1, 2008, that is not subject to a substantial risk of forfeiture and does not specify a payment date or payment deferral. The bonus will constitute a short-term deferral and be exempt from Section 409A if it is paid or made available to the employee on or before March 15, 2009. In contrast, if the employee receives a bonus on November 1, 2008, that is not subject to a substantial risk of forfeiture and provides for a lump-sum payment upon separation of service, the bonus will not qualify for the short-term deferral rule even if paid on or before March 15, 2009, because the plan provides for payment upon an event (separation from service) that may occur after that date. (Treas. Reg. § 1.409A-1(b)(4)(iii), examples 1 and 6.) If a plan complies with the short-term deferral rule but payment is made after the 2½-month period, it may qualify for certain limited exceptions, e.g., unforeseeable administrative delays. (Treas. Reg. § 1.409A-1(b)(4)(ii).)

2.2 When Would an Employer Establish a SAR or Phantom Stock Program?

Before establishing any equity-based compensation program, an employer must assess several threshold issues:

- Which employees will receive the grant? Is the program intended only for executives and key employees or is it intended to be a broad-based program?

- What are the principal objectives of the program, e.g., to encourage retention, increase performance, etc.?

- What is the financial statement (accounting) effect of the program? Does it matter whether the employer is privately held rather than publicly traded?

2.2.1 Key Employee Program vs. Broad-Based Program

Historically, public companies that were interested in providing a broad-based equity compensation program would make stock option grants, create a discounted stock purchase program (under Code Section 423), or contribute company stock to an ESOP (employee stock ownership plan) or 401(k) plan. Under current accounting rules, however, there is no longer an accounting advantage to using stock options; as a result, stock options are less commonly used where a broad-based program is desired. (See chapter 6 of this book for a more complete discussion of equity-based accounting issues.) Also, following a U.S. Supreme Court decision,[7] fiduciary considerations may potentially make it more challenging to offer company stock in 401(k) plans. Therefore, employers desiring a broad-based program are more likely to issue a smaller number of full-value awards, establish a discounted stock purchase program, or establish an ESOP.

SAR and phantom stock awards are typically made only to executives and key employees as part of their long-term compensation packages (in part due to securities law concerns, addressed in section 2.7 of this chapter); however, if such plans are properly designed, they can be made available broadly. Because SAR and phantom stock programs

---

7.   See *Fifth Third Bancorp v. Dudenhoeffer*, 134 S. Ct. 2459 (2014).

often provide for a cash payment at the participant's termination of employment or later, employers would be justifiably concerned that the program could be considered an ERISA retirement plan and, if the program were offered to a broad-based group of employees, it would be subject to all of the ERISA funding, eligibility, vesting, and fiduciary requirements.[8] The more broad-based the program, the more important it will be to ensure that the awards can potentially be exercised or received *during* the grantee's term of employment; heightened ERISA concerns will apply to SAR or phantom plans that allow payout *only* at termination of employment. (The ERISA issues related to SARs and phantom share plans are addressed below in section 2.6 of this chapter.)

2.2.2 Performance vs. Retention

SAR grants and phantom stock awards are generally made to encourage employee retention, provide an incentive to grow shareholder value, or a combination of both.

If the employer's principal objective is to motivate the participants in the program to grow the value of the business, a SAR grant is typically more appropriate. The holder of a SAR award receives no benefit unless the underlying stock value appreciates. As a result, the holder has an incentive to improve financial performance with the expectation of growing the stock value. SAR grants are frequently made subject to a vesting schedule to encourage retention, as well as to provide an incentive to grow value. However, the vesting element of a SAR grant is successful as a retention tool only to the extent that the value of the underlying stock continues to appreciate. If the underlying stock declines in value from the date of grant so that the SARs have no value, the employee might be more willing to entertain an offer to go elsewhere because he or she forfeits no value upon departure. For example, assume an employer makes annual SAR grants with a graded five-year vesting schedule for each grant. Assume further that the underlying stock value appreciates each year during the first four years from $10 to $15, $20, $25, and then $30. If, at the end of five years, the underlying stock is

---

8. "ERISA" refers to the Employee Retirement Income Security Act of 1974, as amended. Section 3(2)(A)(ii) of ERISA defines an "employee pension benefit plan" as any plan that "results in a deferral of income by employees for periods extending to termination of covered employment or beyond."

valued at $40 per share, the employee would have a significant unvested build-up of the early awards. In this case, the annual SAR grants, with their five-year graded vesting schedules, become a valuable retention device. If, however, the underlying stock is more volatile and the value at the end of five years, based on the prior example, drops to $20, the retention value is more limited.

Phantom stock awards are more valuable if the objective is to promote employee retention. Phantom stock awards are typically subject to a vesting schedule for several reasons, not the least of which is to encourage retention. The vesting schedule may be designed with specific objectives in mind. If the employer's sole objective is retention, the forfeiture provisions may be based solely on the passage of time (e.g., a five-year cliff vesting schedule, meaning the award does not vest at all until the end of the fifth year, at which time it becomes 100% vested). In this case, for example, if 500 units of phantom stock are granted when the underlying stock is worth $100 per share, the initial value of the award is $50,000. Even if the value of the stock drops in half to $50 per share, the employee would forfeit significant value if he or she left the company during the five-year period before the units become fully vested. Forfeiture provisions may also be designed to assure that the employee remains in the service of the company during a critical period. For example, the vesting provisions may be tied to the repayment of the company's outstanding senior loan or until the completion of a merger or acquisition. In addition, if the objective is a combination of retention and performance, the size of the award or vesting provisions could be tied to the achievement of certain financial targets (e.g., EBITDA targets). For example, some plans use relatively long vesting schedules (e.g., six to seven years) for grants, but provide accelerated vesting if certain performance measures are satisfied. Alternatively, it would be possible to achieve combined goals of retention and performance incentives by (1) granting a *target* number of phantom shares and then (2) adjusting the number of shares upon which payment will be made based on the company's performance over a specified performance period.

Although it is a broad generalization, it would be more common to see top-level executives receiving SARs (because the executives would be perceived as making policy-type decisions more likely to affect the stock price), next-tier executives receiving a combination of SARs and phantom stock, and still lower-level recipients receiving all phantom stock (to encourage retention).

2.2.3 Public vs. Private Companies

The economic value of a SAR essentially is identical to a stock option. Although SARs do not have the obligation that a stock option holder has to pay the exercise price, today many public company stock option plans have "cashless" exercise (using a broker), "net" exercise, or other features that essentially relieve the option holder from paying cash out of his or her pocket to exercise the shares.

Despite the economic similarities, stock options were historically more popular with public companies because the accounting treatment of stock options was previously much more favorable than the accounting treatment for SARs. Under current accounting rules, however, all companies (public and private) are now required to expense the value of their stock options, which means that SARs may be more attractive for public companies.

- Under the current stock exchange rules, public companies can avoid the shareholder approval requirements by forgoing the issuance of stock if they have a stand-alone, cash-settled SAR program. (However, note that cash-settled SARs trigger additional accounting concerns; see the chapter of this book on accounting.)

- If the SARs are stock-settled SARs, which avoids the need for the holder to produce the exercise price, the plan may use fewer shares than traditional stock options. (See section 2.4 below.)

For private companies, SAR and phantom stock awards are generally more appropriate incentive compensation vehicles than stock options. Closely held businesses (1) may be less concerned about the accounting issues associated with cash-settled SARs, and (2) may have greater concerns about retaining the outstanding shares in the family or a limited group of shareholders for a variety of reasons (e.g., maintaining control within the family) in order to avoid possible securities registration requirements, etc. SAR or phantom stock awards permit a private company to reward employees based on the underlying appreciation in the value of the company's stock but without awarding actual shares of stock.

The use of SARs and phantom stock in privately held S corporations that are owned in whole or in part by an ESOP has increased dramatically.[9] The grant of a SAR or a phantom stock unit is not a grant of an actual share of stock for purposes of the S corporation rules. As a result, such an incentive compensation award does not jeopardize the favorable tax and cash flow structure of an ESOP-owned S corporation, but does motivate management to grow the ESOP's and other S corporation shareholders' value.[10] However, the grant of a SAR or phantom stock unit, or any form of deferred compensation for that matter, must be taken into account in performing certain anti-abuse tests required under Code Section 409(p). Employers that maintain S corporation ESOPs will need to consider the anti-abuse testing requirements when deciding on the level and form of any deferred compensation provided to employees, as the penalties for failure to satisfy those tests are quite severe.

2.3 SAR and Phantom Stock Award Design

Following are a number of plan design issues that must be considered before adopting a SAR or phantom stock award program.

---

9. An employee stock ownership plan (ESOP) is a tax-qualified retirement plan under Code Sections 401(a) and 4975(e)(7).

10. An ESOP trust is an eligible S corporation shareholder and, by virtue of the ESOP trust being a Code Section 501(a) tax-exempt trust and due to a special provision under Code Section 512(e), the portion of the corporate earnings attributable to the ESOP's ownership is not subject to income tax or unrelated business income tax. Because an S corporation is permitted to have only a single class of stock, any S corporation distributions that are made to the taxable S corporation shareholders in order for them to pay the tax on their proportionate share of the corporate earnings must be paid to the ESOP trust even though the ESOP trust is not subject to tax. In order to minimize the required S corporation distributions (and consequent cash outflow), many ESOP-owned S corporations design their management compensation programs to avoid providing a grant of actual stock ownership.

2.3.1 Eligible Participants

The employer (typically through the compensation committee of the board of directors) must determine who is eligible to participate in the program. The employer typically has broad discretion to determine eligibility.

2.3.2 Number of SARs or Phantom Shares

The number of SARs or phantom shares need not be the same for each participant and can be based on any criteria the employer deems appropriate. In setting the number of SARs or phantom shares to be awarded in connection with initial grants, the employer should also consider whether the program will be an ongoing plan, with additional awards being made in the future. The employer may also want to establish a maximum number of SARs or phantom shares that can be granted to all participants in order to limit the percentage interest in future appreciation that will be made available to all participants; public companies will need to do so to comply with the listing requirements of the applicable stock exchange (e.g., NYSE or Nasdaq).

2.3.3 SAR Strike Price

Presuming that the SAR is intended to deliver a benefit from future appreciation only, the SAR strike price would be set at an amount representing the "value" of the employer's common stock at the time of grant. For a 409A-compliant SAR, this value can be set in any manner the employer determines. For a 409A-exempt SAR, this value cannot be less than the fair market value of the employer's stock at the grant date. For this purpose, fair market value is specifically defined under Section 409A.

For publicly traded companies, fair market value can be determined using any reasonable method for deriving fair market value from actual transactions. While the trend is to use the closing price on the date of grant to determine fair market value (particularly for public companies in light of proxy disclosure rules that require additional disclosure for companies that use an alternate approach), the company could also use the last sale price before the grant, the first sale price after the grant, the closing price on the trading day before the grant, or the average of the high and the low sale price on the trading day before the grant or on the grant date. Fair market value can also be determined as the average selling price over a period of up to 30 days before or after the grant, provided that the arrangement specifies the grant recipient, the number of SARs subject to the grant, and the method of determining fair market value (including the period over which the averaging will occur), *before* the averaging period begins. However, an exception applies for grants that must provide for averaging over a specified period pursuant to applicable foreign law.

For companies that are not publicly traded, determining fair market value is more challenging. In general, Section 409A requires use of a reasonable method based on reasonable assumptions. A method will be considered reasonable based on the facts and circumstances as of the selected valuation date, but a reasonable valuation method will likely take into account the value of tangible and intangible assets, the present value of future cash flows, the market value of the company's competitors, and other relevant factors (such as control premiums or discounts for lack of marketability). The final regulations under Section 409A establish three safe harbor methods for determining fair market value:

1. An independent appraisal that meets the requirements for valuing stock held by an ESOP, if that valuation is issued not more than 12 months before the SAR's date of grant.

2. A formula price that is used to determine the price of common stock subject to transfer restrictions, provided that the formula price is used for compensatory purposes and for all transfers of stock to the company or to individuals owning 10% or more of the company's stock. However, use of the formula price is not required for an arm's length transaction constituting the sale of all or substantially all of the stock of the company to an unrelated purchaser.

3. For startup companies with illiquid stock, a reasonable, good-faith valuation that is evidenced by a written report issued by someone with significant training in performing valuations.

The company may use a different valuation method for each separate action; e.g., different methods may be used to determine the SAR strike price and the fair market value of the company stock on exercise. However, once a price or payment amount has been established, it cannot be changed through the retroactive use of a different valuation method.

Many startup and/or pre-IPO companies go through several rounds of financing. As a result, these companies frequently have multiple classes of stock outstanding. Outside investors typically receive preferred stock, while common stock is used for awards to employees of equity-based compensation. When developing the fair market value of a share of common stock for purposes of establishing the exercise price of a 409A-exempt SAR, the value of the company's total equity will need to be allocated between the different classes of outstanding stock. Historically, the fair market value of the common stock was calculated by simply subtracting the aggregate liquidation preference of all classes of preferred stock that were outstanding from the value of total equity (i.e., the common stock was the residual claimant). However, based on current accounting guidance, this approach for allocating equity value (the "current value method") is not considered appropriate for the vast majority of companies.[11] As a result, the use of the current value method may not be considered "a reasonable value method" for purposes of Section 409A.

If the exercise price of a SAR that is otherwise exempt from Section 409A does not meet the above requirements, i.e., if it is less than the fair market value at date of grant, then the SAR will be treated as subject to Section 409A (and will be in violation of Section 409A's requirements) unless the SAR is a 409A-compliant SAR (i.e., it specifies payment dates that comply with Section 409A). However, if the failure to properly set the exercise price is due to an unintentional administrative error, the company may take advantage of relief granted under IRS Notice 2008-113 and reset the exercise price with respect to stock rights that have not yet been exercised to an amount equal to or exceeding fair market value without a violation of Section 409A. To qualify for this relief, the stock price must be reset by the end of the taxable year in which the stock right was granted or, if the affected individual is a non-insider, by the end of the year following the year of grant. Note that any stock

---

11. See the AICPA Practice Aid *Valuation of Privately-Held-Company Equity Securities Issued as Compensation* (AICPA, 2016) for additional detail on equity allocation methods.

rights exercised before reset of the exercise price are not eligible for this relief and will be in violation of Section 409A.

2.3.4 Exercise and Payout Events

A SAR and a phantom stock program differ in the way in which the awards are "exercised" and settled. In addition, the "exercise" of a SAR will differ depending on whether it is a 409A-exempt SAR or a 409A-compliant SAR.

With a 409A-exempt SAR grant, the participant will have the right to exercise vested SARs at any time. Typically, however, the participant will be required to exercise by the earliest of the following events: (1) a fixed or specified date, (2) a certain number of days after termination of employment (e.g., 30 days), (3) a change of control, or (4) an IPO. SARs also frequently expire a short period (although often longer than 30 days) after the holder dies or becomes disabled. Upon exercise, payment will need to be in a lump sum in the same calendar year; i.e., installment payments are not permitted (because that would be treated as an impermissible further deferral).

With a 409A-compliant SAR grant, the participant does not have the right to exercise the SAR freely. Instead, the "exercise" or settlement date must be specified at the time of grant. The SAR program may provide for payment on one or more of the following events: (1) a fixed or specified date, (2) separation from service,[12] (3) death, (4) disability,[13] (5) an unforeseeable emergency,[14] or (6) a change in control (but not an IPO).[15] The program may provide for payment on either the earlier or the later of the specified events. A participant can elect to delay a previously scheduled payment if the participant satisfies the following requirements:

---

12. As defined in Treas. Reg. § 1.409A-1(h), but subject to a six-month wait for specified employees of public companies, as defined in Treas. Reg. § 1.409A-1(i).

13. As defined in Code Section 409A(a)(2)(C) and Treas. Reg. § 1.409A-3(i)(4).

14. As defined in Code Section 409A(a)(2)(B)(ii) and Treas. Reg. § 1.409A-3(i)(3).

15. A change in control may be a change in the ownership of the corporation, a change in effective control of the corporation, or a change in the ownership of a substantial portion of the assets of the corporation, as defined in Treas. Reg. § 1.409A-3(i)(5).

- The election is made at least 12 months before the scheduled payment,

- The election does not become effective until 12 months after it is made, and

- The delay is for an additional period of at least five years. Note, however, that during the five-year period, distributions can be made, if the plan so provides, for any of the other specified distribution events. For example, if the participant is to receive payment on the earlier of age 55 and separation from service, and he or she elects to delay payment (in accordance with the above rules) from age 55 until age 60, payment will be made on the earlier of separation from service and age 60.

Phantom stock awards typically do not give the participant the discretion to elect the timing of payment (unless the phantom stock is a deemed investment of the participant's own deferred compensation). Instead, a traditional phantom stock program will provide that the payments commence on the earliest of: (1) a specified date, (2) a change of control, (3) an IPO, or (4) the termination of employment. However, to the extent that the plan provides for a deferral of payment beyond 2½ months after the later of the end of the employer's taxable year or the end of the participant's taxable year in which the phantom stock award vests, the phantom stock award program must comply with Section 409A (among other things, that would mean that payment could not be made on an IPO because an IPO is not a permissible 409A payment event).

As discussed below, a payout event will only apply to a participant's "vested" SARs or phantom stock awards; unvested awards typically are forfeited for no consideration upon termination of employment (although immediate or continued vesting is provided in certain termination scenarios such as death, disability, retirement, or involuntary termination without cause).

2.3.5 Payout Amounts

For SARs, the amount payable to a participant following exercise or occurrence of a payout event is the product of (1) the number of *vested*

SARs exercised or subject to payout, multiplied by (2) the excess, if any, of the value of a share of the underlying stock as of the date of the payout event over the SAR strike price. As noted earlier, the SAR strike price can be determined in a number of ways. The method used for determining the SAR's value as of a payout event is generally the same as the method used for setting the strike price, but it could be based on different criteria. To be a 409A-exempt SAR, however, the SAR must determine the value as of the exercise date under a valuation method that meets the requirement of Section 409A, as discussed above, and the company must be consistent in its use of a valuation method.

For phantom stock awards, the amount payable is equal to the value of the employer's underlying common stock. If the phantom stock award is payable in a lump sum upon vesting (with no deferral), then typically the employer's common stock is valued on the vesting date. If any portion of the award is deferred beyond the vesting date (either because payments are made in installments or because the recipient has elected to defer receipt), the employer will need to determine the value to be paid at the later date:

- When awards are deferred, many employers opt to determine the award's value by reference to the value of the employer's stock as of the vesting date and then provide for crediting of interest on that value at a specified interest rate; in this case, the participant does not share in increases in the employer's stock value after the applicable vesting or other payment triggering date. (Of course, such a design also protects participants from any subsequent *decreases* in the employer's stock value after the applicable vesting or other payment triggering date, which may not be desirable.)

- Other employers might decide to permit the participant to share in increases in the stock's value while the participant remains employed, but provide for specified interest credits in the event payments are deferred beyond the participant's termination of employment.

Typically, when an award is deferred, the value is transferred to the employer's deferred compensation plan, and the terms of that plan will govern the administration of the award thereafter. The deferred compensation plan should specify the interest crediting rate (if any) to be applied to the award amount, the applicable interest crediting period, and the payment date of the award. Employment (but not income) taxes will be owed (or may have been paid already, depending on the form of the arrangement) on the vested, deferred amounts. However, as long as the interest crediting rate is either the rate on a predetermined actual investment or is otherwise considered reasonable under Code Section 3121(v) and underlying regulations, then the subsequent accrual of interest will not be subject to employment taxes.

Some plans will provide for a different measure of the value of the SARs or phantom stock awards if the payout event is triggered by a change of control (in which case the change of control consideration per share can be substituted for the value based on the method that would otherwise be used) or a liquidity event resulting from an IPO (in which case the market capitalization of the company could be used instead of the general valuation method). Note that a 409A-compliant SAR or phantom stock award must be paid out on a permissible payment date (e.g., a fixed date, termination of employment, or death), and for this purpose an IPO is *not* a permissible payment date. In other words, even though the IPO price could be used for determining the *value* of a 409A-compliant award, the IPO cannot be the trigger for the *payment*.

2.3.6 Vesting

As noted above, a participant typically receives payment only on vested SARs and vested phantom stock awards. Any SARs or phantom stock awards that remain unvested following the employee's termination of employment or other settlement event are typically forfeited for no consideration (although immediate or continued vesting as well as extended exercise periods for SARs is sometimes provided in certain termination scenarios such as death, disability, retirement, or involuntary termination without cause). Vesting schedules can vary by individual in the discretion of the employer.

SARs and phantom stock awards frequently provide for vesting based on the passage of time, meaning the participant will vest on specific dates if he or she remains employed by the employer. However, vesting can also be based on the achievement of company and/or individual performance goals, either alone or in conjunction with a vesting schedule based on the passage of time. Adding a performance feature (e.g., performance-based vesting or adjusting the size of the award based on absolute or relative performance) is becoming increasingly common even for retention awards. For public companies, adding such features can help demonstrate the company's pay-for-performance philosophy and can help reduce the compensation cost for the awards on the company's financial statements if the awards pay out less than originally estimated (see section 2.4 below).

If vesting is based on the passage of time, the vesting schedule should set forth the period over which vesting will occur. This is typically a three- to five-year period, but it can be made longer or shorter if appropriate. The vesting schedule also states whether vesting will occur in equal or unequal installments, and the frequency of vesting (e.g., annually, quarterly, or monthly). In some cases, particularly with awards granted in the technology industry, the vesting frequency may change over time (e.g., annual vesting for the first year, and then monthly or quarterly vesting for the remainder of the vesting term).

2.3.7 Acceleration of Vesting

The employer must determine whether all or part of an unvested SAR or phantom stock unit will automatically vest upon the occurrence of certain events, such as upon a change in control or an IPO. If the vesting of a SAR or phantom stock grant is accelerated upon a change of control of the employer, it may be deemed a "parachute" payment and could possibly expose the employee to an excise tax under Code Section 4999 and may also result in a loss of the deduction for the employer under Code Section 280G. For awards that have been outstanding for at least one year, the Section 280G regulations permit an approach to include less than the full value paid to the employee in the 280G calculations. Awards granted and accelerated all within the same 12-month period frequently require the entire payment amount to be included in the 280G calculations (unless the employer can show that the grant was made in the regular course and not in anticipation of the change of control).

Acceleration of vesting can also occur upon a termination of a participant's employment for certain reasons, such as a termination by the company without "cause," termination by the participant for "good reason," or upon a termination of the participant's employment due to death, permanent disability, or retirement. (The plan document or award agreements should carefully define what constitutes a qualifying "disability" or "retirement" because, absent a clear definition, this could become a point of controversy between the company and a departing employee.) For awards subject to Section 409A, "good reason" terminations may be treated the same as terminations by the company without cause under Section 409A, provided certain conditions are met as described in Treas. Reg. § 1.409A-1(n)(2). If a phantom stock arrangement provides for vesting upon qualifying for retirement but delivery of the cash amount at a later date (e.g., termination of employment or a later stated date), that provision would make the arrangement subject to Section 409A for any participant who will meet the retirement requirements before or during the regular vesting period. This is one very common Section 409A trap because:

- an award can be a 409A-*exempt* short-term deferral when awarded to a younger employee;

- but that same form of award agreement can be subject to 409A when awarded to a retirement-eligible employee.

As a result, employers should carefully consider the consequences of including retirement provisions in their phantom stock awards. For phantom stock arrangements and SARs that are subject to Section 409A, if an acceleration of vesting also accelerates payout to the participant, a violation of Section 409A could occur (particularly if the awards otherwise provided for payment on a specified date), so the employer should consult with its legal advisor in this regard.

2.3.8 Payout Period

Payments of vested SARs and phantom stock units are often made in lump-sum form following the payout event (with or without interest), but installment payments also can be made. Installment payments may be popular for several reasons. First, if payments are made in connection with an employee's termination of employment, paying in installments rather than in lump-sum form can help ensure that the former employee complies with any non-compete, non-solicit, non-disparagement or other restrictive covenants. Second, for payments that are made "in-service" (i.e., to current employees), paying in installments can provide an easy way for the employer to recoup gains if the stock price that formed the basis of a large incentive payment later turns out to be inaccurate (e.g., due to a restatement of the company's financial statements). However, paying in installments will subject the arrangement to Section 409A (and an installment feature cannot be added after the fact to SARs that were originally designed as 409A-exempt).

For arrangements that are subject to Section 409A, the initial election regarding the time and form of payment generally must be specified no later than the time the award is made. If more than one form of payment is available, an employee may change his or her election of the form of payment, subject to the "re-deferral" rules discussed above (see section 2.3.4 of this chapter). By definition, however, a 409A-exempt SAR can make payment only in a lump sum upon exercise of the SAR. Similarly, a phantom stock award that is intended to be exempt from 409A must pay in a lump sum within 2½ months of the later of the end of the employer's taxable year or the end of the participant's taxable year in which the award vests. (See the discussion of the short-term deferral exemption in section 2.1.2 of this chapter.)

The payout form may vary depending on the type of payout event. For example, it is common to provide for a lump sum payout in the event of a change in control or termination of employment due to death or disability. The company sponsoring such a plan might elect, however, to provide for installment payments following separation from service. Under the final Section 409A regulations, an arrangement may not provide for different payout periods for different *types* of separations from service, e.g., voluntary or involuntary (because the IRS perceives potential abuses in the parties changing from installments to lump sums, for example, by how the parties characterize a separation from service as voluntary or involuntary). However, different payout periods may be provided for:

- separations from service either before or after the attainment of a specified age and/or completion of a specified period of service (sometimes referred to as a "toggle" where payment forms will toggle from one form of distribution (e.g., lump sum) to another (e.g., installments), if a participant meets a retirement definition (e.g., attainment of 55 years of age and 15 years of service).

* separation from service within two years after a change in control (as defined in Section 409A).

2.3.9 Forfeiture of SAR or Phantom Stock Award upon Termination for Cause; Violation of Restrictive Covenants

The plan may provide that a participant will forfeit his or her SARs or phantom shares (vested as well as unvested) if the participant's employment is terminated for "cause." Cause can be narrowly or broadly defined.

In addition, the SARs or phantom stock plan can provide for a forfeiture of any remaining installment payouts following the participant's termination of employment in the event the participant violates any applicable restrictive covenants relating to the participant's employment with a competitor, solicitation of employees or customers, or breach of confidentiality requirements following the participant's termination of employment. Note, however, that some states, particularly California, provide very narrow grounds for these "non-compete" clauses (although for the limited number of arrangements subject to ERISA, arguably ERISA would preempt such laws). Note too that courts have ruled that, with respect to such covenants, employment agreements do not automatically also cover agreements for equity awards, which should have their own contractual terms agreed to by both parties.

2.3.10 Dividend Equivalents

A participant can be provided with an additional payout based on any distributions that might have been received by the participant had the SARs or phantom shares been actual shares of company stock.[16] However, such a deemed distribution generally is *not* provided with respect to any actual distributions to the S corporation shareholders

---

16. Any dividends or dividend equivalents that are distributed to the holders of SARs or phantom stock are treated as additional compensation for financial accounting purposes. The employee will be subject to taxation on the dividends or dividend equivalents when the cash is distributed to the employee.

of amounts intended to allow the members to satisfy their tax obligation on allocable income; in other words, if actual shareholders get a
distribution, the SAR or phantom stock holder usually does not get a
distribution nor is he or she deemed to receive one for tax purposes.

If the SARs and phantom share awards (1) are subject to vesting
requirements and (2) carry dividend equivalency rights, then the plan
or award agreement must specify whether the dividend equivalency
rights also will be subject to vesting. If the dividend equivalency rights
are subject to vesting, the amount of dividend-equivalent payments are
usually held in escrow and distributed to the employee when the associated SAR is exercised or the associated phantom share award vests.[17]

Section 409A will apply to dividend equivalents that are credited
after 2004 on unvested awards. To comply with the requirements, the
arrangement must specify the timing of payment of dividend equivalents,
subject to the same general rules as apply to payments of the associated SAR or phantom share award. For a 409A-exempt SAR, however,
the payment of dividend equivalents will not be tied to the exercise of
the SAR but rather will be treated as a separate arrangement subject to
Section 409A for which form and timing of payment must be specified
at the date of grant of the underlying SAR or phantom share award.

2.3.11 Unfunded Plan

No assets need to be segregated or otherwise set aside for payments
under a SAR or phantom stock plan, and participants will be general
unsecured creditors with respect to their interests. This is necessary to
avoid constructive receipt of the SAR or phantom stock award. A "rabbi
trust" could be funded to provide participants with a greater assurance
of payment without triggering constructive receipt. These trusts set aside
funds for employees, but if the funds are needed to satisfy creditors,
they will be used for that purpose before paying employees.

The rabbi trust should be established with the assistance of qualified
legal counsel to ensure the trust does not result in constructive receipt.
(The IRS has issued a model rabbi trust that can be a useful starting

---

17. Shareholder advocacy groups disfavor payment of dividends on performance-
    based awards before the associated performance metrics are satisfied; holding
    such dividends in escrow would be preferred.

point.[18]) In addition, care should be taken when selecting the appropriate funding technique; under Section 409A, certain funding techniques can result in immediately taxation to participants (particularly if the company maintains an "at risk"—i.e., poorly funded—defined benefit plan). Assuming compliance with Section 409A, any funds set aside in a rabbi trust are not deductible by the company until paid out, and any earnings on those funds are taxable to the company.

2.4 Stock-Settled SARs

Under ASC 718, the "fair value" of share-based payment awards must be reported on the employer's financial statements as a compensation expense. The issue is: if an equity compensation expense must be incurred, what is the best or most efficient way to incur that expense?

Stock-settled SARs may be an efficient alternative. A stock-settled SAR is an appreciation right that is settled solely with stock—no cash is paid by the company (or, for that matter, by the employee) other than with respect to any fractional share due the employee. The accounting for stock-settled SARs is as follows:

- If service-vested, this type of award is treated under ASC 718 in the same way as a stock option award, with minor changes.

- If the award is subject to performance-based vesting, the fair value of the award is calculated as if the award were time vested. However, compensation expense is only recognized for the number of awards that actually vest. No compensation expense is recognized for awards that do not vest because the performance goal was not achieved.

- If the performance condition is market-based (based on something related to the price of the company's stock), the fair value of the award will be reduced to reflect the probability that the award may not vest. Unlike the compensation expense for an award that is subject to a performance condition, such as company, unit, or individual economic performance, which can be reversed if the awards do not vest, compensation expense for awards that are subject to market-based vesting cannot be reversed if the condition is not met.

---

18. See IRS Revenue Procedure 92-64.

Table 2-2

	Stock option (cash exercise)	Stock option (cashless exercise)	Stock-settled SAR
Fair market value at exercise	$25	$25	$25
Exercise price	$10	$10	$10
Spread	$15	$15	$15
Number of options/SARs awarded	100	100	100
Aggregate spread	$1,500	$1,500	$1,500
Exercise price paid in cash	Yes	No	N/A
Exercise price paid in shares	No	Yes	N/A
Net shares delivered (taxes not considered)	100	60	60

For purposes of determining the "fair value" of time-vested or performance-vested SARs,[19] the Black-Scholes or lattice valuation analysis is completed in the same manner as for stock options. Thus, 1,000 stock-settled SARs in Company X awarded to employee A on the same date as 1,000 Company X stock options awarded to employee B have exactly the same value for purposes of the earnings charge.

Why would a company consider a stock-settled SAR rather than a stock option? First, it is arguably less dilutive, which is an important consideration at many companies. Consider the three cases in table 2-2.

In the first case, the shareholders have clearly been diluted by 100 shares. In the second case, if the exercise price was paid through a broker-assisted cashless exercise, with 40 shares being sold into the market to cover the exercise price and the employee retaining 60 shares, then again there are 100 new shares in the marketplace. In the case of the stock-settled SAR, the dilution is 60 shares with no possibility of future dilution. Stock-settled SARs also eliminate the need for the optionee to produce the exercise price. Thus, no open market sales are needed to finance the exercise, which most companies would prefer. Similarly, cashless exercise programs would not be needed. Recently,

---

19. The fair value of an award that is subject to a market condition will need to be estimated using a path-dependent valuation model, such as a Monte Carlo simulation. The valuation of awards that are subject to a market condition is highly complex and beyond the scope of this chapter.

many companies have implemented "net-settled" stock options that essentially deliver the same benefit as stock-settled SARs.

There is no economic difference to the employee between a stock option and stock-settled SAR or a net-settled stock option. With each type of award, both the leverage until exercise and the economic benefit (or spread) are the same.

Finally, with a stock option, the company often receives cash for the exercise price. To some extent, therefore, positive cash flow would be adversely affected if stock-settled SARs are used in lieu of stock options. On the other hand, if the exercise price proceeds were used by the company to repurchase shares in the marketplace to minimize the dilution, then the result becomes the same as with the stock-settled SAR.

2.5 Taxation of SARs and Phantom Stock

Assuming a SAR complies with the requirements of Section 409A or is otherwise exempt from those requirements, the SAR does not trigger any taxable income to the employee at the time of grant. Instead, an employee has taxable income when the SAR becomes payable to the employee.

A 409A-exempt SAR is taxed when the employee exercises the SAR and receives payment. The taxation of the income received by the 409A-exempt SAR is governed by the constructive receipt rules under Code Section 451.[20] Treas. Reg. § 1.451-1 provides that "[g]ains, profits and income are to be included in gross income for the taxable year in which they are actually or *constructively* received by the taxpayer" (emphasis added). Treas. Reg. § 1.451-2 goes on to say that "income is not *constructively* received if the taxpayer's control of its receipt is subject to *substantial limitations or restrictions*" (emphasis added). Even though an employee may have the right to exercise and receive payment for a 409A-exempt SAR at any time, in Revenue Ruling 80-300, the IRS held that this right does not result in constructive receipt of income. The IRS reached this holding because it concluded that there is a "substantial

---

20. These rules also continue to apply to grandfathered SARs. While 409A-compliant SARs do not permit free exercise by the participant, the traditional constructive receipt rule also continue to apply to those SARs. The tax result is the same, i.e., payments are taxable to the participant as received.

limitation" on the exercise and payout of a SAR. The economic position of the holder of a SAR is significantly changed after it is exercised and the holder receives payment. Before the exercise and payment, the holder enjoys the prospect of benefiting from all future appreciation in the underlying stock. If, instead, the holder were to exercise the SAR, take his or her profit and immediately reinvest it in the same stock, he or she would be entitled to future appreciation on a smaller number of shares. Suppose, for example, that an employee holds SARs with respect to 1,000 shares whose market value was $10 on the date of grant. The stock's value rises to $20 per share. If the employee were to cash out the SARs, he or she will receive $10,000, with which the employee can purchase only 500 shares. Thereafter, each one-dollar rise in the stock value will gain the employee only $500, compared to $1,000 that he or she had before the cash-out. The IRS concluded that the leverage provided in the SAR creates a substantial limitation to its exercise and, as a result, the employee has no taxable income until the SAR is exercised and payment is made.[21]

The income from a 409A-compliant SAR is taxed only as and to the extent payment is made (even if the employee receives payment for the SAR's value over a period of years).

Phantom stock awards are taxable to the employee when paid, assuming the awards satisfy applicable requirements of Section 409A or are exempt from Section 409A because they qualify as "short-term deferrals." A phantom stock award will be treated as a "short-term deferral" and thus be exempt from Section 409A as long as the award is paid within 2½ months of *the later of* the end of the employer's taxable year or the end of the participant's taxable year in which the award vests, and the arrangement does not require payment upon a date or event that could occur after the 2½-month period. (See the discussion in section 2.1.2 of this chapter.) If the award does not meet the "short-term deferral" rule, then the award must define the date upon which the award will be paid (e.g., the earlier of five years from the date of grant and termination of employment, death, disability, or change in control). The phantom stock award may be designed to permit the employee to elect when to receive payment, but the employer must be careful to ensure that providing such an election does not result in constructive receipt of the

---

21. See PLR 8829070 for the IRS's explanation of this point.

value of the shares and that the election otherwise complies with the deferral requirements of Section 409A.

From the employer's standpoint, the timing of its tax deduction is the same for SARs and phantom stock awards: The employer is entitled to a tax deduction at the time and in an amount equal to the income realized by the employee. However, if the employer's and employee's taxable years differ, then the employer is entitled to a tax deduction in the employer's taxable year in which the employee's taxable year ends.[22]

For Social Security, Medicare, and federal unemployment tax purposes:

- employees are deemed to have compensation income under a SAR when payment is made, and

- employees are deemed to have compensation income under a phantom stock program on the later of the date that the services relating to the compensation are performed or the date that there is no longer a substantial risk of forfeiture.[23]

SARs and phantom stock awards have been attractive forms of equity-based compensation programs for S corporations because they are not treated as outstanding stock and are not deemed to be a second class of stock.[24] For purposes of those rules, SARs and phantom stock are tested under the deferred compensation rules, which provide that a grant will not be deemed to be "stock" if it (1) does not convey the right to vote; (2) is an unfunded and unsecured promise to pay compensation in the future; (3) is issued to an employee or an independent contractor in connection with the performance of services; and (4) is issued under a

---

22. Code Section 162(a). If a SAR is settled in cash, the exercise of the SAR fixes the employer's liability so that an accrual basis taxpayer can deduct the liability under the "all events" test. However, if the payment of cash is not fixed at the time, no deduction is allowed under Code Section 404(a)(5) until the cash is paid. If the SAR benefit is satisfied with the payment of shares of stock, the employer will be entitled to a deduction at the time the service provider has income under Code Section 83(h).

23. Code Sections 3121(v)(2) and 3306(r)(2).

24. Code Section 1361(b)(1)(D).

plan with respect to which the employee or independent contractor is not taxed currently on income.[25]

If the S corporation maintains an ESOP, however, equity-based compensation programs and other deferred compensation are taken into account in determining whether the ESOP satisfies the Code's anti-abuse rules.[26] Section 409A provides some relief by permitting accelerated distributions of deferred compensation in certain instances to avoid a failure of those anti-abuse rules.[27]

2.6 ERISA Coverage

A SAR or phantom stock plan is designed to provide participants with deferred compensation the value of which is tied to the value of the employer's stock. Whether a deferred compensation benefit of this sort is an "employee pension benefit plan" within the meaning of ERISA is a fact-specific determination.

An "employee pension benefit plan" is defined as a plan or program maintained by an employer that by its express terms or as a result of the surrounding circumstances results in a deferral of income by the employees for "periods extending to the termination of covered employment or beyond."[28] An ERISA pension benefit plan must comply with ERISA's strict vesting, funding, and disclosure requirements, as well as ERISA's heightened fiduciary duties of loyalty, care, and prudence.

ERISA provides a frequently used exemption for a "top-hat" plan. Under this exemption, a deferred compensation plan is exempt from the basic ERISA requirements if the plan is unfunded and maintained primarily for the purpose of providing benefits to a select group of management or highly compensated employees.[29] Many SAR and phantom stock plans could comply with this "top-hat plan" exemption.

---

25. Treas. Reg. § 1.1361-1(b)(4); see also PLR 9803023.

26. Code Section 409(p).

27. Treas. Reg. § 1.409A-3(j)(4)(x).

28. ERISA Section 3(2)(A)(ii).

29. ERISA Sections 201, 301, and 401. See Sikora v. UPMC, 153 F. Supp. 3d 820, 830 (W.D. Pa. 2015); see also *Bond v. Marriott International, Inc.* (4th Cir. 2016) (unpublished opinion available at http://www.ca4.uscourts.gov/Opinions/ Unpublished/151160.U.pdf. If the plan is designed as a "top hat plan," the

If, however, the employer desires the SAR or phantom stock plan to benefit a broad cross-section of employees, the "top hat" exemption would not apply. In this case, the key issue is whether the plan has the effect of systematically deferring income until termination of employment or beyond.[30] To avoid ERISA coverage, the employer should design the broad-based SAR or phantom stock plan to compensate participants while they are actively employed rather than deferring the income to termination of employment or retirement. For example:

- A plan that is intended to compensate employees while they are still employed and provides that each year's award pays out five years later should not be considered an ERISA retirement plan.[31]

- On the other hand, a plan that results in the majority of the recipients retaining their benefits through their late fifties and up to their retirement is likely to be an ERISA plan.[32]

- Also, a plan that permits recipients to elect to defer distributions to termination of employment or beyond could be considered an ERISA plan.[33]

2.7 Securities Law Issues

SAR and phantom stock programs have generally been designed so that the holder has only the right to a cash payment at a specified date. SARs

---

sponsor must be sure that the underlying benefit is not considered to be "funded." See *Dependahl v. Falstaff Brewing Corporation*, 653 F.2d 1208 (8th Cir. 1981) (court held excess benefit plan was "funded" with whole-life insurance policies. The court stated: "Funding implies the existence of a res separate from ordinary assets of the corporation . . . [In this case,] the employee may look to a res separate from the corporation in the event the contingency occurs which triggers the liability of the plan.").

30. ERISA Section 3(2)(A)(ii); see also 29 C.F.R. § 2510.3-2(c).

31. See *Murphy v. Inexco Oil Company*, 611 F.2d 570 (5th Cir. 1980); *In re Tucher Freight Lines, Inc.*, 789 F. Supp. 884 (S.D. Mich. (S.D. Mich. 1991); see also DOL Advisory Opinion 95-23A (August 30, 1995).

32. See *Darden v. Nationwide Mutual Insurance Company*, 922 F.2d 203 (4th Cir 1990); *Petr v. Nationwide Mutual Insurance Company*, 712 F. Supp. 504 (D. Md. 1989).

33. See *Tolbert v. RBC Capital Markets Corp.*, 758 F.3d 619 (5th Cir. 2014).

and phantom stock awards that pay out solely in cash do not involve the issuance of any security, so no securities registration is required. However, the following are some securities law issues to consider.

2.7.1 Registration and Disclosure

If the holder of a SAR or phantom stock unit is entitled to elect to receive payment in either stock or cash and controls the time at which the shares or cash will be distributed, the holder is treated as making an investment decision when he or she makes the election.[34] By exercising a SAR and making an election with respect to the form of payment in the case of a SAR or phantom stock unit, the holder is effectively buying the shares received or, if he or she receives cash, selling derivative rights to the stock. Consequently, SARs and phantom stock awards that are potentially payable in stock and for which the holder controls the timing and manner of payment must be registered under the Securities Act of 1933 (the "1933 Act"), unless an exemption from registration exists.

While the SEC has not specifically addressed the registration requirements for SARs and phantom stock that are not eligible for an exemption, the best practice would be to file a registration statement covering a SAR not later than the first date at which the SAR is exercisable and file a registration statement covering a phantom stock award not later than the first date at which the phantom stock is vested or payable. Companies with publicly traded securities may use a Form S-8 registration statement to register the SAR or phantom stock programs. This form offers the simplest method of compliance with the 1933 Act. Under the Form S-8, the actual registration statement merely entails the cover sheet, certain required undertakings, the exhibit sheet, and the signature pages. Although a prospectus is required, the content of the prospectus is limited in scope, generally requiring the disclosure of the material terms of the SAR or phantom share award plan or program. The prospectus, however, is not required to be filed with the registration statement.

Private companies that grant SARs or phantom stock awards that permit the holder to elect a stock or cash payment may rely on one or

---

34. An elective choice of this sort (cash or stock payment) would be an unusual (but not impossible) plan design feature for a SAR or phantom stock program.

more of several exemptions from registration: (1) a private placement;[35] (2) an offering in compliance with Regulation D (commonly referred to as a "Reg D Offering");[36] or (3) Rule 701.[37] Of these exemptions, Rule 701 provides the greatest flexibility with the least amount of burden.

2.7.2 Section 16 Compliance

For public companies, SARs and phantom stock awards are derivative securities that are reportable under Section 16(b) of the Securities Exchange Act of 1934. The grant of a SAR or phantom stock award will be an exempt transaction for purposes of Section 16(b) if granted with the approval of the entire board of directors or a committee of the board consisting solely of two or more nonemployee directors. In addition, the SAR grant is exempt if it is held, or if any shares issued upon its exercise are not sold, for six months from the date of grant.[38]

2.7.3 State Blue Sky Laws

State securities or "blue sky" laws may also affect the design and/or grant to employees of SARs or phantom share awards. Most states have exemptions similar to Rule 701, a Regulation D offering, or a private

---

35. Section 4(2) of the 1933 Act exempts from registration any offer to sell not involving a public offering of the securities.

36. Regulation D is an exemption that provides a safe harbor with respect to a private placement under Section 4(2). Pursuant to Regulation D, securities may be offered for sale to up to 35 nonaccredited investors, plus an unlimited number of accredited investors. 17 C.F.R. §§ 230.501 et seq.

37. Rule 701 allows companies to make offers to sell their securities to employees under compensatory plans with limited restrictions and limited filing requirements. The maximum value of securities that may be sold in a 12-month period in reliance on Rule 701 is an amount equal to the greatest of (1) $1 million, (2) 15% of the employer's total assets, and (3) 15% of the outstanding securities of the class being offered. Offerings in excess of $10 million require the issuer to provide certain disclosure to each purchaser. Note that none of these exemptions provides an exemption from the general provisions of federal common law and state securities laws against fraud or deception in the sale of securities. Thus, disclosure of liabilities and adequate financial information is required to preserve a defense against a claim of fraud if the securities decline in value.

38. 17 C.F.R. § 240.16b-3(d).

placement. However, several states, in particular California,[39] have special requirements that the SAR or phantom share awards must satisfy in order to conform with such exemptions. Some states have requirements that the SAR or phantom share awards must be filed with an appropriate regulatory body. Thus, it is important to make sure that the grant of SAR or phantom share awards not only complies with federal securities laws but also meets the requirements for applicable state securities law exemptions.

---

39. California Corporations Code Section 25102(o) provides an exemption similar to Rule 701. However, the regulations issued under Section 25102(o) contain several requirements that must be contained in the plan in order for the exemption to be met. See California Corporations Code Regulation Section 260.140.42.

CHAPTER THREE

Restricted Stock Awards, Units, and Purchases

Barbara Baksa

Contents

A restricted stock arrangement provides the recipient with the right to acquire a specified number of shares of stock. The recipient may be required to pay for the stock or may receive it at no cost. If the stock must be purchased, the purchase price is typically the fair market value of the company's stock on the date of grant ("grant" here is used in its formal sense in a restricted stock plan and can refer to either the award of shares for no consideration or the award of the right to buy shares).

Privately held companies that offer restricted stock to their employees typically require the employees to pay full fair market value for the stock. While the company is private, the value of the stock is often relatively low, so that this price is not a significant obstacle to the employee's purchase, and requiring payment can alleviate administrative difficulties that might otherwise arise from the tax treatment of these arrangements. In addition, the employee's investment provides the company with additional cash that could be valuable to the operation of the company.

In a publicly held company, however, there is little incentive to employees to purchase restricted stock at full fair market value, since, presumably, they could buy the same stock on the open market at essentially the same price without regard to the restrictions. Because of this, publicly held companies that offer restricted stock to their employees typically offer it at no cost or at a discount from the current fair market value.

Unlike employee stock options, which might provide up to 10 years for employees to purchase stock, the recipient of restricted stock must make a decision with respect to acquiring the shares of stock within 10 to 30 days after the arrangement is granted. Where payment for the shares is required, generally the recipient may purchase the shares of stock with cash, a promissory note, or other consideration approved by the company.

Alternatively, the company may simply award restricted stock at no cost to employees. If the stock is awarded at no cost, it may be issued at grant subject to restrictions or may be awarded in the form of units that convert to shares of stock (usually on a one-for-one basis) upon distribution to the recipient.

In both publicly and privately held companies, the arrangement is granted subject to restrictions or risk of forfeiture. That is, the recipient's right to the shares of stock covered by the restricted stock arrangement (i.e., the "restricted shares") is contingent on continued service or contribution to the company for a specified period of time (the "vesting period"). Alternatively, the recipient's right to the restricted shares may be contingent upon the achievement of one or more specified performance goals.

If shares are issued at grant, the restricted shares are not transferable and are usually held by the company in an escrow or custodial arrangement during the vesting period. The recipient may have some of the rights of a shareholder with respect to the restricted shares during the vesting period, including the right to vote and to receive dividends. If the recipient fails to satisfy the vesting conditions (for example, by terminating employment before the completion of the vesting period or failing to achieve the performance targets), the company has the right to repurchase any unvested (unearned) restricted shares at a price equal to the shares' initial cost to the recipient. If, at the time of forfeiture, the shares are worth less than the recipient's initial investment, the repurchase price is typically the current fair market value of the stock. This repurchase right lapses cumulatively over the vesting period.

If the award is granted in the form of units, no shares are issued until the units are converted into stock (upon distribution to the recipient). The recipient does not have voting or dividend rights with respect to the underlying stock until this time (although some companies pay dividend equivalents on unvested units). If the recipient fails to satisfy the vesting requirements, the units are simply forfeited with no payment to the recipient. Restricted stock units are also sometimes payable in cash, where the cash payment is based on the value of the underlying stock. This chapter discusses awards that are payable in stock only; the tax, legal, accounting, design, international, and administrative considerations applicable to awards payable in cash may differ.

Table 3-1 (see page after next) compares the various forms of restricted stock.

3.1 Advantages of Restricted Stock

From the company's perspective, restricted stock arrangements have many of the strengths of employee stock options. They enhance the company's ability to recruit and retain talented employees. They may

Characteristics of Restricted Stock Plans

- Employees are generally required to accept awards or purchase shares (if payment is required), within 10 to 30 days of grant.

- If offered by a privately held company, the purchase price is usually at or near the fair market value of the company's stock on grant date. If offered by a publicly held company, the shares are usually awarded at no cost or at a discount.

- Shares or units are usually subject to vesting restrictions. If shares are issued at grant, they are usually held in escrow until vested.

- Upon termination of employment, unvested shares are forfeited or subject to repurchase at the employee's original cost.

- Both purchases and awards (of both stock and units) are generally subject to tax upon vesting, at which time the difference between the purchase price (if any) and the fair market value of the stock is treated as compensation income to the employee.

- If shares are issued at grant, an election under Section 83(b) of the Internal Revenue Code (the "Code") can be filed at the time of purchase or award. If a Section 83(b) election is filed, the difference, if any, between the purchase price and the fair market value of the company's stock on the purchase or award date is compensation income to the employee. No taxable income is recognized on the vest date.

- If the award is made in the form of units, it may be possible to defer payment of income tax by deferring distribution of the underlying shares. The deferral and distribution is subject to Section 409A of the Code, and employment taxes (FICA and FUTA) will still be due upon vesting.

- Withholding tax obligations arise at the time compensation income is recognized.

- The company receives a tax deduction equal to the compensation income recognized by employees.

Table 3-1. Comparison of Various Forms of Restricted Stock

Restricted Stock Purchase	Restricted Stock Award	Restricted Stock Units
Price is typically equal to market value at grant.	Price is typically $0 or a nominal amount.	Price is typically $0 or a nominal amount.
Shares are issued at grant and held in escrow until vested.	Shares are issued at grant and held in escrow until vested.	Shares are not issued until distribution.
Underlying shares are considered issued and outstanding before vesting.	Underlying shares are considered issued and outstanding before vesting.	Underlying shares are not considered issued and outstanding until distribution.
Recipient has voting rights even before vesting.	Recipient generally has voting rights even before vesting.	Recipient does not have voting rights until distribution.
Recipient typically receives dividends on unvested shares.	Recipient typically receives dividends on unvested shares.	Recipient does not receive dividends on unvested units but may earn dividend equivalents.
Section 83(b) election can be filed at grant.	Section 83(b) election can be filed at grant.	Section 83(b) election is not applicable.
Taxation cannot be deferred beyond vesting.	Taxation cannot be deferred beyond vesting.	Taxation can be deferred beyond vesting if distribution of underlying shares is deferred (either mandatorily or through a valid deferral election).

be granted to specific individuals in different amounts and subject to different terms and conditions, enabling the company to tailor the arrangements to meet specific corporate objectives. If the arrangements require an immediate purchase of stock, they result in cash inflow to the company (assuming that the employees do not tender payment in the form of a promissory note or previously acquired shares of stock). The company may receive a corporate tax deduction (for compensation expense) when the restricted shares vest. And, as with other equity arrangements, restricted stock arrangements allow the company to align the interests of the employees with those of its shareholders.

In addition, restricted stock arrangements, with the exception of grants where vesting is contingent on market conditions, are much easier to value for financial statement purposes than are stock options or stock appreciation rights. The fair value of service or performance-based restricted stock and units is simply the fair market value of the underlying stock less any amount required in payment under the terms of the grant. No complicated modeling tools or other valuation methods are required, nor is it necessary to estimate future expectations for the company's stock or employee behavior. While companies often feel it is necessary to seek outside assistance to determine the fair value of stock options and stock appreciation rights, it is unlikely that such assistance would be needed for either service or performance-based restricted stock or units.

For employees, restricted stock provides a relatively low-risk way to acquire and maintain an equity interest in the company. It may provide a strong motivational tool, as employees recognize that their individual performance can directly affect the company's prospects and, therefore, the value of the company's stock.

3.1.1 Advantages Distinct to Restricted Stock Issued at No Cost

Restricted stock and units that are awarded at no cost offer a distinct advantage over employee stock options and stock appreciation rights in that, regardless of fluctuations in the company's stock price, these arrangements always retain some value (barring, of course, bankruptcy or some other unfortunate turn of events in which the company's stock becomes worthless). Employee stock options and stock appreciation rights have little value (and do little to retain and motivate employees) when the current value of the company's stock is less than the option price. This disadvantage does not apply to restricted stock and units that are awarded at no cost; because employees do not pay for the underlying stock, whether the company's stock price increases or decreases, the awards always have value.

Some practitioners believe that restricted stock awarded at no cost provides a better incentive for long-term growth since these arrangements are not as leveraged as stock options (and therefore do not benefit as much from short-term spikes in stock value).

Finally, some practitioners believe that employees place a higher value on stock that they receive at no cost than they do stock options or stock appreciation rights, which inherently involve more risk. Where this is the case, restricted awards can be significantly smaller than stock options, reducing the company's overall expense for the plan (even though the per-share expense may be greater than for stock options) and plan dilution.

3.2   Disadvantages of Restricted Stock

There can also be drawbacks to using restricted stock arrangements as a compensation tool. The grant of restricted shares gives rise to a compensation expense if the purchase price is less than the fair market value of the company's stock on the date of purchase. If the shares are awarded at no cost, then the entire value of the grant is treated as a compensation expense. Moreover, if the recipient files a Section 83(b) election in connection with the purchase of the restricted shares at fair market value, the company may forego a compensation expense deduction for income tax purposes. And, as with any equity arrangement, the issuance of restricted stock will dilute the interests of the company's shareholders.

If employees are required to pay for the restricted stock, employees are making an immediate investment decision, and assuming the risk of a decline in the value of the stock before the stock is transferable. Employees may be unwilling to make this investment (especially when their ability to sell the stock is restricted subject to vesting requirements) and may incur substantial risk by doing so. Moreover, if the granting company is privately held, the restricted shares will be illiquid, further limiting the employee's ability to realize any appreciation in the value of the shares.

Unlike employee stock options, restricted stock arrangements offer employees little control over when the stock is subject to taxation. If a Section 83(b) election is not filed, each vesting date under the arrangement is a taxable event to the employee. Upon vesting, employees recognize compensation income equal to the difference, if any, between the purchase price of the restricted shares and the current fair market value of the company's stock, with a commensurate withholding tax obligation. Only with an award in the form of units is there any opportunity for the employee to defer taxation past vesting, and even there the deferral is severely limited by Section 409A of the Code. The stock may vest at a time when the employee is already in a higher than normal tax bracket or when the employee does not have cash available to pay the withholding taxes. In some cases, employees may be forced to sell some of the restricted shares to satisfy this tax liability. When vesting occurs during blackout periods or other periods where employees are not able to sell the stock, satisfying the tax liability can be particularly problematic for employees. For companies that offer restricted stock at no cost, collecting the requisite tax withholding and assisting employees with their tax obligations is often one of the most significant administrative challenges that must be overcome; this is especially true when the plan is offered to a large group of employees.

3.2.1 Disadvantages Distinct to Restricted Stock Issued at No Cost

There are additional disadvantages associated with restricted stock arrangements that are awarded at no cost, the most obvious of which is the lack of cash flow produced for the company. Stock options and restricted stock purchase arrangements will provide the company with capital that can be used for operations or other purposes; restricted stock and units awarded at no cost do not share this advantage.

Where the awards vest solely on continued service, they may be viewed unfavorably by shareholders as a giveaway to employees, since employees will not need to do anything other than remain employed with the company to earn the awards.

3.3 Restricted Stock Plan Design

When a company decides to implement a restricted stock program, management usually instructs the human resources department and/or benefits personnel to design an appropriate plan. Typically, the plan's structure, as well as specific terms and conditions, are determined in consultation with the company's legal counsel, accountants, and outside compensation or benefits specialists. Factors taken into consideration in designing the plan include the cost to the company and proposed participants, the potential liquidity for participants, and the income tax and financial accounting consequences arising from the operation of the plan.

While a few companies adopt a separate plan under which only restricted stock can be offered, most companies adopt "omnibus" plans, under which a variety of equity vehicles, including restricted stock, can be offered. The omnibus plan clearly provides the company with maximum flexibility, allowing the company to determine what types of arrangements to offer to employees as the arrangements are granted.

In most cases, the company's legal counsel prepares the actual plan documents. Once management has approved the restricted stock plan, it is presented to the company's board of directors for consideration and adoption. Under the corporate laws of most states, the board has the authority for all issuances of the company's stock, so board approval is generally required before implementing a restricted stock plan.

Following adoption by the board of directors, the plan is usually submitted to the company's shareholders for approval. Shareholder approval may be a requirement under state corporate law or the company's charter documents. If the company is publicly traded, shareholder approval is almost always required by the exchange where the company's shares are listed. Even where shareholder approval is not required, there may be advantages to obtaining shareholder approval of the restricted stock plan for tax and/or securities law reasons.

Most restricted stock plans expressly provide that the board of directors can amend the plan from time to time, or even suspend or terminate the plan before the expiration of the plan term. Any such action is typically accomplished through a formal board resolution and results in an appropriate revision of the restricted stock plan document.

The restricted stock plan may expressly provide that certain types of plan amendments must be approved by the company's shareholders before becoming effective. These include amendments to increase the number of shares of stock authorized for issuance under the plan, to change or expand the categories of eligible participants in the plan, to extend the term of the plan, to reduce the purchase price at which shares of stock may be sold under the plan, or to increase the benefits available to participants in the plan. Even if not expressly required in the plan, it may be necessary to submit certain amendments for shareholder approval to ensure compliance with relevant laws or listing requirements.

3.3.1 Plan Participation/Eligibility

Restricted stock arrangements are not subject to statutory eligibility restrictions. Therefore, restricted stock can be offered to nonemployees—such as outside directors, consultants, advisors, and other independent contractors—as well as to employees (both full-time and part-time), subject only to any eligibility restrictions contained in the restricted stock plan itself. Moreover, restricted stock can be offered pursuant to a restricted stock plan or as individual arrangements outside any formal plan.

Under a restricted stock plan, both the selection of recipients and the timing of grants are typically at the discretion of the board of directors. Companies use a wide variety of different approaches and/or policies for determining which employees should receive restricted stock. In some instances, only senior management is eligible to receive restricted stock. Other companies grant restricted stock to some or all managers. Still other companies grant restricted stock to all employees, regardless of job description.

3.3.2 Number of Shares Granted

Under a restricted stock plan, the number of shares of stock offered to each employee is typically determined by the board of directors or the compensation committee. Companies use a wide variety of different approaches and/or policies to determine the size of a restricted stock arrangement. For example, the number of shares of stock may be determined on an employee-by-employee basis, by job classification or based on the company's overall performance over a specified period of time.

Many companies use a value-based approach to determine the number of shares of stock to offer to each employee. Under this approach, the company determines an aggregate value of stock that it wishes to grant to each employee. This aggregate value may be a percentage of the employee's salary or overall compensation package or may be determined using another approach (e.g., all employees at a specified salary grade or job code may receive awards roughly equivalent in value). There are no restrictions on how the company determines the aggregate value that will be awarded to employees, nor is there a requirement to treat all employees equally.

The aggregate value allocated to each employee is divided by the value of the stock at the time of grant to determine the number of shares to be awarded. The per-share value of the stock for this purpose may be the same value used for accounting and other purposes, but this is not required. Some companies choose to use a prior day's value for administrative ease; other companies use a multi-day average to mitigate the impact of stock price volatility on award sizes. Of course, where the value used to determine the grant size differs from the value used to determine award expense for accounting purposes, this will result in a discrepancy between the value of the award communicated to employees and the value recorded for financial statement purposes (and, in the case of named executive officers, the value disclosed in the proxy statement).

3.3.3 Purchase Price

Restricted stock can be offered at no cost, or employees can be required to pay for the stock. If employees are required to pay for the stock, the price can be the full fair market value of the stock or can be discounted.

3.3.4 Expiration

If the stock must be paid for, employees usually have a limited period of time in which to complete the purchase. Typically, a decision to acquire the restricted shares must be made within 10 to 30 days after the restricted stock purchase arrangement is granted.

Although not legally required when restricted stock is offered at no cost, for administrative purposes, the company may require employees to accept the offer of stock within 10 to 30 days after the offer is made. While the company could forego requiring acceptance from employees in this situation, it may be advisable to require employees to acknowledge the terms and conditions under which the stock is offered.

3.3.5 Vesting

The process of earning the restricted shares is commonly referred to as "vesting." Generally, a vesting schedule provides that, at the completion of designated intervals, or the satisfaction of established performance criteria, a predetermined percentage or ratio of the restricted shares are earned and thereafter may be transferred by the employee. These interim dates are called "vesting dates." Vesting is typically measured from the date the restricted stock is granted, but it can be measured from any date the company deems appropriate (such as an employee's hire date).

Companies adopt a vesting schedule that best suits the incentive or other objectives of their restricted stock plan. Most restricted stock plans provide for annual vesting schedules; that is, the restricted shares vest in equal annual installments over a period of several years (typically, three, four, or five years). In some instances, monthly or quarterly vesting schedules are used, but because the administrative process of assessing and collecting the taxes that become due as the shares vest can be burdensome, companies may want to avoid vesting schedules where the shares vest in frequent intervals. Where restricted stock is offered at no cost to employees, frequent and/or short-term vesting can be viewed negatively from a corporate governance perspective. A recent survey conducted by the National Association of Stock Plan Professionals (NASPP) and Deloitte Consulting[1] found the following practices with respect to vesting of service-based restricted stock and unit awards:

- 72% of survey respondents report that awards vest on a graded, incremental schedule, rather than all at once, on a "cliff" schedule.

- Of those companies that report using a graded vesting schedule, 44% report that awards vest over three years and 43% report that awards vest over four years; 85% report that awards vest annually over this period.

- Of those companies that report using a cliff vesting schedule, 81% report that awards vest over three years.

Restricted awards can also vest upon the achievement of specified company performance goals (such as earnings per share, revenue, or profitability targets) or based on work unit, individual, departmental, or divisional performance goals. Where restricted awards are performance-

---

1. 2016 Domestic Stock Plan Design Survey, co-sponsored by the NASPP and Deloitte Consulting LLP.

based, the awards are most commonly issued in the form of restricted stock units. Because restricted stock purchases and restricted stock awards involve issuing the stock at grant and would require cancellation of the issued stock in the event that the performance goals are not achieved, it is administratively burdensome to attach performance-based vesting to these arrangements.

3.3.6 Termination of Employment

If an employee terminates employment before the restricted shares have vested, the unvested shares or units are typically forfeited or subject to repurchase by the company. Generally, the terms and conditions of forfeiture and the company's unvested share repurchase right are set forth in the restricted stock agreement. Where repurchase is necessary, the company usually must notify the employee in writing within a specified period of time (60 to 90 days following termination is common) of its decision to repurchase some or all of the unvested shares. To avoid a situation where the notice of repurchase is inadvertently overlooked, some plans provide that the company's repurchase option is automatically exercised unless the recipient is notified otherwise with a specified period (usually 60 to 90 days following termination).

If the employee originally paid for the stock, the company generally repurchases the stock at the lower of the employee's original cost or the current fair market value, since guaranteeing repurchase at the employee's original cost can negatively affect the accounting treatment of the plan (and, where the stock has declined substantially in value, could be a disincentive for continued employment). This payment is made in cash or by cancellation of any outstanding indebtedness of the employee to the company. Where the employee received the stock at no cost, any unvested shares are simply forfeited upon termination, with no payment from the company.

Where employees terminate due to death, disability, or retirement, restricted stock and unit arrangements may provide for some form of additional vesting. Vesting of the remaining shares in the award may be accelerated to the point of termination or may continue under the original vesting schedule. The acceleration or continued vesting may apply to the remaining award in its entirety or may only apply to a portion of the remaining award (e.g., shares scheduled to vest in the next 6 to 12 months or a pro-rata amount tied to the portion of the vesting period that elapsed before termination).

In the case of retirement, employees have theoretically fulfilled their service to the company. Providing for vesting of restricted stock and units in the event of retirement also helps ensure that retirees are not continuing to work merely to vest in their awards when they might otherwise have little motivation remain employed. In the case of death and disability, employees have little control over the termination event. And in all three cases, the additional income provided by the awards could be meaningful to employees and their estates/beneficiaries. According to the NASPP and Deloitte Consulting survey,[2] 75% of respondents provide for full or partial continued or accelerated vesting of service-based restricted stock and unit awards upon death, 71% provide for this upon termination due to disability, and 58% provide for this upon normal retirement (only 28% of respondents provide for full or partial continued or accelerated vesting upon early retirement). For all three types of termination events, a small percentage of additional respondents (5%–7%) provide for accelerated or continued vesting on a discretionary or other basis.

Accelerating or continuing vesting upon retirement can have significant tax considerations for restricted stock and unit arrangements; see the discussion in section 3.4.4 of this chapter.

3.3.7 Additional Restrictions

Privately held companies occasionally impose restrictions on the ability of employees to transfer or dispose of vested restricted shares. These restrictions are intended to discourage employees from leaving the company, and to enable the company to maintain some control over who owns its stock. Such restrictions may also enable the company to regulate and control the development of a trading market in its securities before its initial public offering.

One common type of transfer restriction is a "right of first refusal." A right of first refusal entitles a company to repurchase restricted shares of stock from the employee on the same terms offered, and at their cur-

---

2.   2016 Domestic Stock Plan Design Survey.

rent fair market value, if the employee proposes to sell or transfer the shares to a third party. Typically, the terms and conditions of a right of first refusal are set forth in the restricted stock agreement. A right of first refusal usually terminates when the company's securities become publicly held.

Another device used by privately held companies to restrict the transfer of shares of stock is a vested share repurchase right. As in the case of an unvested share repurchase right, this provision entitles the company to repurchase any vested shares of stock from an employee upon termination of employment. This allows the company to restrict share ownership to current employees and, provided the repurchased shares are returned to the plan, increases the number of shares the company has available to compensate current employees. On the other hand, employees may feel that once they have earned the stock, they should be entitled to keep it upon departure, and, particularly where the restricted stock serves as a substitute for other forms of compensation, may view this restriction unfavorably. If the company does choose to repurchase the vested shares, generally, the repurchase price is an amount equal to the fair market value of the company's stock on the date of termination of employment. Typically, the terms and conditions of a vested share repurchase right are set forth in the restricted stock agreement. A vested share repurchase right usually terminates when the company's securities become publicly held.

Other repurchase provisions may be triggered upon the death of the employee or in the event of a dissolution of marriage.

Both public and private companies might impose further restrictions on selling the underlying shares paid out to employees pursuant to restricted stock and unit awards. Referred to as a "post-vesting holding period," these restrictions prohibit employees from selling the shares for a specified period of time, which could be defined in terms of a number of years or until employees retire. These restrictions are not typically imposed below the executive level. Post-vesting holding periods are generally viewed favorably by institutional investors and their advisors and may result in reduced compensation expense for awards. But the holding requirement may be viewed unfavorably by the executives who are subject to restriction. A full discussion of post-vesting holding periods is outside the scope of this chapter.

3.3.8 Methods of Share Payment

Where payment for the restricted shares is required, a restricted stock plan may provide more than one method for paying the purchase price for the restricted shares. These payment methods include cash (usually in the form of a check), use of a promissory note, or any other consideration approved by the company. Company policy should clarify which methods are available to employees and the relevant guidelines for each.

3.3.8.1 *Restricted Stock Purchase Arrangements*

The most common form of payment for stock issued through a restricted stock purchase arrangement is cash. At the time of purchase, the employee is required to remit the total purchase price for the restricted shares (and any withholding taxes due to the company, if applicable). Generally, payment is made in the form of a check payable to the company. The company should decide whether a cashiers' check is required for payment or if a personal check is acceptable and the permissible time period for remitting payment.

Some companies permit employees to deliver a promissory note to pay the total required purchase price for the restricted shares being purchased. If the use of promissory notes is permitted, such arrangements must provide for the payment of at least the minimum amount of interest required under the Code and current accounting standards. In addition, the promissory note should be a full recourse obligation secured by the restricted shares being purchased or other property acceptable to the company.

If the interest rate charged is less than the applicable federal rate, the Internal Revenue Service (IRS) will treat a portion of the amount repaid as imputed interest, which may have significant income tax consequences to the employee and the company. The applicable federal rates are published by the IRS on a monthly basis. Note that under the Sarbanes-Oxley Act of 2002 public companies are prohibited from offering loans to officers and directors.

3.3.8.2 *Restricted Stock Awards and Units*

Where stock issued through a restricted stock award or unit arrangement is subject to a par value, award recipients may be required to pay this amount since the par value is a minimum payment the company is legally required to collect before issuing its stock. Par value is typically a nominal amount, often only $.01 per share or less. Under the corporate laws of most states, par value can be paid in cash, property, or services. To alleviate the administrative difficulties associated with collecting such nominal amounts from the award recipients, most companies designate the form of payment for units and for non-hire related grants of restricted stock to be past service. (Past service generally cannot be designated as payment for restricted stock granted to new hires because the shares underlying the award are issued at grant, before the newly hired employees have performed any service.)

To avoid this consideration altogether, some companies fund their restricted stock award or unit plan with treasury stock, since par value is not generally required for stock that has already been issued once and reacquired by the company (generally, the company is required to collect par value only on the first issuance of the stock).

3.3.9 Methods of Tax Payment

Restricted stock arrangements are generally subject to taxation upon vesting (except where the employee has filed a Section 83(b) election for a restricted stock purchase or award or where distribution of restricted stock units is deferred). Since the employee's tax obligation upon vesting can be burdensome, the restricted stock plan may provide for more than one method of meeting this obligation. The most common tax payment methods are withholding a portion of the vested stock with a value equivalent to the tax obligation or selling the restricted stock on the open market and applying the sale proceeds to the tax obligation. It is also permissible for employees to pay cash (in the form of a check or, increasingly more common, electronic funds transfer). For employees of privately held companies or employees of publicly held companies who are not officers or directors, it is also permissible to use a promissory note written to the company to pay the taxes. Company policy should clarify which methods are available to employees and the relevant guidelines for each.

If the use of promissory notes is permitted, such arrangements must provide for the payment of at least the minimum amount of interest required under the Code and current accounting standards. In addition, the promissory note should be a full recourse obligation secured by the restricted shares being purchased or other property acceptable to the company. As noted previously, under the Sarbanes-Oxley Act of 2002, public companies are prohibited from offering loans to officers and directors.

If a portion of the restricted shares that are currently vesting are withheld to cover the tax obligation, the tax payments should be limited to the maximum individual tax rate in the jurisdiction applicable to the award holder.[3] Allowing employees to tender shares for payments in excess of the maximum individual tax rate could cause the company to recognize additional compensation expense for the arrangement and could change the accounting treatment applicable to the restricted stock plan. Where this requirement is complied with, however, from an administrative standpoint, this may be the most expedient method of satisfying the tax obligation. It relieves the employee of the sometimes considerable burden associated with making a cash payment, does not require coordination with outside vendors (such as a brokerage firm), and generally is permissible even during a company blackout period. The only significant disadvantage to this tax payment method is that the company must pay over the taxes to the IRS in cash and is reimbursed for this cash expenditure with the shares of stock withheld from the employee's award, rather than with cash.

3.3.10 Dividends

As mentioned above, restricted stock, which is issued at grant, is generally eligible for any dividend payments made to shareholders after its issuance (even those payments made before the stock has vested). Restricted stock units, on the other hand, are not eligible to receive dividend payments until they have been converted to stock (and distributed to employees). However, many companies provide payments on unvested restricted stock units that are equivalent to the dividends paid to shareholders; these payments are typically referred to as "dividend equivalents." Units are designed to track the value of the company's

---

3. Companies that have not yet adopted ASU 2016-09 must limit the shares withheld for taxes to the minimum statutorily required tax payment.

company stock, and dividends paid to shareholders are part of that value. Therefore, although units cannot receive actual dividends, it is reasonable (although not legally required) to provide an equivalent payment to unit holders.

For both restricted stock and units, dividends or dividend equivalents can be paid on either a current or a deferred basis. If paid on a current basis, employees receive the dividend payment at the same time it is paid to shareholders. If paid on a deferred basis, employees receive the dividend payment when the underlying award is paid out; in this case, the dividend payments are typically subject to the same vesting/forfeiture restrictions as the underlying award. This structure ensures that employees do not receive dividend payments until they have earned the award on which the dividends are paid.

Dividends can be paid either in cash or in stock. Where dividends are paid on a current basis, they are most commonly paid in cash. Where the dividends are paid on a deferred basis, they are most commonly paid in stock.

3.3.11 Share Reserve

When adopting any stock plan, the company must designate shares to be issued under the plan. In an omnibus plan, it may be necessary to designate a specified number or percentage of the shares reserved to be used specifically for restricted stock arrangements, particularly where the arrangements will be issued at no cost. This can help address shareholder concerns about plan dilution and share usage and help ensure that the plan will be approved when presented to shareholders.

Rather than designating a specified number or percentage of shares to be used for restricted stock arrangements, some plans incorporate a flexible share reserve (also referred to as a "fungible share reserve"). Under this feature, shares issued at no cost count against the plan reserve at a greater rate than shares issued under stock options, stock appreciation rights, or restricted stock purchase arrangements. For example, for every share issued at no cost, the shares available for grant under the plan might be reduced by two shares (while shares issued under stock options reduce the shares available on a one-for-one basis). This can also address shareholder concerns about plan dilution while offering the company more flexibility in determining how to use the shares available for grant under the plan.

3.3.12 Approval of Awards

Most plans merely provide broad parameters governing grants of awards and further provide the board of directors or plan administrator with authority for determining the terms of individual awards (e.g., the actual award recipients, the number of shares underlying the awards, the effective date, or vesting provisions). Where plans are drafted in this manner, individual awards must be approved by the entity with appropriate authority under the plan and under the laws of the state where the company is incorporated.

Most plans and states allow authority for approving awards to be delegated to a subcommittee of the board, typically the compensation committee, or even to an individual board member. For awards granted to officers and directors who are subject to Section 16, it is generally advisable for awards to be approved by a committee of nonemployee directors, as defined under Section 16, as this can facilitate compliance with this area of the law and also helps address corporate governance and fiduciary considerations. For awards granted to other employees and consultants, authority for approving awards can usually be delegated to a committee of officers who are also board members or a single officer that serves on the board (it is also perfectly acceptable for awards to these individuals to be approved by the full board or the same committee that approves awards to officers and directors).

Under Delaware law, limited authority to approve awards of both stock and units can be delegated to officers who are not board members.[4] The resolution delegating such authority must limit the aggregate number of shares that the officer has authority to grant. In the case of restricted stock, the resolution must also specify the time frame during which the shares must be issued and the minimum consideration for which the shares may be issued (which should not be less than par value,

---

4. Before 2015, there was some question as to whether authority to grant restricted stock awards (as opposed to units) could be delegated to a non-board member. In 2015, Section 152 of the Delaware General Corporation Law was amended to clarify that this is permissible for restricted stock awards as well as units.

if applicable). In the case of restricted stock units, an officer cannot be authorized to grant awards to him or herself.

Where a plan specifies all the terms and conditions of awards on a nondiscretionary basis, such as under a formula plan or automatic grant program, approval of individual award grants should not be necessary. An example of such a plan might be an automatic grant program for outside directors under which all directors receive an annual grant on a specified date, for a specified number of shares, with specified vesting conditions.

3.4 Tax Treatment

As is true of most arrangements that provide for the receipt of stock in connection with the performance of services, Section 83 of the Code governs the tax treatment of restricted stock arrangements. Because restricted stock is subject to Section 83 and because it is paid out immediately upon vesting, it generally is not treated as deferred compensation under Section 409A of the Code (enacted under the American Jobs Creation Act of 2004).

Note, however, that restricted stock units, which represent an unsecured promise to deliver stock at a future date, are treated as deferred compensation under Section 409A. Where the units are subject to distribution (and, therefore, taxation) upon vesting, there should not be any adverse consequences under Section 409A. If the units are subject to deferred distribution, i.e., the units will be paid out sometime after they have vested (either mandatorily or via a deferral election), it is critical for the arrangement to comply with the requirements in Section 409A governing both deferral elections and distributions. A full discussion of Section 409A is beyond the scope of this chapter; companies that wish to offer restricted stock units, especially units subject to deferred distribution, are strongly encouraged to consult qualified tax advisors regarding the Section 409A implications before proceeding.

3.4.1 Tax Treatment of Employee

Since the restricted shares are, by their terms, not transferable on the date of purchase or award and subject to a substantial risk of forfeiture (that is, the restricted shares are not vested), there is no taxable event at this time, and the compensatory element of the transaction remains open until the restricted shares vest. As the forfeiture restrictions lapse (that is, as the restricted shares vest), the difference—if any—between the purchase price and the fair market value on the date of vesting is compensation income to the employee. If the shares were awarded at no cost to the employee, this means that the full fair market value of the stock as it vests is compensation income to the employee. This compensation income is subject to taxation at ordinary income rates. As with other forms of compensation, such as salary and bonus, the employee must include the compensation income arising from the restricted stock in his or her ordinary income calculation for the year of vesting. The employee may elect to close the compensatory element of the transaction and accelerate the time at which compensation income is realized to the date of purchase or award by filing a Section 83(b) election with the IRS.

Where the restricted shares have been purchased at the full fair market value of the company's stock on the date of grant, generally the employee will make this election and recognize no compensation income. If the restricted stock was awarded at no cost to the employee or purchased at a discount, filing a Section 83(b) election causes the employee to recognize compensation income equal to the full fair market value of the stock on the date of award or the amount of the purchase discount. This compensation income is subject to taxation at ordinary income tax rates and must be included in the employee's ordinary income calculation for the year. In the absence of an election, the compensatory element of the arrangement is not determined until the date of vesting, as described above. If a Section 83(b) election is filed and the employee subsequently leaves the company before the restricted shares have been fully earned, the employee is not entitled to a refund of the taxes paid at the time of award or purchase, nor is the employee entitled to take a loss deduction for the amount, if any, previously included in income. Likewise, if the stock declines in value after the award or purchase so that the fair market value of the stock upon vesting is less than the fair market value of the stock when the award or purchase occurred, the employee is not entitled to claim a loss deduction unless the shares are sold at the lower value. Thus, where the stock is purchased at a discount or awarded at no cost, filing a Section 83(b) election could cause employees to pay a higher amount of tax than if the election were not filed; few employees choose to file a Section 83(b) election in this situation. But where the employee is paying full fair market value to acquire the restricted stock, many employees do choose to file the Section 83(b) election, since, in this situation, it eliminates any compensation income associated with the arrangement. The following examples may help clarify the tax treatment.

Example 1: Restricted Stock Purchased at Fair Market Value: An employee is offered the right to purchase 1,000 shares of restricted stock at a price of $10 per share, the fair market value on the date of grant. The stock vests in full one year after the date of grant, when the fair market value is $16 per share. In this example, if the employee does not file the Section 83(b) election, the employee recognizes compensation income of $6,000 in the year the stock vests. If the employee files the Section 83(b) election, the employee does not recognize any compensation income on the stock, since the purchase price is equal to the fair market value at the time the shares are purchased. In this example, the employee would most likely file the Section 83(b) election since it does not present any disadvantages to him or her.

Example 2: Restricted Stock Awarded at No Cost: An employee is awarded 1,000 shares of restricted stock at no cost when the fair market value of the stock is $10 per share. The stock vests in full one year after the date of grant, when the fair market value is $16 per share. If the employee does not file the Section 83(b) election, the employee recognizes compensation income of $16,000 in the year the award vests. If the employee files the Section 83(b) election, the employee recognizes $10,000 of compensation income in the year the stock is awarded, but does not recognize any additional income upon vest. Even in this example, it might be advantageous for the employee to file the Section 83(b) election, since doing so would reduce the amount of compensation income the employee would recognize for the award. But it is impossible for the employee to know that this is the case at the time the shares are awarded to him or her, which is when the Section 83(b) election must be filed. The employee could terminate employment before the vest date, forfeiting the shares, or the stock could subsequently decline in value. Thus, in this example, it is unlikely that the employee would file the Section 83(b) election.

Generally, restricted stock units are subject to the same tax treatment as restricted stock awarded at no cost, with a few important exceptions arising from the fact that stock is not issued at grant under a unit award. For an award to be subject to Section 83, a transfer of property must occur. Because there is no stock issued at grant under a unit arrangement, a transfer of property is not considered to have occurred at grant. Thus, unit awards are taxed under Sections 451 and 409A of the Code rather than Section 83. The first consequence of this treatment is that a Section 83(b) election is not available for unit awards. Some companies consider this to be an advantage, since, as discussed above, it is often inadvisable for employees to file a Section 83(b) election on restricted stock awarded at no cost, yet explaining the election can be cumbersome and confusing to employees.

The second consequence is that the recipient of a unit award does not recognize income for federal income tax purposes until he or she has constructively received the compensation paid under it. Under the Code, compensation is considered to be constructively received when it becomes available to the employee and the employee has control over receipt of it. Compensation is not considered to be constructively received if the employee's control of its receipt is subject to substantial limitations or restrictions. Likewise, compensation is not considered to be constructively received solely because it will be paid out upon termination.

If the unit is converted to stock and distributed at vesting, constructive receipt occurs at vesting, and the employee is taxed in exactly the same manner as if he or she had received restricted stock issued at grant that was not subject to a Section 83(b) election. If, however, the units are subject to a valid deferral election, or a mandatory deferral program, under which they will not be converted to stock and distributed until sometime after vesting, constructive receipt does not occur, and the employee is not subject to income tax, until the actual distribution.

Where units are subject to deferred distribution, employment taxes for FICA and FUTA purposes are still due when the award is no longer subject to a substantial risk of forfeiture (i.e., typically upon vesting), even though income taxes are not assessed until the employee receives the underlying stock.

Example 3: Restricted Stock Unit with Deferral Election: An employee is awarded 1,000 shares of restricted stock units at no cost when the fair market value of the stock is $10 per share. The units vest in full two years after the date of grant, when the fair market value is $16 per share. As permitted under the plan, the employee files a deferral election within 30 days of the grant date, deferring conversion and distribution of the underlying shares until five years after the date of grant, when the fair market value is $23 per share. When the units vest, the employee will recognize $16,000 of income for FICA/FUTA purposes (and the company is required to withhold the payments on this income and make its matching payments) but will not recognize any income for federal income tax purposes. When the units are distributed to the employee pursuant to the deferral election, the employee will recognize $23,000 of compensation income for federal income tax purposes (but will not recognize any further income for FICA/FUTA purposes), on which the company is also responsible for withholding the requisite payments. For capital gains purposes, the stock received under the unit award will have a basis of $23 per share, the fair market value on the date it was distributed to the employee, and the capital gains holding period is measured from the distribution date.

Note, however, that U.S. tax regulations may permit the company to delay reporting income for employment tax (FICA/FUTA) purposes until a later date within the same calendar year, for three months, or until distribution, if awards will be paid out within 2½ months after the end of the calendar year in which the employment tax obligation is triggered. See section 3.8.7.3 below for a discussion of the applicable tax regulations.

There is some question as to whether a short (e.g., a few days) administrative delay in distribution of the shares underlying an RSU following the stated vest/payout date constitutes a delay of constructive receipt and thus delays taxation of the award. There is no bright-line test to determine when constructive receipt occurs; this is a facts-and-circumstances-based determination. Typically, most companies treat a delay in distribution of the shares of a few days beyond the stated vest/payout date as merely an administrative matter and consider the award subject to tax as of the stated vest/payout date. Where a company applies this approach, the shares are valued for tax purposes as of the stated vest/payout date (rather than the actual distribution date), and the deadline to deposit the tax withholding to the IRS is measured as of this date. But reasonable arguments can be made to treat the actual distribution date as the date constructive receipt, and thereby taxation, occurs. Generally, factors to consider in determining when constructive receipt has occurred include the date the shares will be recorded as issued and outstanding in the company's records, the date that voting and dividend (as opposed to dividend equivalent) rights will accrue to the award holder, the length of time that elapses between the stated vest/payout date and the actual distribution, and whether the award holder could request that the shares be distributed earlier. Perhaps the most important consideration is consistency: companies should apply a consistent approach to determining when RSUs are taxable. Note that where the company chooses to treat the distribution date as the taxable event and distribution occurs within a few days or weeks of the vesting date, it should be permissible to delay calculation and collection of FICA/FUTA taxes to the distribution date under the FICA short-term deferral rule noted in section 3.8.7.3 of this chapter.

Nonemployees, such as consultants and outside directors, are not subject to FICA/FUTA and instead pay self-employment taxes. While the self-employment tax system (SECA) typically mirrors FICA/FUTA, there are some differences, one of which is that SECA generally operates on a cash basis, i.e., self-employment taxes generally are not due until income is paid to the recipient. For restricted stock units, this means that self-employment taxes are due when the shares underlying awards are distributed to nonemployees, regardless of when the awards vest.

3.4.1.1 *Deferral Elections for Restricted Stock Units*

The ability to defer distribution is also often perceived as an advantage of unit awards and many companies offer employees the opportunity to elect a deferred distribution. Where this is offered, however, care should be taken to ensure that the deferral feature does not cause the plan to become subject to ERISA. This can particularly be a concern when distribution is deferred to the termination of employment, and it may necessitate limiting the deferral feature to high-level employees.

Also, as mentioned above, the deferral is effective for income taxes only; FICA/FUTA are still due when the awards are no longer subject to a substantial risk of forfeiture (typically the vest date), and income for this purpose is based on the fair market value of the underlying stock at that time.

Finally, any deferral elections must comply with Section 409A, which governs nonqualified deferred compensation. Section 409A restricts the timing of deferral elections, places restrictions on the timing and form of payments of deferred compensation, and generally prohibits acceleration of payments of deferred compensation. The following discussion highlights some of the requirements under Section 409A with respect to deferral elections for restricted stock units. Section 409A is a very complex and lengthy section of the U.S. tax code, and full discussion of all of the requirements therein is beyond the scope of this chapter. Where companies wish to offer deferred payouts for equity awards, they should consult with their own tax advisors. There may be additional requirements that could apply to their equity awards under Section 409A that are not discussed here.

Awards in which payout is made immediately upon vesting or within a short time after vesting are exempt from Section 409A under the so-called "short-term deferral exemption," which applies to awards that are paid out before 2½ months after the end of the calendar year in which vesting occurs (the "short-term deferral period"). Where an award qualifies for the short-term deferral exemption, the award is considered to be outside the scope of Section 409A, and no further compliance with Section 409A is necessary, provided the award is paid out within the short-term deferral period. Where an award is intended to qualify for this exemption, care should be taken to ensure that the award is paid out on a timely basis. While there are some provisions in the regulations that would allow delay of payment beyond the short-term deferral period in limited circumstances where the delay is unforeseeable and unavoidable, failure to pay out on a timely basis could also result in loss of the exemption and imposition of penalties.

It is permissible to allow employees to elect to defer payout of an award that is otherwise intended to qualify for the short-term deferral exemption. The mere ability to make a deferral election does not disqualify an award from the short-term deferral exemption, provided that no such election is made. In the absence of such an election, if the award will be paid out within the short-term deferral period, the award will remain exempt from Section 409A. If, however, the award holder chooses to defer payout of the award beyond the short-term deferral period, the award will become subject to Section 409A and must comply with the restrictions on deferral elections and timing and form of award payouts provide for therein, even if the award ends up being paid out within the short-term deferral period (for example, if the payout is accelerated because of the death of the award holder).

To defer distribution beyond the short-term deferral period, where restricted stock units do not vest for at least one year after grant, an initial deferral election can be made within 30 days after the grant date (provided the election is made at least one year before the units vest). Where restricted units vest in less than one year after grant, the initial deferral election generally must be made before the end of the calendar year preceding the year in which the units are granted.

The following examples may help clarify the limitations on deferral elections.

> *Example 4:* On February 1, an employee is granted restricted stock units that vest in two years. The employee can make an initial deferral election until March 2 (30 days after February 1) of the year in which the units are granted.

> *Example 5:* On February 1, an employee is granted restricted stock units that vest 13 months after the date of grant, on March 1 of the following year. The employee can make an initial deferral election until March 1 (one year before the scheduled vest date) of the year in which the units are granted.

> *Example 6:* On February 1, an employee is granted restricted stock units that vest on February 15 of the following year. The employee can make an initial deferral election until February 15 (one year before the scheduled vest date) of the year in which the units are granted.

> *Example 7:* On February 1, an employee is granted restricted stock units that vest in one year. The employee has only until December 31 of the year before the year in which the units were granted to make an initial deferral election.

Where no deferral election is made at grant, an election to defer receipt of the underlying shares for at least five years can be made up to one year before the date they vest.

> *Example 8:* An employee is awarded restricted stock units that vest as to one-fourth of the underlying shares on each anniversary of the date of grant for four years. The employee would like to defer distribution/payout of the units for several years after they vest. The employee can make a deferral election for any length of time as to the second, third, and fourth vesting tranches within 30 days after the units are granted. Assuming no deferral election is made at grant, an election to defer receipt of the underlying shares for at least five years after the date of vest can be made for each of these same three tranches up to one year before each tranche is scheduled to vest. Any deferral elections with

respect to the first vesting tranche must be made in the calendar year before the year in which the units were granted.

For performance-based unit awards, the deferral election can be made up to 6 months before the end of the performance period. To qualify for this treatment, the following conditions must be met:

- The performance period must be at least 12 months long.

- The award holder must provide services continuously from the time performance goals are established (or the performance period begins, if later) until the election is made.

- The compensation to be paid under the award must not be readily ascertainable when the election is made. Where the amount to be paid under an award is commensurate with the level of performance achieved, the compensation is considered to be readily attainable when the amount to be paid can be calculated and it is substantially certain to be paid.

- The performance goals must be stated in writing no later than 90 days after the start of the performance period.

- Where the performance goals are subjective, the determination of whether the performance has been achieved cannot be made by the award holder, a family member (whole or half siblings, spouse, ancestors, lineal descendants, and spouses of any of these individuals), a person under control of the award holder (or a family member), or a person for whom the award holder (or a family member) determines the compensation.

- Mere increases or decreases in the value of the award are not considered performance goals. Tying performance to stock price targets or increases in stock value are acceptable performance goals, however.

- The awards must be paid out only in the event that the performance conditions are achieved. Awards cannot provide for payout regardless of achievement of the performance goals in the event of retirement, involuntary termination, or any circumstance other than death, disability, or a change in control. Although allowing payout in the event of death, disability, or a change in control does not disqualify an award from be considered performance-based, awards that are paid out as a result of these events will no longer be considered performance-based compensation.

Where an award is subject to a valid deferral election under Section 409A, payout of the award can be deferred to a specified date or dates or certain events (termination of employment, disability, death, a change in control, or a severe unforeseeable emergency). It is also permissible for payout to be deferred to a combination of the allowable payment triggers, such as the earlier or later of multiple events. For example, it is permissible for payout to be deferred to the employee's termination of employment or death, whichever occurs first. Note that each of these permissible payout events is defined within Section 409A; a full discussion of these definitions is beyond the scope of this chapter.

Once an award is subject to a deferral election, Section 409A further restricts the changes that can be made to that election. Any elections to re-defer must be made at least one year before the scheduled distribution date and must defer distribution for at least five additional years. Any changes in the elected form of payment must also be made at least one year before the scheduled distribution date, except that an election to tender or sell shares to cover the employee's tax withholding liability due upon vest or distribution can be made at any time. Generally, distribution of deferred units cannot be accelerated except in limited circumstances, such as death or disability.

3.4.1.2 *Qualified Equity Grants*

Under Section 83(i) of the Code, which was enacted pursuant to the Tax Cuts and Jobs Act of 2017, privately held companies can offer employees an additional opportunity to defer taxation on their RSUs for federal income tax purposes by issuing the RSUs in the form of "qualified equity grants."[5] Under this arrangement, employees can make an election to defer taxation until the earliest of the following events:

- It is five years after the award vested
- The stock becomes transferable

---

5. Qualified equity grants can be in the form of either stock options or RSUs. This chapter discusses the tax treatment applicable to RSUs only.

- The employee becomes an excluded employee (see below)
- The corporation's stock becomes traded on an established securities market
- The employee revokes the election

The election must be made within 30 days after the date the RSU vests. The election defers only the timing of when federal income taxes will be due on the award; the amount of income subject to tax will be based on the value of the stock at the time the award vested, even if the stock is worth less on the date that the award is subject to tax. In addition, the company is required to withhold tax at the maximum individual tax rate, and the employee must agree to comply with the withholding requirements. Finally, the election does not defer taxation for FICA/FUTA purposes. Whether the election defers taxation for state or local purposes will vary by jurisdiction.

RSUs that meeting the following conditions are considered qualified equity grants and are eligible for the associated deferral election:

- The granting corporation cannot ever have been a public company.

- The granting corporation must have a written plan under which 80% of the company's full-time employees receive RSUs with equal rights and privileges (except that the amount of stock granted to each employee may differ, provided all employees receive more than a de minimis amount of stock).[6]

- The RSU must be paid out in stock, and the employee cannot have the right to sell the underlying stock back to the company.

Section 83(i) deferral elections cannot be made if any of the company's stock is publicly traded or if the company has repurchased its own stock in the past year, unless at least 25% of the dollar amount of the repurchased stock was deferral stock (i.e., stock for which deferral elections had been made under Section 83(i)) and the individuals from whom deferral stock is repurchased are determined on a reasonable basis. The 25% requirement is waived if the company repurchased

---

6.   The equal rights and privileges requirement is waived for RSUs granted before January 1, 2018.

all of the outstanding deferral stock. Additional restrictions apply to repurchases, and the company is required to report repurchases to the IRS in years when deferral stock is outstanding at the start of the year.

Qualified equity grants are not considered nonqualified deferred compensation for purposes of Section 409A and thus are not subject to the same restrictions on deferral elections that apply to other forms of compensation under Section 409A. Unlike under Section 409A, however, redeferrals are not permitted.

The following individuals (referred to as "excluded employees") are not eligible to receive or hold qualified equity grants:

- Any employee who is or has been CEO or CFO or has ever acted in that capacity.

- Any employee who own more than 1% of the company's outstanding stock or possesses more than 1% of the total combined voting power of all stock of the company during the during the current fiscal year (referred to as a "1% owner") and any employee who was a 1% owner during the preceding 10 years.

- Any employee who is a family member—spouse, child, grandchild, or parent—of any of the above individuals.

- Any employee who is (or has been during the preceding 10 years) one of the top four highest paid employees, as determined in accordance with the SEC's executive compensation disclosure rules for proxy statement purposes.

Where a company has granted RSUs that meet the conditions to be treated as qualified equity grants, the company most provide a notice to the award holders that informs them of their right to defer income on the RSUs. This notice must be provided at the time the RSUs will be subject to tax (typically at vesting) or a reasonable period before such time. The notice must explain the tax consequences of making the election, including that the taxable income will be based on the value of the stock at vesting (even if the stock subsequently declines in value), that the income will be subject to withholding at the end of the deferral period, and the employee's responsibilities with respect to the tax withholding. Companies that fail to provide the notice can be subject to a penalty of $100 per form, not to exceed $50,000 annually.

Because Section 83(i) is a recently enacted section of the Code, there are a number of areas of uncertainty with respect to implementation of the law. Most significantly, it is not clear whether all RSUs that meet the conditions to be qualified equity grants must be treated as such, even if the company did not intend to issue qualified equity grants. The IRS is expected to issue regulations that will clarify a number of matters related to Section 83(i). Until the regulations are issued, companies may rely on a good-faith interpretation of the requirements.

It is likely that further guidance from the IRS and/or proposed regulations will be issued shortly after publication of this book; before issuing any awards that might be considered qualified equity grants, companies should consult their legal advisors as to the latest guidance that is available.

3.4.1.3 *Performance-Based Awards*

As noted above, performance-based awards are typically issued in the form of units. Where this is the case, they are taxed in the same manner as restricted stock units. The recipient of a performance-based unit award does not recognize income for federal income tax purposes until he or she has constructively received the compensation paid under it, which occurs when the compensation becomes available to the employee and the employee has control over receipt of it. If permitted under the terms of the award, the employee can defer recognition of compensation for federal income tax purposes by making a valid deferral election under Section 409A. Regardless of any deferral election, income for FICA/FUTA purposes is recognized in the year the award vests (or is otherwise no longer subject to a substantial risk of forfeiture). See also section 3.8.7.4 below on special tax considerations applicable to performance-based units.

Although less common, vesting in restricted stock awards can also be tied to performance conditions. This does not change the fundamental tax treatment of the award, however. Performance-based restricted stock awards are taxed under Section 83, just as is the case for service-based restricted stock awards. This is because the shares underlying the award are issued at grant, resulting in a transfer of property at that time. The employee recognizes compensation income, subject to both federal income tax and FICA/FUTA, when the award vests (i.e., the date the shares underlying the award are either transferable or no longer subject to a substantial risk of forfeiture, whichever occurs earliest).

As is the case with service-based restricted stock, the employee may elect to accelerate the time at which compensation income is realized to the date of grant by filing a Section 83(b) election on all or a portion of the award. However, if the award is forfeited for any reason, including failure to meet the performance conditions, the award holder is not entitled to a refund of the taxes paid at the time of grant, nor is the holder entitled to take a loss deduction for the amount, if any, previously included in income. Likewise, if the stock declines in value after grant, so that the fair market value of the stock upon vesting is less than the fair market value of the stock when the award was granted, the holder is not entitled to claim a loss deduction unless the shares are sold at the lower value.

3.4.2 Tax Treatment of Dividend Payments

Dividends and dividend equivalents paid on restricted stock and units are subject to tax at the time they are paid to the employee. Where the dividend is paid in cash, the employee recognizes income equal to the cash received; where a dividend is paid in stock, the employee recognizes income equal to value of the stock on the date it is subject to taxation.

Dividend payments on restricted stock are treated as compensation income, subject to all of the withholding described in section 3.4.3, and are reported on Form W-2 unless a Section 83(b) election was filed on the award. Where a Section 83(b) election was filed on the award, the payment is treated as dividend income, reported on Form 1099-DIV, and is not subject to withholding (note that there is some uncertainty as to whether this treatment applies when the dividends are not paid until the underlying award vests).

Dividend equivalents paid on restricted stock units are always treated as compensation income and will be subject to federal income tax when paid out to employees. In most cases, dividend equivalents are paid on a deferred basis and paid only when the underlying award is paid out. If so, the dividend equivalents are subject to federal income tax when they are paid out, along with the shares underlying the award. Where dividend equivalents are paid on a current basis, they are subject to federal income tax at that time.

The FICA/FUTA treatment of dividend equivalents paid on re-stricted stock units may depend on whether the underlying award has been taken into the employee's income for FICA/FUTA purposes. If the restricted stock unit award has not yet been subject to FICA/FUTA, i.e., is not yet vested or is subject to a substantial risk of forfeiture, the dividend equivalents accrued on the award are clearly subject to FICA/FUTA when they are no longer subject to a substantial risk of forfeiture.

The treatment of the dividend equivalents is less clear when the underlying award has already been subject to FICA/FUTA. Under Treasury Regulations Section 31.3121(v)(2)-(1)(a)(2)(iii), often referred to as the "non-duplication rule," once an award has been included in income for FICA/FUTA purposes, no further income attributable to the award is subject to FICA/FUTA. The term "income" most certainly includes any additional appreciation in the underlying shares; this rule is the reason why restricted stock units are subject to FICA/FUTA at vest only and not again when paid out. Most practitioners believe that dividend equivalents paid on the award are also covered under this rule as "income" attributable to the award (akin to dividends paid on common stock). Thus, dividend equivalents paid after a restricted stock unit award has been subject to FICA/FUTA (e.g., in a situation where a unit award is subject to deferred distribution, those dividend equivalents accrued after the award has vested but before it is paid out) would not be subject to FICA/FUTA.

Note, however, that the non-duplication rule does not specifically address dividend equivalents, which can be viewed as additional compensation (i.e., an additional award) rather than earnings on the underlying shares since, technically, they are not a dividend payment. Of particular concern is Chief Counsel Advice 201414018, issued in April 2014, which addresses a specific scenario in which the IRS staff determined that dividend equivalents paid on vested but deferred RSUs are treated as additional compensation and are subject to FICA when paid. The CCA addresses a situation in which a privately held company pays dividend equivalents on restricted stock units that are subject to deferred payout. The dividend equivalents are paid out to award holders at the same time dividends are paid to shareholders, rather than with the underlying award. In addition, the underlying award is paid out solely in cash. The CCA thus distinguishes the dividend equivalents from earnings on publicly held stock that would be exempt from FICA taxation under the non-duplication rule. While this CCA should be considered when determining the FICA tax treatment of dividends paid on RSUs that have already been taken into income for FICA purposes, it is not clear that it applies to the more common situation where the dividend equivalents will be paid out with the underlying award. Readers should consult their tax advisors on this matter.

3.4.3 Employee Tax Withholding

If the recipient is an employee, any compensation income recognized in connection with a restricted stock purchase, award, or unit arrangement is subject to federal and state withholding obligations for income and employment tax purposes. Relevant withholding taxes include:

- Federal income tax
- Social Security
- Medicare
- State income tax (if applicable)
- State disability or unemployment (if applicable)
- Local taxes (if applicable)

For federal income tax purposes, any compensation income recognized for restricted stock is treated as a supplemental wage payment. Where an employee has received less than $1 million in supplemental payments during the calendar year, this payment is eligible for withholding one of two ways. First, the compensation income may be aggregated with the employee's regular salary payment for the period, with withholding computed on the total amount using a rate determined in accordance with employee's Form W-4 (referred to as the "aggregate procedure"). Alternatively, the compensation income is eligible for withholding at the flat rate for supplemental wage payments. Where an employee has received more than $1 million in supplemental payments (including the current payment) during the calendar year, withholding on the payments, or portion thereof, in excess of $1 million must be at the maximum individual tax rate.

In 2012, the IRS issued Information Letter 2012-0063, clarifying that where a company chooses to withheld taxes on supplemental wage payments at the flat rate, no other rate is permissible. Where employees would like additional withholding on their supplemental wage payments, the company must use the aggregate method of withholding. If the employee would like withholding in excess of his or her W-4 rate, the employee must submit a new Form W-4 requesting the additional withholding far enough in advance of the transaction that it will be effective under the company's policies. Employees who do not wish the new Form W-4 to apply their other compensation will need to submit another Form W-4 after the transaction to reset their withholding rate.

In addition, employment taxes under the Federal Insurance Contributions Act (FICA) and the Federal Unemployment Tax Act (FUTA) may be due. FICA is made up of two separate taxes: old age, survivor, and disability insurance (Social Security) and hospital insurance (Medicare). The Social Security component of FICA is collected up to an annual maximum. The Medicare component is collected against the employee's total earnings, and wages in excess of $200,000 are subject to withholding at a higher rate. The employer must match these taxes, except that the employer's match for Medicare purposes is always at the regular rate, not the higher rate that applies to wages in excess of $200,000. The FICA rates and their applicable ceilings, if any, are subject to change annually. The company's payroll department should be contacted for notification as to when rate changes occur.

Under Section 6672 of the Code, a 100% penalty may be imposed for failing to withhold and pay over taxes.

In the case of restricted stock purchases and awards, all withholding obligations arise at the time of vesting (or grant, if a Section 83(b) election is filed). Restricted stock units are subject to federal income tax withholding upon distribution (which may occur at vesting or later, if the unit arrangement is subject to either a mandatory or elective deferral) and are subject to FICA withholding (Medicare and Social Security) and FUTA at the time of vesting (regardless of whether distribution occurs at that time).

The withholding taxes collected by the company are only an estimate of the employee's ultimate tax liability. It may be necessary for the employee to make additional quarterly tax deposits depending upon his or her personal tax situation (or to remit additional amounts owed when tax returns are filed).

In addition to the company's withholding obligation, the company must furnish an employee (or former employee) receiving restricted stock with a Form W-2 for the year of vesting (or grant or distribution) reporting the compensation income recognized as "wages." If the recipient is a nonemployee, the compensation income is not subject to withholding but must be reported on a Form 1099-MISC for the year of vesting (or grant or distribution).

Most states follow the federal treatment for income tax purposes and may require withholding of state disability or unemployment taxes. Generally, state taxes are determined on the basis of the employee's state of residence. The company may also be required to withhold certain local taxes in addition to federal and state taxes.

Taxes should not be withheld for outside directors and nonemployees, even if the nonemployee requests such withholding. Where taxes are withheld from nonemployees, the taxes cannot be deposited and reported to the IRS via the processes and forms used for taxes withheld from employees; doing so would make it appear that the income is subject to FICA. Compensation paid to nonemployees is subject to self-employment tax (SECA) instead of FICA. Failure to collect FICA on income that otherwise appears, because of the manner in which it is reported to the IRS, to be subject to FICA, however, is likely to trigger tax penalties. Moreover, collecting FICA on compensation paid to nonemployees does not relieve the nonemployees of the obligation to pay SECA. The company's matching payments under FICA further compound this issue. In addition, penalties can apply for improperly withholding and reporting taxes.

Nonemployees are responsible for paying their own taxes to the IRS and, in most cases, should make estimated payments to the IRS on a quarterly basis. These estimated payments should be adjusted for income resulting from restricted stock and unit arrangements.

3.4.4 Tax Treatment of Arrangements Subject to Acceleration of Vesting Upon Retirement

Offering restricted stock arrangements where vesting will accelerate (or continue) upon an individual's retirement can result in unexpected tax consequences for those individuals who are already retirement-eligible or will become eligible to retire before the arrangement vests.

Under Section 83, both restricted stock awards and restricted stock purchase rights are subject to tax when they are either no longer subject to a substantial risk of forfeiture or transferable, whichever occurs first. If an individual who is eligible to retire receives an award or purchase right in which vesting will accelerate (or continue) upon retirement, for all practical purposes, that award or right is not subject to a substantial risk of forfeiture. Presumably, virtually any termination by the individual at that point would be considered retirement, triggering the acceleration of vesting (or vesting would simply continue as scheduled). Because there are few, if any, situations in which the individual would forfeit the award or right, it is taxable upon grant.

Where an individual is not eligible to retire when the award or right is granted, but achieves this status before the arrangement vests, the arrangement will be subject to tax at the time the individual becomes eligible to retire.

This consideration also applies to restricted stock units, but it is limited only to employment (FICA/FUTA) taxes (which apply only to employees, not to consultants or outside directors), since restricted stock units are not subject to income taxes until award recipients realize constructive receipt of the underlying shares. Thus, where restricted stock units that include a provision for acceleration (or continuation) of vesting upon retirement are granted to employees who are retirement-eligible, the units are subject to FICA/FUTA taxation upon grant but are not subject to income taxation until the underlying shares are distributed to the employees. Units with vesting acceleration (or continuation) upon retirement that are granted to employees who are not yet retirement-eligible but who achieve this status before the scheduled vesting dates are subject to FICA/FUTA taxation when the employees become retirement-eligible (but are not subject to income taxation until distribution).

In the case of restricted stock units, however, U.S. tax regulations may permit the company to delay reporting income for employment tax (FICA/FUTA) purposes until a later date within the same calendar year, for three months, or until distribution, if awards will be paid out within 2½ months after the end of the calendar year in which the employment tax obligation is triggered. See section 3.8.7.3 below for a discussion of the applicable tax regulations. Because, for restricted stock units, the taxes due upon achieving retirement eligibility are limited to FICA/ FUTA and because it may be possible to delay collection of these taxes until a time when it is more administratively convenient, it generally is more administratively feasible to offer acceleration of vesting upon retirement on restricted stock units than on restricted stock awards.

3.4.5 Disposition of Stock

Upon a sale or other disposition of the restricted shares, the employee generally recognizes a capital gain or loss equal to the difference be-tween the employee's adjusted tax basis in the restricted shares and the sale price. An employee's tax basis in the restricted shares is equal to the total purchase price paid (if any) for the shares plus the amount of compensation income recognized by the employee. Generally, this means that the restricted shares have a tax basis equal to the fair market value of the company's stock on the date of vesting/distribution (or the date of grant, if a Section 83(b) election is filed).

The holding period for long-term capital gains purposes generally commences on the date of vesting. Where a Section 83(b) election is filed, however, the holding period commences on the date of grant or purchase, and where a unit award is subject to deferred distribution, the holding period commences on the date of distribution.

3.4.6 International Tax Considerations

Outside of the United States, the tax treatment of restricted stock can vary greatly from country to country. Some countries assess income based on any value at the time of grant or purchase (regardless of vesting), but other countries may defer taxation until the arrangement vests or until the underlying shares are sold. In countries where restricted stock awards are taxed at grant (which is generally undesirable), this outcome may sometimes be avoided by granting restricted stock units instead. In some countries, it may be necessary for participants to complete filings with the local tax authorities to defer or accelerate the time at which the stock is taxed. The tax rates applicable to restricted stock may be substantially higher than the tax rates that apply in the United States.

Payment of dividend equivalents on restricted stock units may cause the award to be taxable at grant or result in other adverse tax consequences because employees may be viewed as having received benefits commensurate with stock ownership. Where the company wishes to provide for dividends or equivalent payments on awards, it may be desirable to grant restricted stock awards, as some jurisdictions offer favorable taxation of dividends that may not be available for dividend equivalents.

There may also be significant obligations imposed on the company for the restricted stock. The company may be required to fulfill reporting obligations for the income recognized by participants and may also be required to withhold taxes on this income. Where withholding is required, there may not be a flat withholding rate applicable to stock compensation (as exists in the United States), in which case companies will need to work closely with local payroll offices (or apply to the local tax authorities for a flat rate) to determine the appropriate tax withholding rates. Many countries also have substantial social insurance taxes that can apply to stock compensation, often with matching payments required from the company. In some cases, the company's matching payments may not be subject to any maximum and could ultimately become a significant burden for the company.

Many countries provide some form of qualified stock option that is subject to lower tax rates, yet only a few countries provide the same benefit to restricted stock arrangements. Thus, offering restricted stock could be significantly more costly to both participants and the granting corporation (which may have to make matching social insurance contributions that would not apply under a qualified option plan).

The company should review the tax treatment applicable to the plan in each country where it will be offered carefully with its legal advisors before offering restricted stock to any employees outside the United States. Failure to comply with local laws could ultimately be very costly to the company; it can be difficult to correct errors or minimize the cost to the company after the stock has been granted.

3.4.7 Tax Treatment of Employer Company

The company receives a corporate tax deduction (for compensation expense) under Code Section 162 equal to the amount included as compensation income in the gross income of the employee. The company generally is able to take the deduction in the taxable year that includes the close of the taxable year in which the employee recognizes income.

Under IRS regulations, an employer is allowed a deduction only for the amount of compensation "included" in the employee's gross income. This "included" amount is the amount reported by the employee on an original or amended tax return, or the amount included in the employee's gross income as the result of an IRS audit.

The regulations stipulate that timely compliance with the Form W-2 or Form 1099 filing requirements, reporting the amount includible in the employee's income, is deemed "inclusion" of the amount in gross income. The employer company is not required to establish that the employee actually included the reported amounts in his or her income tax return. Where the amount of compensation income recognized meets the requirements for exemption from reporting for payments aggregating less than $600 in any taxable year, or is eligible for any other reporting exemption, no reporting is required for the employer company to claim the deduction.

Section 162(m) limits the corporate tax deduction available to public companies for compensation, including stock-based compensation. For public companies that are not health insurance providers, the limitation is $1,000,000 per covered employee; for tax years beginning on or after January 1, 2018, Section 162(m) applies only to compensation paid to the chief executive officer, chief financial officer, and the three most highly compensated executive officers (other than the CEO and CFO). All forms of restricted stock awards and units granted after November 2, 2017—whether service- or performance-based—are subject to the limitation.[7]

---

7. The Tax Cuts and Jobs Act of 2018 significantly expands the scope of Section 162(m) as it applies to companies that are not health insurance providers. Before this act, CFOs were not subject to the limitation, and performance-based compensation was also exempted from the limitation. Under a grandfather provision included in the act, arrangements granted on or before November 2, 2017 may be exempt from the expanded provisions of the Section 162(m). Thus, performance-based restricted stock and units granted on or before November 2, 2017, may be exempt from the limitation, if specified conditions are met and the awards are not materially modified after this date. Likewise, both service and performance-based restricted stock and RSUs granted to

The Patient Protection and Affordable Care Act expands the application of the deduction limit under Section 162(m) as it applies to health insurance companies. The limitation for health insurance companies is $500,000 per employee. In addition, the limitation applies to both public and private health insurance companies, to compensation paid to all employees and most nonemployees of the company, and regardless of whether the compensation is service- or performance-based.

3.5 Securities Law Considerations

Federal and state securities laws affect restricted stock plans of both privately held and publicly held companies. Securities law considerations may arise in connection with a restricted stock plan in at least two situations: (1) at the time of grant or purchase of restricted stock and (2) upon disposition of the shares of stock acquired under the restricted stock plan.

When presented with a securities law question, companies must consider both the federal securities laws, which include the Securities Act of 1933 and the Securities Exchange Act of 1934, and state securities laws, which include the laws of the state of the company's principal place of business and each state in which the company proposes to grant restricted stock arrangements to its employees and sell shares of stock. In addition, if the stock will be offered to employees residing outside the United States, companies must also consider the securities laws of the countries in which the employees receiving the stock reside.

3.5.1 Registration

Before implementing a restricted stock plan, the company must address the question of whether the offer and sale of securities under the plan is subject to registration under applicable securities laws. It is the offer to sell a security that triggers coverage under securities laws, not the actual purchase. Generally, registration requires that the proposed issuance involve both a "security" and the "offer" or "sale" of the security.

CFOs before November 2, 2017, may be exempt from the limitation, if certain conditions are met and the awards are not materially modified after this date.

The Securities Act of 1933 governs the offer and sale of securities for federal securities law purposes. Generally, the Securities Act of 1933 provides that it is unlawful to offer or sell a security unless a registration statement containing detailed information about the company and the terms of the proposed offering is in effect or an exemption from registration is available. Registration of restricted shares of stock is required to the extent that a "sale" is involved and there is not an exemption available to cover the sale.

3.5.1.1 *Private Companies*

The process of registering securities for offer and sale under the Securities Act of 1933 can be expensive. Accordingly, most privately held companies design their restricted stock plans to fit within one of the available exemptions from registration under the Securities Act of 1933. Most private companies rely on Rule 701, which provides an exemption from the registration requirements of the Securities Act of 1933 for offers and sales of securities pursuant to compensatory employee benefit plans exclusively for privately held companies, to cover their employee stock plans. Rule 701 covers offers and sales of restricted shares.

Under Rule 701, a company may offer and sell securities to its employees, officers, and directors, as well as to consultants and advisors to the company under certain circumstances, if made pursuant to a written plan or contract (a copy of which is provided to the employee or other participant).

The amount of securities that can be offered and sold during any rolling 12-month period in reliance on the exemption cannot exceed the greater of (1) $1 million, (2) 15% of the total assets of the company (measured at the end of the last completed fiscal year) or (3) 15% of the outstanding securities of the class being offered. Shares acquired under restricted and unit arrangements are taken into account under this limitation at the time of grant. Shares acquired under restricted stock purchase arrangements are valued at their purchase price; shares acquired at no cost under restricted stock award and unit arrangements are valued at the fair market value at the date of grant.

When relying on Rule 701, the company must provide employees purchasing stock with a copy of the plan or contract under which the stock is issued. Where more than $10 million worth of securities are offered and sold during a 12-month period, the company must provide additional disclosures to employees, including the company's financial statements and information about the risks associated with purchasing the securities.

Shares of stock acquired pursuant to Rule 701 are deemed to be "restricted securities" for purposes of the federal securities laws. Generally, the employee cannot resell these shares of stock unless they are subsequently registered under the Securities Act of 1933 or are sold pursuant to an exemption from registration, such as Rule 144. Ninety days after the company becomes subject to the reporting requirements of the Securities Exchange Act of 1934, however, shares of stock acquired pursuant to Rule 701 may be resold by non-affiliates without regard to Rule 144[8] and by affiliates in reliance on Rule 144 (but without regard to the holding period condition).

3.5.1.2 Public Companies

Generally, publicly held companies register the shares of stock to be offered pursuant to their restricted stock plans on Form S-8, a simplified registration statement available exclusively for the employee benefit plans of companies subject to the reporting requirements of the Securities Exchange Act of 1934. Form S-8 reflects an abbreviated disclosure format and incorporates by reference information contained in the company's other publicly available documents. Shares of stock acquired under a restricted stock plan registered on Form S-8 are not considered "restricted securities" for securities law purposes and gener-

---

8. Rule 701 expressly provides that, 90 days after the company becomes subject to the reporting requirements of the Securities Exchange Act, nonaffiliates may sell under Rule 144 without regard to the current information requirement (Rule 144(c)) and the holding period requirement (Rule 144(d)). However, the other requirements for resale under Rule 144, including the volume limitation (Rule 144(e)), manner of sale (Rule 144(f)), and notice (Rule 144(h)), do not apply to nonaffiliates. Thus, 90 days after a company's IPO, nonaffiliates can freely sell any stock acquired pursuant to Rule 701. Note that the seller must have been a nonaffiliate for at least three months as of the date of the sale to rely on this 90-day exemption.

ally can be more easily resold by employees. Even for restricted stock awards that will be issued at no cost, where registration may not be legally required since the offer does not involve a "sale" of stock, most publicly held companies register the restricted stock plan on Form S-8 to alleviate the resale restrictions that might other otherwise apply to the stock awarded under the plan.

3.5.1.3 *State and International Securities Laws*

Most states follow the pattern of the federal securities laws and treat restricted stock plans as involving the offer and sale of securities that must either be registered under state law or exempt from registration. Thus, it may be necessary for a company to register its restricted stock plan in each state where restricted stock arrangements are to be offered to employees or to locate suitable exemptions for the arrangements. Many states have specific exemptions from registration that cover the offer and sale of securities pursuant to an employee benefit plan, such as a restricted stock plan. These exemptions may impose specific (and often minor) filing requirements on the company.

The securities laws of other countries can vary significantly from U.S. securities laws. It may be necessary to register the plan (which can sometimes be costly) with the local authorities before offering the restricted stock to employees. In some cases, exemptions from registration may be available for stock offered to certain types of employees or under certain circumstances. If an exemption is available, it may be necessary to seek approval from the local authorities to qualify for it. In addition to the registration requirements, the company may be required to provide a prospectus or make other disclosures to the employees receiving the stock. The securities laws of some countries prohibit ownership of foreign securities, making it difficult or impossible for employees of those countries to receive restricted stock.

Before awarding restricted stock arrangements, a company must take steps to ensure that the restricted stock plan and the proposed offering comply with current federal, state, and/or local securities laws. Particularly when a company is experiencing significant growth and expansion, it is important to make sure that the securities laws of each state and country in which the company intends to extend its restricted stock plan have been reviewed and compliance procedures are in place. Advance planning is critical in this area, since certain exemptions may require filings and/or approval from local authorities in advance of when the restricted stock is granted and adequate time must be allowed to register an offering, if required.

Aside from meeting any applicable registration requirements, companies must provide antifraud disclosure statements to anyone receiving an offer to buy securities. These documents provide the purchaser with the information needed to assess the company's financial conditions and risks. The level of detail required varies from state to state as these laws are at the state, not federal, level. These statements may not be required if the offer is made only to top executives or others meeting the definition of "sophisticated" investors.

3.5.2 Resale

Rule 144 may limit the ability of an employee to resell shares of stock acquired under a restricted stock arrangement.

In the case of restricted shares that are acquired under an exemption from the registration requirements of the Securities Act of 1933, such as Section 4(2), Rule 506 of Regulation D, or Rule 701, such shares are considered to be "restricted securities." Generally, restricted securities must be sold in reliance on Rule 144.

In the case of restricted shares registered on Form S-8, the shares may be resold by non-affiliates without regard to Rule 144 and by affiliates in reliance on Rule 144 (but without regard to the holding period condition).

3.5.3 Officers, Directors, and Principal Shareholders

Under Section 16 of the Securities Exchange Act of 1934, restricted stock is subject to both the reporting requirements of Section 16(a) and the "short-swing profits" recovery rule of Section 16(b). Consequently, transactions involving restricted stock offered to directors and officers who are subject to Section 16 ("corporate insiders") must be considered in light of compliance with these provisions. Section 16 applies only to directors, officers, and principal shareholders of companies with registered securities (i.e., publicly held companies).

3.5.4 Reporting Requirements

Both a restricted stock purchase by a corporate insider and an award of restricted stock to a corporate insider are reportable events for purposes of Section 16(a).The purchase or award of restricted stock is reportable on Form 4 within two business days after the purchase or award occurs.

Under the Section 16 rules, neither the vesting of a right to receive a security nor the lapse of restrictions relating to a security are subject to Section 16. Consequently, the vesting of restricted shares is neither a reportable event for purposes of Section 16(a) nor subject to the "short-swing profits" recovery rule of Section 16(b).

If restricted shares are forfeited or repurchased by the company while the insider is still subject to Section 16 (e.g., when the insider fails to achieve performance targets required for vesting), the transaction is reportable for purposes of Section 16(a). The forfeiture or repurchase is reportable on Form 4 within two business days after it occurs. If the forfeiture or repurchase occurs after the insider is no longer subject to Section 16 (e.g., after the insider has terminated employment), it is not necessary to report it, provided that the forfeiture or repurchase is exempt from the operation of Section 16(b).

3.5.4.1 Application of Reporting Requirements to Restricted Stock Units

The grant of restricted stock units to a corporate insider is also subject to Section 16(a) and must be reported on a Form 4 within two business days of the date of grant. Where the units must be paid in stock and are convertible to common stock on a one-for-one basis, the grant can simply be reported as a direct acquisition of common stock. If reported in this manner, there is no further reporting obligation when the units vest and are converted to stock.

Alternatively, the grant can be reported as the acquisition of a derivative security. If reported in this manner, the conversion of the units to common stock upon vesting or release must also be reported. Both the grant and the subsequent conversion are reportable on a Form 4 within two business days. This alternative approach is required for units that do not convert to common stock at a one-for-one ratio or that are payable in cash.

Regardless of how the initial awards are reported, forfeitures of restricted stock units are not reportable because units are considered a derivative security. Forfeitures or cancellations of derivative securities for no consideration are not reportable.

3.5.5 "Short-Swing Profits" Recovery

Under Section 16(b), a purchase or grant of restricted stock or units is considered a "purchase" of the shares of stock unless the arrangement is exempt from the operation of Section 16(b) pursuant to Rule 16b-3. Thus, a nonexempt restricted stock purchase or grant can be matched with any sale of company stock occurring within six months either before or after the date of purchase/grant to trigger the operation of the "short-swing profits" recovery rule.

Rule 16b-3 exempts certain transactions by corporate insiders conducted under employee benefit plans, such as a restricted stock plan, from the "short-swing profits" recovery rule of Section 16(b) where the conditions of the exemption are satisfied. Under the Rule 16b-3 exemption, a restricted stock purchase or award can be exempted from the operation of Section 16(b), provided that the transaction satisfies *one* of the following conditions (only one condition must be satisfied, not all of the conditions):

- The purchase or award must be approved in advance by either the company's board of directors or by a committee of two or more nonemployee directors.

- The purchase or award must either be approved in advance or ratified after the fact by the company's shareholders.

- The restricted shares cannot be disposed of within six months from the date of purchase or award. If this alternative is relied on, a sale of the restricted shares within six months of the date of purchase or award will cause the retroactive loss of this exemption for the grant. A corporate insider may sell shares of stock other than the restricted shares, however, without affecting the exempt status of the restricted stock purchase or award.

The repurchase or forfeiture of restricted shares (such as where a corporate insider terminates employment) is considered a disposition to the company and, unless exempt, can be matched with any nonexempt purchase of company stock occurring within six months either before or after the repurchase/forfeiture date to trigger the operation of the "short-swing profits" recovery rule. A repurchase or forfeiture of restricted shares is exempt if it is approved in advance by the company's board of directors, a committee of two or more nonemployee directors, or the company's shareholders. Where the original grant of the restricted stock was approved by one of these three entities, the initial approval covers the subsequent repurchase or forfeiture without any further action.

3.5.6 Disclosure and Reporting

The Securities Exchange Act of 1934 requires that a publicly held company disclose detailed information about the compensation of its executive officers, including compensation under any restricted stock plans in its proxy and information statements, periodic reports, and other filings. In addition, the proxy solicitation rules of the Securities Exchange Act of 1934 require tabular disclosure of the shares outstanding and available for grant under the company's restricted stock plans (additional disclosures are required when a plan is being submitted for shareholder approval).

3.6　Financial Statement Impact

The accounting treatment of restricted stock plans may have a direct effect on the company's financial results. Companies are required to account for most forms of stock compensation, including restricted stock and units, under Accounting Standards Codification Topic 718 (ASC 718), which treats restricted stock plans as compensatory arrangements that give rise to a compensation expense that must be reflected in the company's financial statements. This expense is generally equal to the fair value of the award on the "measurement date" for the arrangement.

The measurement date is the date the terms of the arrangement are mutually understood by both the company and the award recipient.[9]

9.　For companies that have not yet adopted ASU 2018-07, the accounting treatment of awards issued to nonemployees (other than outside directors) will differ from that which is described here.

This typically is the date of grant, provided that the awards are payable only in stock. Where awards are payable in cash, the measurement date would be the settlement date. Awards payable in cash are beyond the scope of this chapter.

For restricted stock or units where vesting is contingent on continued service or performance goals that are not related to the company's stock price (such as earnings or revenue targets), the fair value of the arrangement is generally equal to its intrinsic value—that is, the difference between the purchase price, if any, and the fair market value of the underlying stock on the measurement date. Where dividends are paid on the underlying stock but will not be paid on the unvested restricted stock or units, the fair value can be reduced by the present value of the dividend stream that is expected to be paid to shareholders over the vesting period of the arrangement. For restricted stock where vesting is contingent on market conditions (e.g., stock price targets or shareholder return), the fair value is adjusted based on the probability that the targets will be met. This adjustment must be computed with an option pricing model, most commonly the Monte Carlo Simulation.

If the restricted stock is offered to employees at a price equal to the fair market value on the date of grant, the company does not recognize any expense for the arrangement. Where a company grants restricted stock purchase arrangements with a purchase price less than the fair market value of the company's stock on the date of grant, or awards the stock at no cost to the recipients, compensation expense results under ASC 718. This expense must be amortized, or "accrued," over the service period for the arrangement. The service period is generally the vesting period for the arrangement, but other factors, such as automatic acceleration of vesting upon retirement, may have an impact on the determination of the service period. Where the arrangement is subject to vesting contingent on performance goals or price targets, the service period is derived based on the time period in which the goals or targets are expected to be achieved.

Where restricted stock is subject to vesting that is contingent on service conditions, companies can choose to apply an estimated forfeiture rate to expense recorded for the awards, thus accruing expense only for the portions of the arrangements that are expected to vest. If the expected or actual vesting outcome varies, the expense accrual is adjusted to reflect the new expected or actual outcome so that expense is recorded only for those awards that actually vest. Alternatively, companies can choose to accrue the full amount of expense recorded for the award and, when forfeitures occur, reverse the previously accrued expense attributable to the forfeited awards.[10] This is a policy election companies must make upon adoption of ASU 2016-09; the same policy must be applied to all awards issued by the company. Changes to this policy are considered a change in accounting principle, which must be adopted on a retrospective basis and which must be accompanied by a preferability assessment performed by the company's auditors.

Where restricted stock is subject to vesting that is contingent on non-market performance conditions, the expense accrued for the award should be adjusted based on the likelihood that the performance conditions will be achieved. If the expected and actual outcome of the performance-contingent vesting requirements varies from the prior expectations, the expense accrual is adjusted to reflect the new expectations or the actual outcome.

Where restricted stock is subject to vesting that is contingent on market conditions, the expense is not adjusted for expected or actual forfeitures. Because the initial fair value of the arrangement is adjusted to reflect the market conditions, expense is recorded for the arrangement regardless of whether those conditions are met.

3.6.1 Disclosure

To accurately represent a company's financial condition and capital structure in its financial statements, certain disclosures are required under generally accepted accounting principles and the rules of the Securities and Exchange Commission. ASC 718 sets forth the specific financial statement disclosures that are required with respect to a company's employee stock plan.

Under ASC 718, the following information must be disclosed about a company's restricted stock plans:

- A description of the restricted stock arrangements, including vesting conditions, price, and the number of shares authorized for issuance under the plan.

---

10. This alternative is not available to companies that have not adopted ASU 2016-09.

- The weighted average grant date fair value of arrangements granted under the plan.

- A description of the method used to calculate the fair value. Where restricted stock vests based on market conditions, this should also include a discussion of how the effect of these conditions on fair value was determined.

- The total compensation cost recognized for the company's equity compensation plans, including restricted stock.

- The remaining unrecognized compensation cost for the company's equity compensation plans, including restricted stock, and the period of time over which it is expected to be recognized.

- A description of any modifications to previously granted restricted stock arrangements, including the terms of the modifications, number of employees affected, and additional incremental cost resulting from the modification.

- The amount of cash received from payments for restricted stock and/or tax benefits realized by the company.

- The method the company uses to account for forfeitures due to failure to meet service-based vesting conditions.

- The company's policy for issuing restricted stock, including the source of shares (i.e., authorized but unissued shares or treasury shares) and the number of shares the company expects to repurchase in the following annual period.

The company should provide the following additional information for restricted stock purchase and award plans:

- The number and weighted average grant date fair value of shares unvested at the beginning of the period.

- The number and weighted average grant date fair value of shares unvested at the end of the period.

- The number and weighted average grant date fair value of shares granted, vested, and forfeited during the period.

The company should provide the following additional disclosures for restricted stock units:

- The number and weighted average conversion ratio of units outstanding at the beginning of the period.

- The number and weighted average conversion ratio of units outstanding at the end of the period.

- The number and weighted average conversion ratio of units convertible at the end of the period.

- The number and weighted average conversion ratio of units granted, forfeited, or converted during the period.

- The number, weighted average conversion ratio, aggregate intrinsic value, and weighted average remaining term of units outstanding (for fully vested units and those expected to vest during the current period).

- The number, weighted average conversion ratio, aggregate intrinsic value, and weighted average remaining term of units currently convertible (for fully vested units and those expected to vest during the current period).

- The total intrinsic value of units converted during the period.

3.6.2 Accounting for Tax Effects

The expense that companies recognize for restricted stock differs from the tax deduction they are entitled to for the arrangements both in terms of timing and the amount of the tax deduction. The expense recognized for the arrangement is equal to the fair value of the arrangement (typically the intrinsic value of the underlying stock) at grant and is recorded over the arrangement's service period, typically the vesting schedule. The company's tax deduction, however, is generally realized only once the arrangement vests (and, in the case of restricted stock units subject to deferral, not until the shares are distributed) and is equal to the intrinsic value of the stock at this time. These differences must be accounted for in the company's financial statements.

Assuming that a Section 83(b) election has not been filed for the award, the company records an estimated tax benefit (sometimes referred to as a deferred tax asset) as it recognizes expense for the award. This estimated benefit is always equal to the amount of expense recognized multiplied by the company's statutory tax rate (regardless of the current intrinsic value of the stock), and it reduces the company's reported tax expense. Upon recognition of a tax deduction (at either vest or release of the shares), the actual tax savings resulting from the deduction is compared to the estimated benefit recorded earlier. Any difference in the two amounts is recorded to tax expense.[11] Where the actual tax savings exceeds the previously recorded estimate (an "excess tax benefit"), tax expense is reduced. Conversely, where the actual tax savings is less than the previously recorded benefit (a "tax shortfall"), tax expense is increased.

For example, assume a company grants a restricted stock award for 10,000 shares when the fair market value of the underlying stock is $10 per share. The award vests in full two years after the date of grant, and the employee does not file a Section 83(b) election. The total expense for the award is $100,000 (10,000 shares multiplied by $10 per share). This expense is recorded over the two years that the award is vesting. During this same period, the company records an estimated tax benefit of $40,000 (assuming a combined corporate tax rate of 40%) and reduces its reported tax expense by this amount as well.

Now assume that the fair market value is $17 per share when the award vests. At this fair market value, the company recognizes a tax deduction of $170,000, which, at the same 40% tax rate, produces an actual tax savings of $68,000. This tax savings exceeds the previously estimated tax benefit by $28,000; thus, the company's reported tax expense is reduced by this amount for the period in which the award vests.

On the other hand, if the fair market value when the award vests is only $8 per share, the company's tax deduction will be only $80,000,

---

11. For companies that have not yet adopted ASU 2016-09, differences between the estimated tax benefit recorded over the service period of the award and the actual tax savings recognized for the award at vest/payout are generally recorded to paid-in capital (unless, in the case of a shortfall, there is insufficient paid-in capital from excess benefits from prior stock plan transactions to absorb the shortfall, in which case it increases tax expense.)

and the resultant tax savings is only $32,000. This is $8,000 less than estimate benefit recorded for the award. In other words, the company reduced its reported tax expense by $40,000 for the award but only realized a tax savings of $32,000; the tax expense reflected in the company's financial statements is less than the amount of tax it actually paid. This $8,000 shortfall increases the company's reported tax expense in the period in which the award vests.

Where a Section 83(b) election is filed for a restricted stock purchase or award, there will generally be no difference between the expense recognized for the arrangement and the tax deduction realized for it. In addition, the company's actual tax savings will be known at grant; thus, there is no need to reduce tax expense based on an estimated amount. As expense is recorded for the arrangement, the company will simply reduce tax expense based on the amount of actual tax savings received at grant. Assuming the company's tax deduction equals the expense recognized for the award, no further adjustments to tax expense will be necessary.

3.6.3 Accounting for Dividend Payments

Under ASC 718, dividends and dividend equivalents paid on restricted stock and units are charged to retained earnings. This applies regardless of whether the dividends are paid on a current basis (i.e., at the same time the dividend is paid to other shareholders) or on a deferred basis (i.e., not until the underlying award is paid out). It also applies whether the dividends are paid in cash or stock and whether they are paid on restricted stock or restricted stock units.

When the award is granted, the fair market value of the underlying stock already includes the value of the future dividend payments (i.e., when investors are buying and selling the stock, the prices they agree on should take into account the future dividend stream the buyer will be entitled to and the seller is giving up). Since the expense the company recognizes is based on this fair market value, when the dividends are actually paid there is no need for the company to recognize any further expense.

As mentioned above, for restricted stock arrangements that are not entitled to dividends before vesting but where the company does pay dividends on the underlying stock, the fair value of the award is reduced by the present value of the dividends that will be paid over the vesting period of the award. For example, assume that restricted stock units are granted when the fair market value is $40 per share and that the present value of the dividends the company expects to pay over the vesting period of the award is $2 per share. If the company pays dividend equivalents on the unvested restricted stock units, the fair value of the unit award is $40 per share (the fair market value on the date the award is granted). If the company does not pay dividend equivalents on the unvested units, the fair value of the award is reduced by the present value of the future dividend stream, to $38 per share.

Note, however, that where dividends are paid on awards that are ultimately forfeited, the company will recognize compensation expense for the dividends. In this situation, because of the forfeiture, the company will not recognize any expense for the award itself. However, the employee has received compensation in the form of the dividend payment; that compensation should be recognized as an expense. Another way to think of it is that the original award encompassed both the underlying shares and the future dividend stream that would be paid on them; both of these components contributed to the award's fair value. Now that the underlying shares have been forfeited but the employee retains the dividend payments, the company still must recognize expense for the portion of the award that was not forfeited, i.e., the dividend payments. Thus, the portion of the award's fair value that is attributable to the dividends is recognized as compensation expense.

This scenario is much more likely to occur with dividends that are paid on a current basis. For example, assume that on January 1, 2014, a company grants a restricted stock award that cliff vests in four years. The company pays a dividend to the grantee in 2015, and then the grantee terminates in 2016, forfeiting the award. In 2015, when the dividend is paid, it is charged to retained earnings. But in 2016, when the award is forfeited, unless the company makes the employee pay back the dividend (highly unlikely), the company will have to recognize compensation expense equal to the amount of the dividend. Where the company applies an estimated forfeiture rate to expense recorded for awards under ASC 718, the company would have to estimate forfeitures up front and record expense for dividend payments based on the estimate, truing up for actual outcome. Or rather, the "haircut" that the company applies to its overall expense for estimated forfeitures is reduced by the amount of the dividends that are expected to be paid out on awards that ultimately will be forfeited.

This is less likely to be a concern with dividends that are paid on a deferred basis because they are typically subject to forfeiture if the vesting conditions of the underlying award are not met.

Where performance-based awards are eligible for dividends before vesting, the dividend payments should be subject to the same performance conditions as the underlying award. If any portion of a performance award is forfeited and the dividends accrued on the award are not commensurately adjusted for the forfeiture, this results in a situation in which dividends have been paid on an award that was forfeited, causing the company to recognize expense for the dividends, as described above.

In addition to the expense considerations, where dividends are paid on unvested awards and the dividends are not subject to forfeiture, the company is required to use the two-class method when reporting earnings per share. The two-class method is typically used by companies with multiple classes of common stock or with other securities that participate in dividends paid to common stockholders. The method uses a formula to allocate earnings (the numerator of the EPS equation) to each security. Thus separate EPS calculations would be required for the company's unvested awards vs. the rest of its common stock. A full discussion of the two-class method of reporting EPS is beyond the scope of this chapter.

3.6.3.1 *Accounting for Tax Effects of Dividend Payments*

Where employees receive dividends on unvested restricted stock arrangements that are not subject to a Section 83(b) election, as mentioned earlier, the dividend is treated as compensation income. Consequently, the company recognizes a tax deduction equal to the amount of income reported for the dividend; the tax savings attributable to this deduction are recorded to tax expense.[12]

---

12. For companies that have not yet adopted ASU 2016-09, where the dividend payment itself is charged to retained earnings (rather than compensation expense), the tax savings attributable to the dividend are recorded as additional paid-in-capital. If the dividend is later treated as compensation expense (due to

3.7 International Considerations

In addition to the tax and securities law implications of offering restricted stock to employees located outside the United States, there are many legal and administrative issues that must be considered when a restricted stock plan is extended overseas.

3.7.1 Cultural and Language Differences

It can generally be assumed that employees in the United States understand what stock is and how the stock market works; it can also usually be assumed that they have some experience with stock compensation. This may not always be true for employees located outside the United States. While it is certainly true that in some countries, employees have an understanding of these concepts equaling that of U.S.-based employees, it is also likely that in some countries the concepts of stock and stock compensation are completely new to employees. Even in those countries where employees are familiar with these concepts, one may find that the forms of stock compensation they are familiar with differ from restricted stock. Often, the terminology used in reference to stock compensation, even in English-speaking countries, is different than the terminology used in the United States. Where employees are not familiar with the concept of restricted stock, it is necessary to provide additional education to ensure that employees fully understand the arrangement and the restrictions associated with it. Where employees are required to pay for the stock, it is critical that they understand the risks associated with such purchases. It may be necessary to translate plan documents and other educational materials into local languages or dialects.

3.7.2 Labor Laws

Just like any other form of compensation, restricted stock can be subject to labor laws. These laws may provide specified rights to certain groups of employees (such as part-time employees or employees on leave of absence), create entitlements to future awards of stock, or provide

---

forfeiture of the underlying award), the tax savings attributable to the dividend are deducted from paid-in-capital and reported as a reduction in income tax expense.

certain entitlements and rights upon termination of employment. The restricted stock plan must be reviewed for compliance with local labor laws, and, in some cases, it may be advisable to include language in the plan relinquishing these rights.

3.7.3 Data Privacy Regulations

Many countries, especially members of the European Union, have regulations governing the collection and transmission of personal data, such as name, address, compensation, and so on. Where such data is collected and transferred between corporate entities, countries, or third-party service providers, the company must ensure that the transmission of such data complies with any relevant data privacy regulations.

3.7.4 Currency Exchange Controls

Where employees are required to pay for the restricted stock, the purchase may be subject to local currency exchange controls. These controls govern the transmission of funds into and out of the country. Where currency exchange controls limit the funds that can be transmitted to the United States, it may be necessary to ensure that the purchase price does not exceed these limitations or to structure the purchase in a manner that is permissible under the exchange controls. In some cases, the currency exchange controls may prohibit the purchase altogether.

In addition, for unit and stock awards, as well as for purchases of restricted stock, where employees receive shares upon vesting, i.e., where the vested shares are not immediately sold, shareholder reporting may be required under local laws or repatriation of funds when the shares are eventually sold may be required.

3.8 Administrative Matters

Many companies establish formal policies and procedures to facilitate the efficient administration of their restricted stock plan. Formal policies enhance the plan administrator's ability to operate the plan consistent with the company's objectives for the restricted stock purchase program. They also enable the plan administrator to resolve problems that arise during the course of operating the plan. Formal guidelines for processing restricted stock transactions can serve as an effective means for ensuring that all company procedures are properly followed.

A comprehensive restricted stock plan policy should address:

- How recipients are determined
- How the number of restricted shares offered to each employee is determined
- How often restricted stock is granted
- How the vesting schedule is determined
- The handling of restricted stock in special situations
- How applicable withholding taxes are calculated and collected
- The different treatment for directors and officers subject to Section 16 of the Securities Exchange Act of 1934 (applicable to publicly held companies only)

A written procedure should address:

- The company's internal approval process
- The tasks of the plan administrator
- The grant transaction recordation
- The purchase/award agreement preparation and completion process
- Transfer agent communications
- Interdepartmental communications

3.8.1 Internal Approval Process

Companies often find it beneficial to establish internal approval procedures for grants of restricted stock. These procedures should address such matters as who will be recommended for a restricted stock grant, what the size of the grant will be, and whether any special terms and conditions will be incorporated into the grant. The human resources department and/or other benefits personnel usually make these decisions, possibly with input from various management-level employees.

Following internal approval, all restricted stock arrangements—regardless of origin—are incorporated into a formal proposal and submitted to the company's board of directors for review and approval. If the board of directors has delegated responsibility for restricted stock arrangements to a subcommittee, such as a compensation committee, the recommendations are considered and approved. Alternatively, the committee may make its own recommendations that are submitted to the full board of directors for review and final approval. Restricted stock arrangements generally become effective as of the date of board action.

3.8.2 Restricted Stock Agreement

Most companies document a restricted stock arrangement by preparing a written agreement that sets out specific terms and conditions. The agreement typically contains:

- The correct name of the employee
- The effective date of the grant
- The number of shares of stock covered by the arrangement
- The price, if any
- The vesting schedule for the shares of stock covered by the arrangement
- The expiration date of the right, if any
- Permissible forms of payment (if payment is necessary)
- Permissible forms of tax payment
- Provisions governing the treatment of the award in the event of termination of service, including retirement, death, and disability

Since the agreement usually also specifies the obligations of the employee and any restrictions imposed on the restricted shares, most companies require that the employee sign the agreement. Where this is the case, grant agreements that have not been signed before award vesting events can be problematic. The vest date may be a taxable event regardless of whether the agreement has been signed. In addition, for restricted stock units, refusing to pay out vested awards until the associated agreements have been signed could trigger consequences under Section 409A. Companies should set a time limit within which employees must sign and return agreements, and address whether there is a penalty for failure to return an executed agreement.

The majority of companies that issue equity awards distribute grant agreements electronically: according to NASPP surveys, 92% of respondents distribute awards agreements electronically for U.S. employees[13] and 81% for non-U.S. employees.[14] The predominant practice is also to require employees to acknowledge acceptance of the grant; according to the NASPP, 76% of companies require separate acknowledgement of award agreements.[15] Where grants are not acknowledged by award recipients, the most common response is to follow up with employees until they acknowledge the award or to suspend issuance of the shares upon vesting (note, however, that suspending issuance of the shares can be problematic for tax purposes, as described above.) Only 22% of companies cancel awards that are not accepted within a specified period.[16] Where companies distribute award agreements electronically, the majority also allow employees to accept the agreement electronically: 83% of companies that distribute agreements electronically allow U.S. employees to sign the agreements digitally[17] and 99% consider a digital signature binding in some or all countries in which their non-U.S. award recipients are located.[18]

3.8.3 Collateral Materials

In addition to the agreement, other materials may be provided to an employee in connection with a restricted stock arrangement. For purposes of compliance with applicable federal and/or state securities laws, it is customary for the company to provide each employee with a copy of the company's restricted stock plan or with a document that

---

13. 2014 Domestic Stock Plan Administration Survey, co-sponsored by the NASPP and Deloitte Consulting LLP.

14. 2015 Global Equity Incentives Survey, co-sponsored by the NASPP and PwC.

15. 2014 Domestic Stock Plan Administration Survey.

16. 2014 Domestic Stock Plan Administration Survey.

17. 2014 Domestic Stock Plan Administration Survey.

18. 2012 Global Equity Incentives Survey.

summarizes the principal terms and conditions of the plan, describes the tax consequences of participation, and advises employees where to obtain additional information about the company. This document is sometimes referred to as the plan "prospectus." Where restricted shares have not been registered with the Securities and Exchange Commission, it may be necessary to provide investment representation letters or statements and related materials to employees.

It is common for companies to provide additional educational materials in the form of printed or online award/plan summaries and FAQs, recorded or in-person presentations, interactive tools, and videos. These materials explain the objectives and benefits of the award program to employees, summarize the terms and conditions of awards, describe the applicable tax treatment, and address common questions. It is critical to educate employees on their awards to ensure that they understand that the awards are an important and valuable component of their compensation. The company has made a significant investment in the award program in terms of both financial and administrative costs; providing education to ensure that employees understand and value the program only makes sense. An educational program can also minimize poor decisions employees make with respect to their awards (thereby increasing the benefit delivered to employees), dispel common misperceptions about the program, and proactively address employee questions (reducing administrative costs).

At the time that restricted stock purchase, award, or unit arrangements vest and again when the underlying shares are distributed to employees (if this does not occur upon vesting), most companies provide employees with a statement reporting the number of shares vested and/or distributed, the value of the shares, the employee's taxable income, any required tax withholding, how the shares will be issued, and any shares sold or withheld to cover the employee's tax liability.

For stock acquired after 2010, brokers are required to report the tax basis of securities that are sold on the Form 1099-B issued for the sale. For restricted stock purchase arrangements, brokers are required to report only the purchase price of the shares as the tax basis. Although the tax basis also includes any compensation income that employees recognize in connection with the acquisition of the shares, brokers are not permitted to include this income in the basis reported on Form

1099-B.[19] This income increases the tax basis (employees will recognize compensation income on restricted stock purchases if the purchase price is discounted or if they do not file Section 83(b) elections on the purchase) and reduces employees' capital gains when the shares are sold (or increases their capital loss, as the case may be). Employees will have to report an adjustment to their gain on their tax return using Form 8949 to take this income into account when computing their capital gain/loss. Companies may find it advisable to provide instructions to employees on how to report this adjustment so as to ensure that employees do not overestimate the tax they owe as a result of their sale.

Securities that do not require a cash investment from employees, including shares acquired under restricted stock and unit awards issued at no cost, are considered non-covered securities under the tax-basis reporting regulations. As such, when these shares are sold, brokers are not required to report a tax basis for them on Form 1099-B, but they may voluntarily choose to do so. Where brokers voluntarily choose to report a basis for these shares, for sales of shares acquired after January 1, 2014, the reported basis must be $0 (or the nominal amount paid for the stock, if any).[20] Employees will then have to report an adjustment to their gain on their tax return using Form 8949 to take the compensation income recognized in connection with their award into account when computing their capital gain/loss. Where the broker does not report a basis for the shares on Form 1099-B, employees simply report the correct basis when recording the sale on their tax returns; it is not necessary to report an adjustment to their gain/loss. For this reason, it may be pref-

---

19. For shares acquired from January 1, 2010, until December 31, 2013, brokers could choose to voluntarily include the compensation income recognized in connection with the acquisition of the restricted shares in the tax basis reported on Form 1099-B. For shares acquired on or after January 1, 2014, however, this is no longer permissible. Companies should contact the brokers that service their stock plans to determine their reporting procedures for shares acquired through December 31, 2013, to ensure that any educational materials provided to employees appropriately reflect the brokers reporting procedures. Where employees hold shares at brokers that the company does not have a relationship with (and thus where the company has no insight into the brokers' reporting procedures), it may be necessary to provide employees with additional education on this topic.

20. See note 7.

erable for brokers to choose to not report a basis, rather than reporting an incorrect basis. In any event, companies should contact the brokers that service their stock plans to determine their reporting procedures so that employees can be provided with educational materials explaining the tax basis reported on Form 1099-B. Where employees hold shares at brokers that the company does not have a relationship with (thus meaning it has no insight into their reporting procedures), it may be necessary to provide additional education on this topic.

3.8.4 Amendments

Generally, the agreement provides that the terms of the restricted stock arrangement can be amended or terminated by the board of directors at any time. To the extent that the amendment or termination has any adverse effect on the employee, however, the amendment or termination is not effective without the consent of the employee.

3.8.5 Purchase Procedures

If payment is required for the restricted shares, the employee must follow the procedures established by the company to purchase the stock. Typically, these procedures are set forth in the employee's restricted stock agreement. At a minimum, these procedures require that the employee provide written notice to the company stating his or her intention to purchase the restricted shares. This written notice may also contain other information, such as:

- Specific representations and/or statements by the employee deemed necessary by the company to ensure compliance with all required federal and/or state securities laws.

- Information relevant to the form of payment that the employee has selected to pay the total required purchase price for the number of restricted shares being purchased.

- Specific statements pertaining to the tax withholding obligations of the employee if any, arising in connection with the purchase and/or vesting of the restricted shares.

- Specific statements with respect to any restrictions and/or conditions imposed on the restricted shares.

Generally, the written notice must be submitted to the plan administrator or other designated representative of the company in person, or by registered or certified mail with return receipt requested, before the expiration date of the restricted stock purchase arrangement. The notice should be accompanied by full payment of the total purchase price for the number of restricted shares being purchased and any other required documents.

3.8.6 Filing of Section 83(b) Election

If the employee wishes to file a Section 83(b) election, it must be filed within 30 days of the purchase or award date. The election is filed with the IRS office where the employee files his or her tax return and must include the name, address and tax ID number of the employee, a description of the property for which the election is filed and the restrictions applicable to it, the date the stock was purchased or awarded, the fair market value of the stock on the purchase or award date, the amount paid for the stock, and a statement that all required copies of the election have been provided to the appropriate parties. A copy of the election must be provided to the company. Previously, the employee was also required to file a copy with his or her tax return for the year in which the election was filed. In 2016, however, the IRS amended Treasury Regulations Section 1.83-2(c) to eliminate this requirement. The new regulation is effective for transfers of property occurring on or after January 1, 2016, but taxpayers were permitted to rely on the proposed regulation, which was the same as the final regulation, for transfers of property in 2015. Moreover, failure on the part of the employee to file a copy of the election with his/her tax return in the past did not invalidate the election. IRS Rev. Proc. 2012-29 provides a sample Section 83(b) election form.

3.8.7 Withholding Taxes

If the recipient is an employee of the company, upon the vesting/distribution of the restricted shares (or the purchase or award, if a Section 83(b) election has been filed and the purchase or award price of the shares is less than the fair market value of the company's stock on the date of purchase or award), the company is obligated to withhold applicable federal and state income tax. In addition, withholding is required for purposes of the Medicare Insurance portion of FICA, and may be required for purposes of the Social Security portion of FICA to the extent that the employee has not already satisfied his or her annual obligation.

Arrangements must be made to satisfy any withholding tax obligations that arise in connection with the vesting (or purchase or award) of the restricted shares. In accordance with Section 83 of the Code, the applicable taxes will be calculated based on the fair market value of the company's stock on the vesting/distribution date (or the purchase or award date, in the event that a Section 83(b) election has been filed).

Most companies provide employees with notification of this tax liability in advance of the vesting/distribution date. In most cases it is not possible to accurately calculate the employee's tax liability until the vesting/distribution date, but the advance notice might estimate this liability based on the current fair market value of the company's stock and offer the employee several alternatives for paying the taxes. Subject to the terms of the restricted stock plan, these alternatives might include payment in cash (usually by check), additional withholding from the employee's paychecks before the vesting/distribution date, sale of the shares, loan, or withholding a portion of the shares vesting.

As mentioned earlier, withholding sufficient shares to cover the employee's tax withholding liability is often the most expedient method of dispatching this obligation. Where feasible for the company from an administrative and cash-flow standpoint and where permissible under the terms of the plan, it may be advisable for the notice to provide that this method will be applied in the absence of any other election and to set a firm deadline for making a different election. In addition, the notice usually states the time period within which the company must receive the withholding tax payment, generally before or very shortly after the vest date. The company generally holds the certificate for the vested shares of stock until full payment of all amounts due is received. Where feasible and permissible, it may also be advisable to provide that if full payment is not received by the required deadline, a portion of the vested shares will be applied to the tax payment. This can alleviate a situation where employees procrastinate making the required tax payments and the company has no recourse but to continue holding the shares for an indefinite period.

3.8.7.1 *Withholding Shares to Cover Taxes*

Under this tax payment method, the company withholds some of the shares currently being released to the employee to cover his or her tax obligation. The withheld shares are not sold on the open market; essentially, the shares are sold back to the company.

Share withholding offers considerable advantages to both the company and employees: it relieves the employee of the sometimes considerable burden associated with making a cash payment, and it does not require coordination with outside vendors (such as a brokerage firm).

> *Example 9:* An employee is granted a restricted stock award for 1,000 shares. When the award vests, the shares have a fair market value of $16 per share. The employee recognizes $16,000 of compensation income on the vest date ($1,000 shares multiplied by $16 per share). This income is subject to federal tax withholding as follows:* $3,520 of federal income tax, $992 of Social Security, and $232 of Medicare. The aggregate tax withholding for the transaction is $4,744. The company withholds 297 shares to cover the taxes ($4,744 divided by the $16 per share fair market value, rounded up to the nearest whole share). The withheld shares have a total value of $4,752, which is slightly higher than the tax withholding obligation; the company can refund the excess $8 in value to the employee or can aggregate it with the employee's tax payment and deposit it with the IRS on the employee's behalf. The employee receives 703 shares (1,000 shares released less the 297 shares withheld to cover the taxes).
>
> * Based on 2018 withholding rates, including a flat rate for federal income tax purposes of 22%, a Social Security tax rate of 6.2%, and a Medicare tax rate of 1.45%. Assumes the employee has not yet reached the wage cap for Social Security tax purposes (and, likewise, the threshold at which the additional Medicare tax applies). State taxes may also be applicable.

Under some plans, the withheld shares are returned to the plan reserve and can be regranted to other participants, referred to as "share recycling." Under the ISS Equity Plan Scorecard, where a plan provides for share recycling, points are deducted from the plan's score (ISS considers this to be a "liberal share counting policy"). Some plans may earn enough points elsewhere in the scorecard that the loss of points for this provision is not important; other companies may be forced to choose between retaining the share recycling provision and reducing their share request. Other proxy advisory firms and institutional investors likewise may not view share recycling favorably.

Withholding shares to cover tax payments is not considered an open-market sale. As such, the transaction is not subject to Rule 144 and is generally exempt from the short-swing profits recovery provisions of Section 16(b). For purposes of Section 16(a), the cancellation of the shares is reportable on a Form 4 within two business days, but it is a reported as an exempt sale of stock to the company rather than an open-market or similar non-exempt transaction. Because the transaction does not occur on the open market, withholding shares to cover taxes is generally is permissible even during a company blackout period. This is, however, a matter of company policy; some companies choose to restrict share withholding to open window periods because the value of the shares is based on the current stock price. Where insiders are allowed to have shares withheld shares to cover their taxes during blackout periods, it may be advisable to require the share withholding election to be made during an open window period or to be made pursuant to a Rule 10b5-1 trading plan.

The most significant disadvantage to share withholding is that the company must pay over the taxes to the Internal Revenue Service in cash but is reimbursed for this cash expenditure with the shares of stock withheld from the employee's award. This creates a cash outflow for the company; where cash flow is a concern, this payment method may not be viable.

Under ASC 718, as amended by ASU 2016-09, withholding shares for tax payments in excess of the maximum individual tax rate in the applicable tax jurisdiction triggers liability treatment for the award.[21] In addition, allowing share withholding for tax payments when there is no statutory requirement to withhold taxes also triggers liability treatment. Where a company establishes a pattern of allowing share withholding for tax payments in excess of the applicable maximum individual rate or allowing share withholding when there is no legal requirement to withhold taxes, liability treatment could apply to the entire restricted stock plan. Note also that ASC 718 provides guidance only on how the

---

21. Companies that have not yet adopted ASU 2016-09 must limit the shares withheld for taxes to the minimum statutorily required tax payment.

transaction must be accounted for; the procedures for withholding taxes must comply with the regulations promulgated by the relevant tax authority, as described earlier in this chapter (i.e., U.S. federal income taxes must be withheld using the aggregate method or at the flat rate, no other rate is permissible). Generally, taxes should not be withheld for outside directors and other non-employees. In addition to the penalties for doing so that could apply under the Code, allowing share withholding for these individuals will trigger liability treatment under ASC 718 because there is no statutorily required withholding for non-employees. At a minimum, liability treatment will apply to the award in question. Where the company establishes a pattern of allowing share withholding for non-employees, or where it seems likely that the company will allow this in the future, liability treatment could apply to all awards granted to outside directors and other non-employees under the plan.

In most cases, the per-share value of the shares will not evenly divide into the tax withholding obligation for the transaction. Because shares must be issued in whole amounts, companies will have to decide whether to round the shares withheld up or down to the nearest whole share. If rounded down, the employee will have to provide a small cash payment to the company to make up for the shortfall. This payment is typically deducted from the employee's next paycheck.

Alternatively, the shares withheld may be rounded up, causing the value of the withheld shares to exceed the employee's tax withholding obligation. The excess can be refunded to the employee or can be included with the tax withholding for the transaction and paid over to the IRS as an additional tax payment on behalf of the employee. Most respondents to the NASPP's 2016 Domestic Stock Plan Design Survey (cosponsored by Deloitte) indicate that the shares withheld are rounded up, with 62% of respondents including the excess with the employee's tax withholding and 13% of respondents refunding the excess to employees. Where U.S. federal income tax is withheld at the maximum individual tax rate (as is the case for employees who have received over $1 million in supplemental payments during the year), there is some concern that rounding the shares withheld up to the nearest whole share constitutes a cash payout (because this results in a payment in excess of the applicable maximum individual tax rate or a cash payment to the employee) and thus triggers liability treatment for accounting purposes. This can particularly be a concern where an employee has multiple awards vesting on the same day and thus the additional tax payment or refund to the employee is in excess of the price of one share. Companies should consult their accounting advisors when deciding on their rounding approach in this situation.

3.8.7.2 *Sale of Shares to Cover Tax Withholding*

This tax payment method is similar to a same-day-sale exercise of a stock option: the employee's broker is directed to sell a portion of the vested shares on the open market, and the sale proceeds are applied to the employee's tax withholding obligation. Generally, just enough shares are sold to cover the tax withholding and associated brokerage fees; the remainder of the shares are deposited in the employee's brokerage account. The shares necessary to cover the taxes are issued directly to the brokerage firm and are sold—and the proceeds remitted to the company—before the remaining shares are released to the employee. Just as with a same-day-sale exercise of a stock option, the shares may be sold before they are issued.

> *Example 10:* Assume the employee in example 9 sells shares on the open market to cover the tax withholding, instead of tendering shares back to the company. The shares are sold at $17 per share, and the employee pays a brokerage fee of $25 on the sale. Two hundred eighty-one shares will be sold to cover the tax withholding ($4,744 tax liability plus the $25 brokerage fee, divided by the $17 per share sale price). The employee will report a short-term capital gain of $256 on the sale. This represents the difference between the amount realized on the sale ($4,777 sale proceeds less $25 brokerage fee) and the fair market value of the shares sold on the vest date (281 shares multiplied by $16 per share fair market value). The remaining 719 shares are deposited in the employee's brokerage account, along with the $8 left over from the sale ($4,777 sale proceeds, less $4,744 tax liability and $25 brokerage fee).

This payment method relieves employees of the burden of making cash payments to cover their tax withholding while also eliminating any cash outflow for the company. It is marginally more expensive for employees, since they will generally pay a fee to the brokerage firm executing the sale. It also is more dilutive than if shares were withheld to cover the tax withholding.

Where a large number of awards or units will be released on the same day, the trading volume in the company's stock must be sufficient to provide a market for the sales, or this tax payment method will not be practical. Where there is insufficient trading volume, the sales may need to be spread over several days and could cause the company's stock price to decline, resulting in losses for some employees.

And, of course, the sale is an open-market transaction. For insiders and company affiliates, the sale is subject to both Rule 144 and the short-swing profits recovery provisions of Section 16. The acquisition of shares pursuant to the vesting/payout event is generally exempt from the short-swing profits recovering provisions, so the combined transactions (vesting/payout and associated sale) do not trigger short-swing profits recovery, but it is necessary to ensure that that insiders do not have any other nonexempt acquisitions of company stock during both the six months before and after the sale. The sale is reportable on a Form 4 within two business days. Finally, the sale will be prohibited during company blackout periods unless executed pursuant to a Rule 10b5-1 trading plan.

The timing of remittance of the sale proceeds to the company may also be of critical importance. Sale transactions such as this are generally subject to a settlement period of three days, yet, as described above, where the cumulative withholding exceeds $100,000, it must be deposited with the IRS within one business day. An IRS field directive provides that the one-day period is measured from the settlement date for nonqualified stock option exercises (where a sale is involved), but it is unclear whether this directive can be relied on for restricted stock awards.

3.8.7.3 *FICA Taxes Due at Vest for Deferred RSUs*

Where a restricted stock unit is subject to a valid deferral election, income taxes are deferred until the underlying shares are released. In this situation, the FICA taxes that are due from the employee can be a particular challenge because these taxes are triggered when the award is no longer subject to a substantial risk of forfeiture—typically, the vesting date, as noted above in section 3.4.1. Thus, even though the underlying shares have not yet been paid out and income tax has not been assessed for the award, the employee may be subject to FICA once the award has vested. (In general, FUTA, which is paid entirely by the company, is subject to the same rules regarding timing, assessment, and collection as FICA. Thus, where employees have not met the maximum wage threshold for FUTA purposes, FUTA taxes are due at the same time that the company collects FICA taxes.)

Where the award will be paid out within the same calendar year or within 2½ months after the end of the year in which the award vests, it may be possible to delay collection of FICA taxes until the distribution event. Under Treasury Regulations Section 31.3121(v)(2)-(1)(b)(3)(iii), often referred to as the "FICA short-term deferral rule," if the award will be paid out within 2½ months after the end of the calendar year in which the award vested, collection of FICA taxes can be deferred until the underlying shares are distributed. Under this rule, the value of the shares for FICA purposes is based on the fair market value of the stock on the distribution date. Where the stock increases in value from the vesting date to the distribution date, the FICA taxes will be higher (but the reverse is also true—if the stock decreases in value, the FICA taxes will be reduced). This rule offers the advantage of allowing the company to wait to collect the FICA taxes until income taxes are assessed and collected on the award, which is likely easier from an administrative standpoint. It also enables employees to sell or have shares withheld to cover both the FICA and income tax payments without affecting their tax consequences. There is some question, however, as to whether this rule can be relied on for restricted stock unit awards. An IRS ruling issued on October 9, 1999, Technical Advice Memorandum 199923045, seems to support application of the rule to unit awards, but companies that wish to rely on this rule should verify its applicability with their legal advisors. In addition, where this rule is relied on, it must be applied to all employees participating in the plan and in substantially similar plans.

If the FICA short-term deferral rule cannot be relied on, another rule may help. Under Treasury Regulations Section 31.3121(v)(2)-1(e)(5), often referred to as the "rule of administrative convenience," collection of FICA taxes can be delayed to any later date in the same calendar year in which vesting occurs (but in no event can collection of FICA taxes be delayed beyond the distribution date). Where the award will be paid out within this same calendar year, e.g., if distribution is deferred for only a short period, such as for a trading blackout period, this rule could be relied on to delay collection of FICA to the distribution event. As under the FICA short-term deferral rule, under the rule of administrative convenience, the value of the stock for FICA purposes is based on the fair market value of the stock on the distribution date.

Where restricted stock units will not be paid out within 2½ months after the calendar year in which the awards vest, FICA taxes will have to be assessed and collected before distribution occurs. While, technically, FICA taxes are due when unit awards vest, there are two tax regulations that can be relied on to defer collection of the FICA taxes to a later date:

- As previously mentioned, the rule of rule of administrative convenience (Treasury Regulations Section 31.3121(v)(2)-1(e)(5)) allows the collection of FICA taxes to be deferred to any later date within the same calendar in which vesting occurs. Where the award will be paid out after the end of this calendar year, this rule could be relied on to defer collection of FICA until very late in the year, e.g., the last payroll period. Assuming employees meet the maximum wage threshold for the Social Security portion of FICA, only the Medicare portion of FICA would then be required to be collected— a significantly smaller and easier amount to collect (it might even be feasible to simply withhold this amount from employees' final paychecks for the year). Where this rule is relied on, the value of the stock for FICA purposes is based on the fair market value of the stock on the collection date.

- Treasury Regulations Section 31.3121(v)(2)-1(f)(3), often referred to as the "lag method," allows the collection of FICA taxes to be deferred for up to three months after the vesting event. This rule might be useful where awards vest late in the year, e.g., on December 31, and the rule of administrative convenience is of less benefit. Under the lag method, the value of the shares for FICA purposes is based on the fair market value of the stock as of the vesting date but the tax payment must include interest for the period of the delay, thus increasing the payment.

Regardless of the rule relied on to delay collection of FICA taxes, under no circumstances can the collection of FICA be delayed beyond the distribution event.

Section 409A permits employees to elect to sell or tender a portion of the underlying shares to cover the FICA payments, without any restrictions as to when the election to do so must be made. The employee will realize constructive receipt of any shares sold or tendered and will therefore recognize income tax on these shares. If these shares would not otherwise have been paid out at this time, this increases the employee's tax liability. Section 409A permits sale or tender of a further portion of the underlying shares to cover this additional tax liability, but doing so will further increase the employee's tax liability.

For awards where FICA must be collected before the distribution event, because sale or tender of the underlying shares increases the employee's tax liability at the time FICA is collected, some companies find it preferable to require that employees pay the FICA amounts in cash, via either a check or via payroll deduction.

3.8.7.4 *Special Tax Withholding Considerations for Performance-Based Unit Awards*

Unlike the typical restricted stock unit award, performance-based units frequently have bifurcated vesting and payout events. In the typical performance-based award, performance is measured over a specified period (referred to as the "performance period"). Once the performance period has concluded, the compensation committee of the board of directors will generally be required to certify that the performance goals have been achieved before the award can be paid out. This process can take several weeks to a few months. Once performance has been certified, there may be a further administrative delay while the company prepares for the distribution. In some cases, an additional service requirement must be met before the awards can be paid out, while other companies treat the awards as vested and earned as of the end of the performance period. All of these factors can affect when performance-based unit awards are subject to taxation.

The following examples illustrate common performance-award arrangements and discuss how each is taxed.

Example 11: A company grants a performance-based unit award for which performance is measured over a three-year period. Upon conclusion of the performance period, the compensation committee must certify achievement of the performance goals before the award can be paid out. This certification will occur within two months after the conclusion of the performance period, and the award will be paid out within one week of when performance is certified. The award will be subject to taxation for FICA/FUTA purposes when it is considered vested (i.e., the date the award is no longer subject to a substantial risk of forfeiture) but will not be subject to federal income tax until it is paid out.

As a practical matter, however, because the performance period concludes, performance is certified, and the award is paid out within a short period (less than two and half months, in our scenario), the company would likely rely on the FICA short-term deferral rule (discussed in section 3.8.7.3) to delay payment of FICA/FUTA until the payout date. In the fact pattern described, this is a viable strategy regardless of whether the award is considered vested as of the end of the performance period or at the time performance is certified. Moreover, this strategy is viable even if the award is considered to have vested in one calendar year but is not paid out until early in the next calendar year. The FICA short-term deferral rule allows FICA/FUTA taxation to be deferred to the payout date so long as the payout occurs no later than two and a half months after the end of the calendar year in which the award vests. If, for some reason, the FICA short-term deferral rule is not available, the company might be able to rely on the lag method (discussed in section 3.8.7.3), which allows payment of FICA/FUTA to be delayed for up to three months after the vesting date, to delay FICA/FUTA taxation until the payout date.

Example 12: Assume the same facts as in example 11 except that instead of the award being paid out once performance has been certified, the award is subject to a one-year service-based vesting requirement (meaning that if the employee terminates with a year after performance is certified, the award will be forfeited). The award will be paid out immediately at the conclusion of the one-year vesting period. In this scenario, the award is subject to both federal income tax and FICA/FUTA at the conclusion of the one-year vesting period.

Example 13: Assume the same facts as in example 11, but further assume that the award holder has made a valid election to defer payout of the award for five years after conclusion of the performance period. In this case, the award will be subject to federal income tax only when the award is paid out at the end of the five-year deferral period. The award will be subject to FICA/FUTA in the year that it vests (this could be the end of the performance period or the date achievement of the performance goals is certified, depending on the terms of the award). The company might choose to rely on either the rule of administrative convenience or the lag method to delay taxation of the award for FICA/FUTA purposes, but both of these taxes would need to be paid well before the end of the deferral period.

3.8.8 Issuance of Shares

The plan administrator must provide instructions to the company's transfer agent for the preparation and issuance of a certificate for the restricted shares purchased or awarded for no consideration. The instructions should include the number of shares of stock to be issued, the number of certificates to be issued, the correct name under which the shares are to be registered, and appropriate mailing instructions. Generally, the transfer agent's instructions require the signature of an authorized company representative.

In anticipation of the initial purchase or award of restricted shares, the plan administrator should provide the company's transfer agent with a list of the relevant legends to be placed on certificates for the restricted shares. Transfer agents or legal counsel are usually able to assist with the drafting of these legends. Legends may be required by applicable federal and/or state securities laws to prevent transfers of the restricted shares that are not in compliance with such laws. In addition, where the restricted shares are subject to repurchase rights or transferability restrictions set forth in the restricted stock plan or imposed by the company, the certificates should include appropriate legends to notify potential grantees of these restrictions.

CHAPTER FOUR

Performance Award Plans

Dan Walter

Contents

4.1 What Is Performance Equity?

The use of performance-based equity continues to grow as equity compensation evolves. This growing popularity is being driven primarily by a perceived lack of alignment between corporate performance and the compensation received by executives. "Performance-based equity" is a term used for a wide variety of equity instruments and design techniques. To properly understand performance-based equity, we must first establish what is meant by the term.

Performance conditions can be applied to almost any equity instrument. Knowing when performance goals are used, what the performance goals are, and how performance goals modify an award is essential to understanding performance-based equity.[1] The lack of a common lexicon for performance-based equity has led to much of the disparate data on its use.

Performance metrics are applied to equity compensation in a variety of ways. Pre-award performance can determine eligibility, the award size, or the grant price. Post-award performance is commonly used to accelerate vesting, determine eligibility for vesting, and determine the amount to be earned, vested, or paid out. At a corporate level, metrics may be aligned with the company's stock value or its financial or operational performance. Metrics may also be set at group and individual levels.

Performance awards can take the form of equity that has been granted as a result of meeting performance criteria before the award date. For these awards, the performance metrics often determine both eligibility and award size. Performance awards often require additional time-based vesting to be met, but sometimes they are fully vested as of the award date. These awards can result in miscommunication between the process used to create them and the process used to administer and report on them. Many stock administration and accounting professionals are unaware of the pre-award goals that play into these awards, and thus the awards are often classified simply as restricted stock or restricted units.

Performance awards can also take the form of equity that has been granted with metrics that apply after the initial award date. These types of awards come in many variations. Currently, the most common structure requires both a period of time and a performance metric to be satisfied for vesting to occur. Another popular design uses a standard time-based vesting schedule that allows for acceleration if certain goals are met. For some programs, there is only a performance metric. The accounting for performance-only plans can be tricky in a volatile mar-

---

1.   For purposes of this chapter, the terms "award" and "grant" will be interchangeable unless otherwise noted.

ket. Goals may be met much faster or slower than is initially planned. In still other programs, the underlying equity can be earned based on meeting incremental performance goals and subsequently vested or released pursuant to a time-based schedule.

Table 4-1 lists the 11 types of performance equity.

The most common use of performance metrics is as a vesting modifier on full-value awards such as restricted stock shares and units. Full-value awards have no purchase cost to the participant, but some performance awards may require an initial investment. While there is no consistent naming convention used by all companies, most use some variation of "performance shares" or "performance units." Equity is awarded in a manner similar to time-based awards, but the timing and/or amount of vesting is determined by pre-defined metrics. These awards usually allow for multiple levels of potential vesting. Common terminology includes the following: "Threshold" is the minimum performance level that must be met. "Target" is an acceptable middle payout. "Maximum" is the cap on the amount of equity that can be earned from the award. The terms used by companies vary widely; however, most external data use the above terms fairly consistently.

Performance shares are restricted stock shares that are issued at the time of award and may be earned, vested, or paid out based on performance metrics. Performance units are split into two categories. The first category of performance units is generally granted on a one-unit-to-one-share basis. This is most commonly used by public companies and is usually used in coordination with other types of equity awards. The second category of performance units is a company-defined denomination for each unit. One of these units may be worth several shares or may be based on a specific dollar amount that is then converted to shares in the event of earning, vesting, or payout. This type of unit is most often used in private companies or in companies that only peripherally link these awards to other equity plans. In both categories earning, vesting, or payout is determined by performance metrics and, in some cases, a period of time.

Performance-based stock options also come in many variations. The most typical type of performance option program accelerates vesting based on a performance metric. Another common type of performance-based option is the premium-priced option (PPO). PPOs

Table 4-1. The 11 Types of Performance Equity

Type	Description
Performance-awarded shares	Award of restricted outstanding shares. Award size based on meeting defined goals. Vesting is typically based on time.
Performance-awarded units	Award of restricted stock units. Award size based on meeting defined goals. Vesting is typically based on time.
Performance-leveraged units	Award of restricted stock units. Spread at vest is typically multiplied or divided by factors of between 1 and 5, based on performance against goals.
Performance-earned units	Award of restricted stock units. Shares at payout are determined as a percentage of shares awarded, as related to threshold, target, or maximum goals.
Performance-accelerated units	Award of restricted stock units. Award vesting is time-based, but can be moved forward if goals are met.
Performance-priced units	Variable-priced units. Award price is set according to performance against defined goals or index of companies.
Indexed options	Variable-priced stock options. Exercise price linked to performance to a present index or group of peers.
Performance-granted options	Grant of stock options. Grant size based on meeting preset goals. Vesting is typically based on time.
Performance-accelerated options	Grant of stock options. Grant vesting is time-based, but can be moved forward if goals are met.
Premium-priced options	Grant of stock options. Exercise price is set to a price higher than current FMV. Typical plans set price at a 10%-15% premium.
Performance-earned options	Grant of stock options. Options available to be exercised are determined as a percentage of total granted, as related to threshold, target, or maximum goals.

have a grant price that is higher than the stock price on the date of grant. The most common threshold is a 10% premium. This means that if the stock price on the grant date is $50, the grant price will be $55. This ensures that the stock price must rise significantly before there is any intrinsic value for the participant. PPOs can be effective for companies with low to average volatility, but provide little to those companies with highly volatile stock prices. Less popular designs allow for performance-based modifications of the number of options or an exercise price that varies against a preset index of peer companies. Performance-based stock options are less popular than shares or units. Since the exercise price of stock options creates an initial hurdle to value creation, the additional hurdle for a vesting event is often seen as having two separate and perhaps unrelated performance measures on the same equity award.

When an award is given for meeting goals, such as in a performance award, generally those goals are part of a company's short-term incentive (STI) plan. Designed properly, performance awards can link short-term performance to long-term retention. Equity awards with performance goals that apply after the award date are generally part of a company's long-term incentive (LTI) program. In today's compliance and governance environment, it is important for companies to clearly define the purposes of their plans and ensure that goals are not unintentionally additive, meaning they are essentially based on the same metrics.

The flexibility of performance-based equity is one of the more intriguing and frustrating aspects of these plans. The multiple variations in terminology, structure, application to different equity instruments, and metrics create a complex environment without many definitive rules. This same flexibility can create program successes and issues that are unusual, even for the world of equity compensation. Great care must be taken to avoid the potential for mistakes and misunderstanding. Adding to the difficulty of creating effective plans is the fact that administration systems are still in their evolutionary stages. The use of performance equity is certain to continue to grow, and companies must prepare for both the strategic and tactical effort required for these plans.

4.2 The Growing Interest in Performance Equity

Until very recently, performance equity was used sparingly in the United States. Since 2005, the use of these plans has steadily risen. Surveys show that more than 50% of U.S. companies have some form of a performance equity program. Outside the U.S., performance equity has been widely used for at least a decade, mainly in executive programs. More than 90% of companies in the U.K. and Australia have some form of performance equity. Use of performance-based equity has largely been driven by growth in shareholder "management say on pay" (MSOP) provisions that have become mandatory across much of the Western world. With the inclusion of an MSOP provision in the Dodd-Frank Wall Street Reform and Consumer Protection Act that was signed into law in August 2010, the U.S. will have mandatory MSOP for most public companies beginning in 2011. If the U.S. follows the pattern shown by countries in Europe that already have mandatory MSOP, companies will move quickly to use executive equity programs that are tied to explicit performance goals.

The extreme volatility of the stock market since the year 2000 is another driver in the growing use of equity compensation. Volatile stock prices result in unpredictable equity payouts. Underwater stock options and stock option exchanges have received a great deal of attention, most of it negative. There is a growing argument that the significant amount of underwater options, combined with companies feeling a need to replace them, is proof that stock options are a flawed compensation device. Companies increasingly turned to restricted stock shares and units, also known as "full value" shares, to help combat the impact of volatility. During the most recent steep market decline in 2008 and 2009, even these full-value awards received less than positive support from employees at many companies. Employees felt that the market's decline was not indicative of their individual or their company's performance, i.e., their compensation was being affected by forces beyond their control. Shareholders, on the other hand, have been decrying the use of time-based full-value awards for decades. Their argument is that time-based awards retain value even when the shareholder stock does not. This conflict between employees and shareholders is not likely to end, but properly designed performance equity may provide a compromise for both sides of the argument.

The design of a performance equity program can help moderate the volatility of the stock market. Performance equity can also compensate individuals fairly when corporate or individual performance is not in line with market performance. This moderating factor can be performed through indexed performance; relative performance; and performance that is explicit to internal, financial, or operational goals. In the end, it is important to remember that shareholders see corporate performance delivered in the form of rising or falling stock prices. Any plan design, metrics, and communications must keep this basic premise in mind.

Institutional shareholders and proxy advisory firms have become increasingly demanding with regard to linking corporate performance to compensation. Evolving guidance on compensation structure seeks more explanation and evidence of the alignment between executive pay and corporate performance. For example, the ISS 2010 Pay for Performance Policy describes not only the need for this alignment but suggests possible metrics to be used:

ISS Pay for Performance Policy 2010:

Evaluate the alignment of the CEO's pay with performance over time, focusing particularly on companies that have underperformed their peers over a sustained period. From a shareholders' perspective, performance is predominantly gauged by the company's stock performance over time. Even when financial or operational measures are utilized in incentive awards, the achievement related to these measures should ultimately translate into superior shareholder returns in the long-term.

Focus on companies with sustained underperformance relative to peers, considering the following key factors:

- Whether a company's one-year and three-year total shareholder returns ("TSR") are in the bottom half of its industry group (i.e., four-digit GICS – Global Industry Classification Group); and

- Whether the total compensation of a CEO who has served at least two consecutive fiscal years is aligned with the company's total shareholder return over time, including both recent and long-term periods.

The advent of MSOP in the U.S., combined with increasing shareholder scrutiny and a stock market that continues to be volatile, will continue to spur growth in the use of performance-based equity. Employee dissatisfaction with time-based equity during volatile markets is another driver of change. It is essential that companies design, communicate, and administer these programs in a way that supports the understanding and acceptance of everyone involved.

4.3   Designing a Performance Equity Plan

4.3.1   Purpose and Intended Consequences

The most important aspect of any performance equity plan is that it aligns the goals of the participant with those of the company and its shareholders. This requires a thorough understanding of your business and the factors that drive its success. It may also require an understanding of your peers, stock market conditions, and what motivates your staff.

Performance equity plans most often fail for three reasons.

1.   The goal structure or progress to the goal was not properly communicated, and participants did not understand or were not focused on the goal.
2.   Goals did not ensure that participants had to stretch to attain them.
3.   Goals did not properly account for market or other volatility and became unattainable or too easily satisfied.

The first step in proper alignment is to clearly define the purpose of the plan. Compensation programs are designed to attract, motivate, and retain staff members. It can be difficult to design a single program that equally meets the needs of all three of these objectives. Most often performance plans are designed to first motivate staff and then to retain them. At present, these programs are seldom used to attract new staff. Once you have defined your programs' high-level objectives, you must then clarify the specifics of what you are trying to motivate and who you are trying to retain. You must also define how you will link these individuals to the intended objectives of the plan (see table 4-2).

Companies with successful performance equity plans have completed a thorough analysis and evaluation of the elements that relate directly to performance at their company. Unlike many other types of equity plans, it is very difficult to determine the proper metrics to use based

Table 4-2. Intended Objectives of a Performance Equity Program

Objective	Goals to consider
Increase shareholder value	Higher stock price Better dividends Increased market capitalization
Better align participants' goals with those of investors	Long-term investment growth Market-leading presence
Reduce "lottery" aspect of equity compensation	Reduce impact of market volatility, including underwater stock options, over-leveraged stock option value, and restricted stock that holds value even when the company performs poorly.
Focus participants on those metrics that best support long-term corporate success	Financial metrics Operational metrics Customer relations/satisfaction metrics
Obtain shareholder buy-in for current and future share usage	Defensible argument for purpose of approved shares. Link to metrics that shareholders use to base buy/sell decisions.

on a simple review of competitive market data. With the exception of total shareholder return (TSR), the specific metrics used in these plans are usually as unique as each individual company. A thorough analysis requires a review of financial, operational, and human resources metrics and objectives from the past. This analysis must then show a link between those metrics and objectives and their impact on both corporate performance and (hopefully) the stock price.

As discussed above, most plans allow for a range of potential payouts. The lowest number of shares that can be earned is based on a threshold or minimum goal. The base amount of the award is expressed as the target, and the highest number of shares is based on a maximum goal. The target of the award is usually expressed as the 100% goal. This is the number of shares or units that is communicated to the participant as his or her award amount. If performance is somewhere between the target and the threshold, the participant receives less than 100%. If performance is above the target, the payout is above 100%. Many plans have a minimum threshold that pays out regardless of performance. This allows for the company to have a guaranteed retentive value for the award. Payouts between each defined level can be calculated linearly or in predefined steps. Because we are discussing only equity-based awards, the maximum amount refers only to the number of shares, units, or options and not the cash value.

Some awards incorporate "negative discretion" for some performance metrics. Essentially, negative discretion allows the company to reduce or eliminate any shares or units that may have been otherwise earned pursuant to a more formulaic method. For example, a company may set a payout of 100% of units based on a quantitative absolute TSR goal and allow for modification of the final payout based on a subjective goal, such as the board's evaluation of total job performance. The final payout could then be modified downward if the TSR goal was met but the board determined the CEO's overall performance to be below expectations. Awards that allow for negative discretion may have unexpected accounting considerations.[2] Metrics incorporating negative discretion are generally qualitative in nature and are often combined with other, more quantitative, goals that must also be met. Essentially, negative discretion allows the company to reduce or eliminate any shares or units that may have been otherwise earned pursuant to a more formulaic method. For example, a company may set a payout of 100% of units based on a quantitative absolute TSR goal and allow for modification of the final payout based on a subjective goal, such as the board's evaluation of total job performance. The final payout could then be modified downward if the TSR goal was met but the board determined the CEO's overall performance to be below expectations.

4.3.2 Determining Metrics and Goals

Accounting rules on share-based compensation separate metrics into two categories: market conditions and performance conditions. These goals have different accounting properties.[3] Market conditions are metrics that are tied directly to the company's stock price. TSR, since it is based on a combination of stock price and dividends, is a good example of a market goal. Performance conditions are metrics that are not tied directly to the company's stock price. EBITDA and revenue are

---

2.   See section 4.1.5 in "Expense Recognition for Market, Performance, and Service Conditions," chap. 4 in Takis Makridis, *Advanced Topics in Equity Compensation Accounting*, 8th ed. (NCEO, 2019).

3.   For details on accounting, see Barbara Baksa, *Accounting for Equity Compensation*, 15th ed. (NCEO, 2019).

examples of performance goals. It is not uncommon to see these two categories of goals combined in a single award. The metrics used for performance equity plans generally fall into one of several categories, as summarized in table 4-3.

Table 4-3. Metrics Used for Performance Equity Plans

External metrics	Absolute total shareholder return (A-TSR) Relative total shareholder return (R-TSR) Stock price
Internal financial metrics	Revenue, earnings per share (EPS) Return on invested capital (ROIC) Earnings before interest, taxes, depreciation, and amortization (EBITDA)
Operational metrics	Production volumes Delivery timing
Group, team, and project metrics	Departmental year-over-year customer satisfaction Delivery of new software program FDA approval
Individual metrics	Performance appraisal Sales goals Project/task success factor

The measurement of performance for most metrics can be relative or absolute. A relative goal is also defined by reference to the same performance measure in another entity or peer group. For example, a relative goal could be attaining a growth rate in earnings per share (EPS) that exceeds the average growth rate in EPS of other companies in the same industry. Relative goals generally flatten the volatility of a company's individual performance and provide a moving benchmark outside of company analysis. Levels for these goals may be easier for a company to set since they require less accuracy in predicting a future outcome.

While the levels of these goals may be easier to set, choosing and managing a representative peer group can be difficult. When choosing a peer group, a company must take into consideration several factors. The company must evaluate past and potential future performance of each peer for the metrics in question. The data required for measurement must be available in an accurate and timely manner. Rules must be defined for how to handle the exit of companies from the defined peer group. Peers may be acquired, grow to a size that no longer fits the group parameters, change business focus, or go out of business altogether. Too small a peer group at the start can result in too few peers to properly measure results at the end. Too large a peer group may make the administration and tracking of some metrics administratively unfeasible.

Absolute goals do away with the complexity of peer group definition and analysis. These goals instead require a company to accurately project their future performance. For well-established companies, this may be a task that can be accomplished with confidence. For companies that have little history or are in rapidly growing industries, predicting a performance metric two or three years into the future may not be possible. Absolute goals can provide the best alignment to plan participants, but also provide the greatest possibility for large-scale errors. Whether a company chooses a relative goal, an absolute goal, or some combination of both, determining the right metrics to be measured is critical.

TSR is a metric that shareholders feel strongly reflects the performance of a company. Because of this, TSR is easy for shareholders to recognize as a useful goal for equity compensation. In a world where MSOP is mandatory, using metrics that shareholders value is an excellent way to help elicit their approval. In addition, TSR receives fixed grant date accounting under Accounting Standards Codification (ASC) 718 and International Financial Reporting Standards 2 (IFRS 2). These positive factors have helped fuel the growth of the use of this metric.

Relative total shareholder return (R-TSR) is the most common performance metric applied against equity around the world. Total shareholder return (TSR) is expressed as an annualized rate of return that reflects appreciation in stock price plus the reinvestment of any dividends and the compounding effect of any dividends that are paid on the reinvested dividends. For an R-TSR plan, a company measures its TSR against a group of peers. Shares are earned, vested, or paid out based on the ranking of the company against the peer group. An R-TSR plan allows shares to vest even if the company's stock price is falling. These plans also moderate the leveraging effect of the stock price if the market is pushing all companies upward.

TSR also has downsides and risks. Very few employees, even at the executive level, can clearly link the work they do with a direct impact on TSR. This lack of alignment makes TSR a weak goal for driving performance even though it is a strong goal for rewarding it. An R-TSR plan can also have the capacity to pay out when performance is poor. If the plan is designed to pay out the maximum amount if the company is the 85th performance percentile or above, and the company's peers perform poorly, then the company may end up paying out at the maximum levels even when its stock price and/or corporate performance are far below expectations. Properly incorporating dividends into a TSR calculation can also be difficult. The design should account for both when the dividend was paid, and the impact it had on the stock price. Finally, many companies are in industries where individual stock prices can be very volatile relative to their peers. Picking a specific point in time for a TSR measurement may not be reflective of the company's ongoing performance over a span of time. Payouts may be significantly higher or lower than shareholders or employees will believe are justified. A key variable is the amount of leverage included when a company under- or over-performs its goals. Improperly designed leveraging can result in participants being delivered shares that are inconsistent with relative peer group performance in other areas such as revenue and profit.

R-TSR offers clear benefits and risks. For these reasons, many companies combine R-TSR with other performance metrics or implement multiple awards, each with its own metric. This "portfolio" approach allows companies to customize their programs to meet the goals of the shareholders, the company, and the employees. Table 4-4 provides an example of an R-TSR plan.

The stock price is another metric with fixed grant date accounting. Historically, stock price has been used in various ways to trigger the vesting or accelerate the vesting of performance equity awards. In some cases, a stock price threshold is created. The threshold must be exceeded for a defined period, usually 30 to 60 days, for the underlying equity to vest. The threshold price is most often set to a level believed to be reachable in a historically similar period of time, as was used for time-based stock options. In a volatile stock market these types of price-based thresholds are very difficult to accurately predict, and they may pay out far too soon, or never. For this reason, many companies use only a price threshold in combination with some other type of goal, if they use it at all.

Table 4-4. Example of a Relative TSR Plan

Metric: TSR
Peer group: S&P 500
Performance period: 3 years
Measurement period: Annually

Ranking criteria and amount earned	Year 1	% Earned	Year 2	% Earned	Year 3	% Earned
	<25th Percentile	50%	<35th Percentile	50%	<50th Percentile	50%
	25th-50th Percentile	75%	35th-60th Percentile	75%	50th-70th Percentile	75%
	50th-75th Percentile	100%	60th-80th Percentile	100%	70th-85th Percentile	100%
	>75th Percentile	150%	>80th Percentile	150%	>85th Percentile	150%

The past 10 years have seen an explosion in the use of sophisticated financial metric analysis to evaluate past performance and predict future performance. An entire field has been created around business intelligence (BI) and corporate performance management (CPM). More companies have moved to include internal financial metrics for their performance equity programs. These metrics can be seen as stand-alone goals but more often are seen in combination with other goals. A popular combination is R-TSR and a broad financial goal such as revenue or EBITDA. A combination of an explicit internal financial metric and a relative external metric allows a company to design a program that directly relates to the understanding and focus of the staff member and shareholders.

Recently there has been a growing use of operational metrics in addition to financial metrics. Some of this is driven by the unpredictability of financial markets over the last two to three years. Much of it is driven by the difficulty of communicating a direct link between operational staff performance and financial goals. Proper performance analysis and the valuation can often identify operational metrics that have a direct impact on financial metrics. Companies have found that the goals that work are the ones that are communicated well and understood by the recipients.

Relatively few companies use group, team, project, or individual metrics for their equity programs. The process for determining metrics that align to shareholder focus can be complex and time-consuming. Since most performance equity programs are still generally restricted to executives, these types of goals are not yet a priority for many companies. It is expected that as performance equity evolves, these programs will become more broad-based and these more granular goals will become more common. In the end, the most important aspect of any performance equity program is that the payouts are aligned to the actual and expected performance of the company.

When the underlying performance is volatile, awards with performance conditions may result in large swings in financial reports. The expense amortized is a combination of the fair value of each share and the probability the shares will vest.[4]

---

4. For more information, see Barbara Baksa, *Accounting for Equity Compensation,* 15th ed. (NCEO, 2019).

4.3.3 Planning for Risk and Unintended Consequences

The risks of performance equity include earning large numbers of shares, based on historic performance, but paying these out when the company is doing poorly. Goals are meant to motivate individuals and executive teams to stretch their capabilities. This stretching can inadvertently result in motivating recipients to put themselves or the company in positions that are potentially more risky than desired. It is essential that a company clearly define its risk profile and understand the risk impact of potential metrics. One often sees companies working only with expected scenarios. It is essential to consider the possibility of worst-case and best-case scenarios. A company must evaluate the impact of each metric individually and in conjunction with other metrics, including those used for non-equity programs. An understanding of the impact must be quantified in the forms of dilutive impact, potential monetary gain (or loss), and post-vesting retentive power. A qualitative analysis should also be performed.

A company must understand potential shareholder reactions, the media-worthiness of the program, and its visibility to employees. Consider the case where a company is in the 90% percentile of its R-TSR peer group and pays out the maximum number of shares to its executives while at the same time battling costs and being forced to reduce its overall corporate headcount. Plan designs must also consider how any goal, or combination of goals, may motivate individuals to focus on a specific metric to the detriment of others. There must be an understanding of goals across different compensation programs that may have an unintended additive effect. Understanding the full risk potential of these programs is a basic requirement of the governance and reporting environment (see table 4-5).

4.3.4 Design Elements Beyond the Metrics

Once a company has chosen an equity vehicle and metrics, it must design a plan that can be understood and administered while allowing for flexibility and evolution. While administrative concerns should not define a plan, consideration must be made for how these plans will be supported, reported, and managed. A stakeholder team that includes representatives from the compensation committee of the board of

Table 4-5. Unintended Consequences of a Performance Equity Program

Unintended consequence	Example of misalignment reasons
Pay executives well when company is cutting pay or reducing headcount for broad-based staff	Shares are earned for prior year's performance and vested when current performance is poor.
Disengage participants due to unreachable goals	The metrics may be correct, but goals associated with them may not be due to change in strategy or market forces.
Disengage participants via misunderstood or poorly communicated plan details	The goals may be arcane and provide little in the way of alignment to participant deliverables. Communication may not be provided on a frequent and consistent basis.
Orient participants on specific goals at the risk of others	Focus on profit without a link to cost or risk may result in goals being met at the expense of actual success.
Losing retentive value due to early payout	The goal is not properly calibrated to potential performance, and vesting occurs before new awards can be granted.
Magnified payout when short-term and long-term goals are too similar	Example: The bonus program is based on revenue, while the equity program is based on EBITDA.

directors, management, legal, finance, compensation, payroll, human resources, and whoever is responsible for equity compensation administration should be involved before finalizing a plan. It is important to define and document (1) the metrics associated with the plan; (2) award conditions such as eligibility, service period before measurement, and change-in-control (CIC) provisions; and (3) termination and retirement rules, and flexibility regarding missed goals. There should also be care taken in defining what happens in the event that a peer group materially changes or metrics no longer apply to a group or individual due to change in strategy or individual status.

Performance plans require carefully crafted plan and award documents. Many plan provisions will be similar to those found in time-based plans. Provisions regarding the purposes of the plan, the definition of fair market value, eligibility, transferability, and corporate actions are likely to follow familiar structures. Other provisions, specifically the sections covering the administration of the plan, terms and conditions of the awards, participant terminations, and shareholder rights, may need to take into consideration unique aspects of performance-based equity. Global considerations must also be defined carefully.

The formal administration of the plan, by the board of directors or its appointed compensation committee, will need to take into account risk factors, clawback contingencies, and how to handle unexpected results. The terms and conditions of the awards must clearly define the possible equity instruments that may be used and the potential vesting rules. They must also define who will make the final determination of performance and when that decision will be made. Termination rules need to account for a participant leaving the company when he or she is partway through a performance measurement period. The plan document must also define how earned but unvested shares will be handled, how clawback provisions can be applied to former employees, and much more. It is essential that the company's compensation, legal, finance, and equity compensation professionals work closely together to create plan documentation that clearly supports the stated goals of the plan, maintains legality, and allows for proper administration.

The careful integration of equity instruments, performance metrics, and plan rules determines the potential of a program. The plan design and correct application of metrics are essential to success, but companies with successful performance equity report that the implementation, rollout, and communication of the plan differentiate the effective from the ineffective.

Companies that pay dividends must include details on how they will be applied to performance equity. Since the final number of shares will not be known until performance is measured and certified, tracking dividends becomes a more difficult task than for time-based equity. The company must first determine whether it will calculate dividends as they are paid, or perform a single calculation when the number of shares has been finalized. If the decision is made to calculate dividends during the performance cycle, the company must also determine whether the dividends will be paid out or held until performance has been certified. This interim calculation of dividends can result in income and taxation issues, as well as administrative concerns. Waiting to pay dividends until the end of the performance cycle can also be problematic. These would not be paid as dividends, but rather are a payment from the company to make a participant "whole" for dividends missed. These payments are generally subject to the rules and taxation associated with ordinary income rather than with dividends.

Plans must also clearly define the rules for potential deferral of payout. See section 3.4 in chapter 3 of this book for a discussion of deferral elections and other tax issues. At the minimum, a company must define whether deferrals are allowed, when deferrals can take place, and how many times a group of shares can be deferred. The plan may also cover the interaction between deferral and retirement or termination provisions.

4.3.5 Planning for a Potential Incorrect Payout and Clawbacks

Occasionally a payout will be made on a goal that is later determined to have been missed. Plan design must include provisions for this possibility. Corrections may be due to accidental circumstances or some type of impropriety. Accidental circumstances may include miscalculations, data that was inadvertently missed at the time of vesting, or data that was initially included in totals but had to be rolled back for some reason. An example would be a large transaction that was included in revenue totals for a given period and then subsequently fell through, with the deal never resulting in income to the company. The most visible example of circumstances that are not considered accidental are those resulting in a restatement of financial statements called out specifically by Section 954 of the Dodd-Frank Act. This law requires companies with securities listed on a U.S. exchange to adopt a clawback policy applicable to executive officers in the event of an accounting restatement due to material noncompliance with financial reporting requirements.

It is critical that a plan clearly document the correction policies for all types of corrections. Many plans allow, but do not require, the company to demand repayment of funds associated with errors. In the event that the error is immaterial, most companies will not make a correction. Where an accidental mistake was material but due mainly to the timing of data collection or to a transaction that will be included in a future measurement, many companies will incorporate adjustments at a later date. Policies regarding corrections to performance equity payouts are not yet, and probably will not be anytime soon, universal. The most important consideration is clear and unequivocal documentation of the company's approach to these types of errors.

Other common triggering events for clawbacks related to performance awards include an individual being terminated for "cause" or an individual violating restrictions clearly defined in the plan, agreement, or related employment agreement, such as a noncompete clause. Anything that may lead to a clawback should be clearly documented in advance. Attempting to correct a payout or have it returned is very difficult without unambiguous and agreed-upon language.

On July 1, 2015, the SEC proposed the long-awaited set of clawback rules under Section 954 of Dodd-Frank. Section 954 requires companies to create, design, and execute an executive compensation clawback policy. It is unique in that it requires a company to claw back compensation without regard to an individual executive officer's wrongdoing or fault. Partly in anticipation of the details of these new rules, many companies have already taken the preemptive action of adding clawback provisions to new equity plans. For many years, institutional shareholders and their advisory firms, such as ISS and Glass-Lewis, have been pushing companies to adopt formal clawback policies as a corporate governance best practice.

The proposed rule, 10D-1 has not yet been finalized as of this writing (fall 2016). It defines the listing requirements that exchanges will be directed to establish under Section 10D of the Exchange Act. The proposal also includes amendments to Regulation S-K and Forms N-CSR and 14A. The combination of these amendments requires the disclosure of the issuer's policy on the recovery of incentive-based pay and its recovery actions under its recovery policy.

Once the rule is finalized, a company will be required to adopt its new clawback policy no later than 60 days following the date each national securities exchange and national securities association publishes its rules that comply with Section 10D. Companies will be required to disclose their recovery policy in the first annual report after the effective date of the new rules. For any fiscal period following the effective date of Rule 10D-1, companies will be required to claw back excess incentive-based compensation that was received by current or former executives on or after the effective date.

The language for the proposed rule provides the following definition of incentive-based compensation. "For purposes of Section 10D (15 U.S.C. 78j-4), *incentive-based compensation* is any compensation that is granted, earned or vested based wholly or in part upon the attainment of a financial reporting measure. Financial reporting measures are measures that are determined and presented in accordance with the accounting principles used in preparing the issuer's financial statements, any measures that are derived wholly or in part from such measures, and stock price and total shareholder return. A financial reporting measure need not be presented within the financial statements or included in a filing with the Commission."

The SEC's summary of the proposed rule and rule amendments is included below (footnotes omitted):

> We are proposing new Rule 10D-1 under the Exchange Act and amendments to Items 601, 402 and 404 of Regulation S-K, Schedule 14A, Form 20-F, Form 40-F, and Form N-CSR to implement the provisions of Section 954 of the Dodd-Frank Wall Street Reform and Consumer Protection Act of 2010, which added Section 10D to the Securities Exchange Act of 1934. Section 10D requires the Commission to adopt rules directing the exchanges and associations to prohibit the listing of any security of an issuer that is not in compliance with Section 10D's requirements concerning disclosure of the issuer's policy on incentive-based compensation and recovery of erroneously awarded compensation. In accordance with the statute, proposed Rule 10D-1 directs the exchanges to establish listing standards that, among other things, require each issuer to adopt and comply with a policy providing for recovery, under certain circumstances, of incentive-based compensation received by current or former executive officers and to file all disclosure with respect to that policy in accordance with Commission rules.
>
> To implement Section 10D(b)(1), we are proposing to add new disclosure provisions to Items 601 and 402 of Regulation S-K, Schedule 14A, Form 20-F, Form 40-F, and Form N-CSR. The new disclosure provisions would require each listed issuer to file the issuer's policy, if applicable, regarding recovery of incentive-based compensation from its executive officers as an exhibit to its Exchange Act annual report or, in the case of a listed registered management investment company, its Form N-CSR annual report. A new instruction to the Summary Compensation Table would require that any amounts recovered pursuant to the listed issuer's policy reduce the amount reported in the applicable column and total column for the fiscal year in which the amount recovered initially was reported.

In addition, if during the last completed fiscal year, either a restatement was completed that required recovery of excess incentive-based compensation pursuant to a listed issuer's recovery policy, or there was an outstanding balance of excess incentive-based compensation from the application of the policy to a prior restatement, proposed Item 402(w) would require the listed issuer to disclose:

- For each restatement,
  - ○ The date on which the listed issuer was required to prepare an accounting restatement;
  - ○ The aggregate dollar amount of excess incentive-based compensation attributable to the restatement;
  - ○ The estimates used to determine the excess incentive-based compensation attributable to such accounting restatement, if the financial reporting measure related to a stock price or total shareholder return metric; and
  - ○ The aggregate dollar amount of excess incentive-based compensation that remained outstanding as of the end of the last completed fiscal year;
- The name of each person, if any, from whom during the last completed fiscal year the listed issuer decided not to pursue recovery, the amount forgone from each such person, and a brief description of the listed issuer's reasons for not pursuing recovery; and
- The name of, and amount due from, each person from whom, at the end of its last completed fiscal year, excess incentive-based compensation had been outstanding for 180 days or longer since the date the issuer determined the amount the person owed.

We propose that the same disclosure requirements apply to listed U.S. issuers and listed foreign private issuers, including MJDS filers. These disclosure requirements would increase the amount of information that listed U.S. issuers and listed foreign private issuers must compile and disclose in their schedules and forms. For listed U.S. issuers, other than registered management investment companies, the proposed amendments to Items 402 and 601 of Regulation S-K would require additional disclosure in Exchange Act annual reports and proxy or information statements filed on Schedule 14A or Schedule 14C relating to an annual meeting of shareholders, or a special meeting in lieu of an annual meeting, at which directors are to be elected and would increase the burden hour and cost estimates for each of those forms. For a listed management investment company registered under the Investment Company Act of 1940, the proposed amendments to Form N-CSR and Schedule 14A would require additional disclosure and would increase the burden hour and cost estimates associated with Form N-CSR and Rule 20a-1, if the registered investment company pays incentive-based compensation. For a listed foreign private issuer filing an annual report on Form 20-F, Form 40-F or, if a foreign private issuer elects to use U.S. registration and reporting forms, on Form 10-K, the proposed amendments to those forms and the proposed amendment to Item 402(a)(1), respectively, would require additional disclosure in annual reports and would increase the burden hour and costs estimates for each of these forms. The disclosure required by proposed Item 402(w), proposed paragraph 22(b)(20) to Schedule 14A, proposed new Item 12 to Form N-CSR, and proposed Item 6.F of Form 20-F would be required to be block-text tagged in XBRL.

4.4 Implementation and Rollout of a Performance Equity Plan

4.4.1 Determining Processes

Successful implementation and rollout of a performance equity plan may require new internal communication and data integration techniques; the communication regarding the entire life of each award must be seamless. Unlike time-based awards that require little in the way of regular management, unless there is a major corporate or individual event, performance equity requires integration at the time of the award, at regular intervals (at least quarterly) during the measurement period, at the time of final measurement, and at the time of vesting and payout. Building these processes at the outset will afford focus on the effectiveness of the plan, rather than the process.

Awards with market conditions require complex valuation upon grant. While the financial reporting after the award date is fixed, the progress toward the goal is not. Implementation should include a method and frequency for determining proximity to the goal. Communication of this proximity must also be defined to ensure that the award is fulfilling its intended objectives.

Awards with performance conditions can be valued in a manner similar to time-based equity. The expense for these awards must be evaluated every quarter, based on the probability of attaining the goal(s) associated with the award. A company must always amortize expense based on no less than the number of shares that are probable to vest. Depending on the nature of the goal, this may be a simple formula or it may require interaction between multiple departments and data sets. The values used in the probability to vest may not always coincide with the proximity details being communicated to the staff.

Finally, the company must detail the process for calculating and approving the final performance measurement for the awards. There should be a clear process for determining goal proximity, obtaining the required sign-off, and processing the vesting or payout event. The timing of this process should be accounted for in determining the actual vesting date for the award. This will ensure that there is ample time to obtain sign-off before the participant has an income and tax event.

Managing a performance-based equity plan requires significantly more data than managing basic equity plans. Regardless of the performance metric being used, a company must determine how it will collect data and apply it to awards. Many companies neglect this critical step until the deadline for measuring performance is near. Failing to define this process at the onset of the plan reduces the potential impact of the plan. Companies must be able to accurately track goals for both financial reporting and participant communications purposes.

Table 4-6 lists the stages of implementing a performance-based equity plan.

4.5 Communicating a Complex Topic in Simple Terms

Performance-based equity plans are more difficult to communicate than most other compensation instruments. Combining the difficult topic of equity compensation with complex performance goals makes proper communication essential to the success of these plans. Participants must understand the purpose of the plan and how they can affect the metrics being used. Initial communication should focus on explaining why specific goals were chosen and applied to specific awards and individuals, and participants must understand what they must do to meet the goals and what will happen when the goals are met (or not met). Once the initial awards have been properly communicated, a new level of communication begins.

Interim progress must also be communicated. If the purpose of the plan is to meet a revenue goal, participants must understand where they are at consistent periods along the way. An effective performance plan will not result in any surprises to the company or the participants. The company must communicate the potential of the plan and provide

Table 4-6. Performance Equity Design Project Flow

Project milestone	Details
Corporate compensation philosophy and intent	Executive management, the compensation committee, and key stakeholders should define the company's approach to equity compensation and its purpose within the overall compensation structure.
Data analysis	Review historic data for the company and its peers as well as general market data to determine possible performance drivers.
Plan goals	Determine the specific purpose of the plan for the current grant cycle. Example: Retain staff during sustained underperformance, drive efforts toward one or two long-term end goals.
KPI/metric selection	Determine the underlying metrics that support the plan goals.
Equity instrument selection	Define the type(s) of equity instruments that best fit the compensation philosophy and plan goals.
Measurement selection	Evaluate and define the level of performance against each metric that must be met to attain minimum, target, and maximum performance levels.
Plan structure	Create the plan rules for terminations, missed performance targets, corporate actions, missed goals, etc.
Review by external and internal stakeholders	Provide detailed presentation of plan aspects and allow for thorough evaluation before finalizing the plan.
Plan documentation	Plan document. Grant agreements. Basic reporting needs.
Approval	Review and approval by compensation committee and shareholders.
Data integration	Process for collecting required data for metrics and calculating progress to goals.
Rollout and implementation	Initial communication to managers and participants. Implementation on stock administration and/or financial reporting system.
Communication—ongoing	Progress toward goal. Detailed metric tracking. Performance of peers. Potential shares to be earned.
Administration and reporting	Tracking, managing, and reporting goals. Calculating the probability of attaining goals. Expense reporting. Tax calculations.

realistic updates to this potential. Proximity to goals must also be communicated to the participants. This communication is often dependent upon the goals being used. Effective programs will incorporate words, charts, reports, and examples to ensure understanding. An investment in participant education is usually worth the cost as the payout potential of performance-based equity is often very high.

Communication excellence is achievable by any organization. Among the key aspects of any effective communication program are messaging, branding, data, and delivery. The following are five guidelines to keep in mind when communicating a plan.

1. It is essential that any communication of performance equity incorporate stock prices and growth rates that reflect realistic expectations, rather than hopes. Companies should also avoid using unrealistic numbers simply because they make communications and examples easier.

2. It is best to provide examples of both up and down performance. While discussing underperformance is never fun, participants in performance equity programs need to understand the actual potential of their award if they are to act on achieving goals.

3. Clearly communicate the what, why, and how of each equity instrument and the goals related to it. Always remember that performance equity works only if you monitor performance closely and consistently recognize achievement.

4. Consider delivering brief communications at frequent intervals. These are more likely to be read and understood by participants than larger, infrequent communications.

5. Most importantly, maintain a predetermined communications schedule, regardless of performance.

4.6   Integrating and Tracking Data and Managing Goals

It is essential that a company build a process to consistently monitor the progress of metrics. Most performance, for equity awards, is measured over a period of three to five years. During this time, the expense for these awards needs to be reported on a quarterly basis. Generally, the expense for awards with market conditions does not change once it has been calculated, but the difference between what is being reported on financial reports and what may actually vest can vary materially. Depending upon the nature of the performance conditions used for an award, the probability of achievement can change during any quarter. These basic requirements make it necessary to accurately and efficiently track performance on an ongoing basis.

In addition to financial reporting requirements, a company must be able to regularly communicate progress to award recipients. Market condition data (e.g., the stock price or dividends) changes every day and can materially affect the potential payout in a matter of days or weeks. R-TSR is too complex a goal for most staff members to calculate, but for most companies the calculation can be automated fairly well. The TSR data must then be linked to appropriate awards, and calculations of goal proximity must be made. This management often requires integration of an external data source or sources, a system that calculates the goals against specific awards, and a system that takes this information and applies it to financial reporting and potential vesting events.

The possible combination of data sources and calculation frequency for performance conditions can be infinite. The metric will define the data collection frequency. It is also quite common for a single metric to require data inputs from more than one source. Most data for these performance conditions change monthly, quarterly, or annually. In extreme cases such as sales data, information may change on a daily basis.

Regardless of the metrics used, a company should clearly identify the sources of the underlying data. It may take multiple systems and stakeholders to document both the process and calculations to support the tracking and managing of goals. Clear processes will allow for smoother administration and communication for the life of the award. This best practice also allows the company to more accurately project and plan for potential payouts. When possible and appropriate, the company should also make this data accessible to participants.

This regular measurement and dissemination of metrics keeps both the company and the plan participants focused on the stated goals. It also allows for proper adjustments when considering new goals.

4.7 Stock Plan Administration of Performance Equity

4.7.1 Administration Overview

As mentioned previously, performance-based equity usually requires the integration of multiple systems. Metric data may come from external sources, finance, HRIS, compensation, performance management, or other systems. All of this data must then be linked or aligned to a performance metric tracking system, stock administration system, and perhaps financial reporting solutions. As the use of performance equity grows, companies must thoroughly evaluate their internal needs against the systems available to support them. Processes must bridge the gap between current functionality and company necessity. In some cases this may require linking multiple systems and manual processes to create a compliant and efficient environment.

Plans with only a few participants and limited metrics can likely be managed effectively through a combination of manual and systematic process. As the number of participants and metrics grow, these plans quickly require automated solutions. Depending upon the plan design and the metrics used, a performance equity program with 50 participants may require as much work as a traditional time-based program with 500 to 1,000 participants. This is due in part to the complex nature of these programs and the emerging functionality of the administration systems.

When a plan is being designed, ease of administration should be considered, but it must not impede an effective plan design. It is unlikely that any current stock administration system will fully automate or support every aspect of a plan. Today's stock administration systems generally have limited functionality to support performance-based equity; the functionality tends to focus primarily on the financial reporting functions and general transactional support. Financial reporting is more likely to be supported for market conditions than for performance conditions, and complex goal interdependency or codependency is often outside the scope of these systems. It is not uncommon for companies to use a specialized financial reporting system to support their performance equity. Where a manual approach is chosen over a systematic solution, processes must be documented carefully to ensure financial reporting, vesting processing, and taxation calculations are performed correctly.

Companies should engage their providers as early as possible during the plan design process. Even without plan specifics, communicating with your provider may allow you to understand system capabilities and shape a program to work well without affecting the intent of the plan. Complex internal goals and performance conditions will usually require a separate metric tracking system. Market conditions such as TSR may be provided from external sources, but applying a metric to an individual award will likely require a tightly controlled spreadsheet or a software solution expressly designed for this purpose.

4.7.2 Administration Process Flow

The administration process flow may be summarized as follows:

1. Obtain a list of participants, approved by the board's compensation committee.

2. Meet with other stakeholders to discuss metrics and goals.

3. Work with outside counsel to draft new agreements specific to current metrics, goals, and rules.

4. Enter award details into the equity administration system.

5. Prepare and deliver participant agreements and related communications.

6. Prepare and file SEC Form 4.

7. Support the award valuation.

8. Work with stakeholders to determine the probability of achieving the performance goals.

9. Prepare and support quarterly financial reports.

10. Prepare and deliver pre-vesting communications.

11. Obtain final certification of performance from management or board of directors.

12. Process the release of vested shares.

13. Calculate taxes and send data to the payroll department.

14. Instruct the transfer agent on share distribution and delivery.

15. Send confirmations to participants.

4.7.3 Common Limitations of Equity Administration Systems

Many systems do not yet have the ability to support awards that pay out at greater than 100% of the target. Systems may require bifurcating the awards into a "base award" and "performance award." This can complicate both participant communication and financial reporting and can put an additional burden on the stock administration department to determine a method to link these two awards for tracking and reporting purposes. Applying multiple metrics against a single group of shares can be challenging. Currently most systems allow for only one metric against any tranche of shares and may not allow for multiple metrics for a single award. The type of equity instrument used can also be problematic. Some systems may support performance units but not offer support for performance options or shares. Best practices are still being developed, and systems will continue to evolve as more plans are rolled out. It will likely be several years before the same level of automation and support is available for performance equity as currently exists for time-based equity.

4.8 Global Issues

Performance equity awards are subject to all the same legal and tax issues as time-based equity. Performance equity may also be subject to additional tax considerations, labor law issues, and communication hurdles. As noted above, performance equity has been commonly used in many countries for several years. In these countries, regulations may be more detailed and less open for interpretation than the rules in the U.S. In still other countries there has been little or no use of performance equity; these countries may not have yet created specific rules for performance equity, and implementing a plan may be a combination of regulations, negotiations, and art.

4.8.1 Securities Laws

As with all equity programs, a company must be careful not to run afoul of securities laws in any country where it grants equity. Performance equity requires additional considerations since many countries have little experience with it and the facts and circumstances of an individual award may require specific interpretation or additional filings. Before a company grants awards to residents of any country, it should thoroughly evaluate the immediate and long-term impact to both the company and the participant. It may not be advisable or even feasible to award performance equity in every country in which the company has employees.

4.8.2 Labor Law

Labor law issues outside the U.S. are commonly linked to whether compensation can be considered part of the company's commitment to the employee and how the compensation relates to work performed by the individual. Time-based equity can often be viewed as only indirectly related to work performed. It can also be documented in a way that clearly indicates that the eventual vesting is dependent upon the employee's continued service. This strategy may also work for metrics that are tied to corporate performance, but goals that are tied to individual performance may result in labor law issues. In addition, creating individual goals, or even group goals, may require more interaction with the local entity, resulting in a more complex and time-consuming plan design process.

Considerations that companies must address for non-U.S. employees include acquired rights and entitlement issues, and the possibility of earned amounts being considered part of local compensation. In the case of acquired rights or entitlements, a company may not be able to enforce cancellation or forfeiture provisions when the individual terminates service. Companies may also be faced with being held accountable for issuing new grants in the future, based on their past practices. The issue of payments being considered local compensation can create difficulties with termination provisions. Local compensation may also be subject to additional social insurance contributions by the individual and/or the company.

4.8.3 Global Taxation

Taxation rules for performance equity do not always follow the model structured in the U.S. Income and associated taxes may be calculated and due before the actual payment date. This is most likely when a performance goal has been met but payout or vesting is delayed. Termination and retirement provisions may also trigger income and tax before the participant has access to the underlying shares. In some countries it may also be possible to deliver performance equity as a tax-qualified program. Obtaining professional tax guidance should be included in the budget for any performance equity program.

It should also be noted that the timing of social taxes varies widely around the world. Some countries do not recognize the concept of vesting restrictions at all and may require social taxes to be due at the time of award. Other countries may trigger social taxes when the performance goals are met, even though payout is designed to occur at a later date. It is best to consult a qualified international tax law advisor before offering performance awards outside the U.S.

4.8.4 Cultural Concerns

Cultures around the world view individual, small group (team) and large group (corporate) performance differently. The most important aspect of a performance equity program is that it meets the initial philosophy and goals defined in the early planning stages. Metrics, communications, and overall plan structure should account for the best practices in any locality. Some cultures view the emphasis on individual performance as counterproductive, while others view any focus on explicit performance to be a negative comment on their work product or effort. These cultural considerations should also be taken into account when designing a performance equity program.

It is essential that a company obtain professional advice before granting performance equity outside the U.S. Plans may need special documentation or acknowledgements from employees beyond what the company uses for time-based awards. Analysis by an expert may be required in order to determine the plan or process changes required for international employees. Qualified tax treatment may be available in some countries. As with any equity plan, expert guidance should be sought before granting performance equity outside the U.S.

CHAPTER FIVE

Selling Stock Directly to Employees in a Closely Held Company

Corey Rosen

Contents

Business owners often want to allow some or all employees the opportunity to purchase shares in their company. They may want to do this to provide some liquidity for their own shares, to raise capital by selling new shares, and/or provide employees with a stake in the outcome. This chapter provides a brief overview of the issues involved in this. Its focus is on closely held companies not planning to go public.

Selling shares raises a variety of issues. How will they be valued? How will employees finance the purchase? What are the tax consequences of the sale? How will employees be able to sell their shares? Do securities laws apply to the sale? This chapter looks at each of these issues.

This chapter does not look at qualified employee stock purchase plans (ESPPs, also called Section 423 plans for their location in the tax code). These plans allow employees to purchase shares, usually via ongoing payroll deductions. At the end of an offering period of between 3 and 27 months, they can purchase shares with the accumulated funds, generally with a discount of up to 15%, usually with a "lookback" feature that allows them to buy based on the lower of the current price or the price when the offering period started. These plans can, in theory, be used by closely held companies, but because of their intersection with securities laws, administrative requirements, and the need for regular valuations to determine a price, they are rarely used in closely held companies other than those who plan to go public in the next year or so.

5.1   Where Will the Shares Come From?

Imagine that ABC Enterprises has 10,000 shares, all presently owned by Sam Smith. Sam would like to allow two key executives to buy shares. There are two ways to make that possible. Sam could sell some of his shares, or the board could authorize the issuance of additional shares. Company bylaws authorize a certain number shares, and in most cases, not all these shares are issued so that they are available for future sale. If additional shares are issued, Sam's percentage of ownership will be diluted, but the equity value of the company will increase by the new investment. In other cases, employees may own shares already, or there may be outside investors who want to sell.

In many cases, owners have buy-sell agreements in place that specify when shares must be sold and at what price, often based on a formula.

5.2   How Will Shares Be Valued?

If the shares are sold from an existing owner to a new buyer, they can be sold at a price they agree to, although an excessively low price might trigger a gift tax and an inflated price might trigger a lawsuit down the road. If new shares are issued, they have to be assigned a value. So how should companies determine a fair price?

Many companies just use a proxy, such as book value or some formula (a multiple of sales or earnings) they have heard about. These estimates are almost certainly wrong, for reasons explained below. As a result, Sam is selling shares at either too low or high a price (most often, too low, since book value is a common metric). It is not illegal to sell shares at a formula price, however. Both parties need to understand, however, how this differs from what an appraised value would yield.

Ideally, Sam hires an appraiser to calculate value. The appraiser first looks at how much the entire company is worth. To do that, the appraiser asks how much a hypothetical willing buyer would pay for the right to assets and future earnings of the company. Earnings are usually calculated as EBITDA (earnings before interest, taxes, depreciation, and amortization, a measure of free cash flow). The earnings are normalized, meaning they are adjusted for any annual expenses or savings (if Sam has a vacation home paid for by the company, this presumably is not something the buyer would give to the new CEO, so this can be added back to earnings; if Sam receives a salary far below the market rate, the added needed costs for a new CEO are added).

The appraiser takes these earnings and, using data from the company, projects what they will be for, typically, five years out. They are then discounted each year based on how risky they are, interest rates, returns on other forms of investments, and other factors to determine the rate of return on these earnings the buyer expects. The riskier the future earnings, and the better alternative investment returns, the less the buyer will pay. That yields a number that can be expressed as a multiple of annual earnings, usually between two and seven, a buyer will pay.

The appraiser also looks at the asset value of the company and, if applicable, any data on comparable company sales. These three approaches to value are weighted, almost always with the earnings multiple getting most of the weight. The final number may be adjusted for debt or assets held but not needed for the business to produce a final value.

Now the appraiser has to calculate the share value, which is arrived at by applying minority and non-liquidity discounts, discussed in the following paragraphs.

You can see why book value usually underestimates value—it is essentially saying a company is just worth what its net assets are, rather than what all its tangible and intangible assets are capable of producing in terms of earnings.

In any case, however, Sam needs to understand how selling a minority of shares should be priced. Sam's perception will probably be that if the $10,000 shares are worth $100 each, if he issues 100 new shares, or sells 100 shares, they will also be worth $100, but that is probably not correct—they should be worth less.

Share ownership represents a separable bundle of rights. Owners can have the right to dividends, control, and liquidity preference. In addition, the shares may have easy liquidity (as shares in a publicly traded company would have) or could be more difficult to sell when you want to sell (as would shares in a closely held company).

ABC has what is called an enterprise value—how much the entire company could be sold for. A buyer now gets full control over its assets, including the right to use profits as desired. The shares are, because the company is being sold, now fully liquid. ABC shares have a share value—how much each share in the enterprise is worth. If all the shares are sold, each share is worth a pro-rata part of the price. If there are 10,000 shares in a $1,000,000 company, each share is worth $100.

But what if someone buys, say, 10% of the shares? They do not have control rights, may or may not have dividend rights, and the buyer cannot easily sell the stock. So per share, these shares are worth less than Sam's, which have all these features (Sam can choose to sell the company, for instance; the buyer can't). The buyer should then pay for the shares on a non-control, non-liquid basis. These discounts are calculated by an appraiser based on data from other investments. Each can add 20% to 30% or more in discounts, so the buyer might end up paying half, more or less, of what the shares are worth to Sam.

Most direct sales are for the issuance of new shares. Employee buyouts of companies through direct share purchases are also used, but this book focuses on equity as a compensation tool, so we will not discuss how this can done (see the NCEO publication *Selling Your Business Directly to Employees* for details). Sam can sell a minority of his shares to get liquidity, but he needs to realize he will take a "haircut" on the sale.

If ABC sells new shares at this discounted price, Sam will suffer both share dilution (he will own a smaller percentage of the company) and value dilution (because he has sold shares at less than their control price). But Sam presumably has decided that this is an acceptable tradeoff in order to get more capital and more commitment from key employees.

While the shares should be valued as non-control, illiquid shares, in practice, many companies just use whatever price they have determined all the shares to be worth. While this may be common, it is important to understand it is neither theoretically nor financially correct.

5.3   Share Purchase Mechanics

There are three typical ways employees buy shares:

1. The employees buy them directly out of their savings. The purchase is not tax-deductible.

2. The employees take part of their bonus in the form of shares. The shares are taxable just as if the employee had been paid in cash.

3. The employees take a recourse or non-recourse loan from the company to buy the shares. The purchase is again not deductible. The interest rate has to be non-compensatory (a rate below the applicable federal rate (2.76% as of December 2018) or the difference is taxable. Typically, this will be a short-term loan, such as two to five years.

Employees may purchase all the shares in a single transaction or be given periodic opportunities to buy more shares. The former appears to be the most common method.

5.4   Rules

Employers can set rules for the stock. If these rules limit employee rights, then the price they pay for the shares should reflect that. Employers we at the NCEO have talked to sometimes see the right to buy stock as a privilege, even if it is at full fair value, rather than an economic exchange. Employees may see that differently if they have to pay full value but their ownership is subject to constraints the owner's stock is not. Common rules include:

*   *Vesting:* Employees may be required to work a certain number of years or meet performance or other criteria in order to have a vested right to what they purchased. That makes the shares restricted stock, discussed in detail in a separate chapter in this book.

- *Repurchase:* Employers normally have a right of first refusal on the shares and may additionally require that employees sell back the shares at departure. If a formula is used to buy the shares, the price used to sell back the shares would normally be based on the same formula, such as book value (this is called a non-lapse provision). If, however, the shares are sold in a sale of the company, they would have the full value at sale if the non-lapse provision is waived.

- *Noncompete agreements:* Employers may require that employees buying shares agree to a noncompete clause. While this is understandable, it may not be enforceable in many states (such as California). It also limits the employee's future income opportunities, and thus makes the share purchase less valuable.

The stricter the rules, the less value the shares have, and the less motivated employees might be as a result, so employers need to weigh the tradeoffs carefully.

5.5 Taxes

Employee purchases, as noted above, are made with after-tax money. The sale of the stock normally qualifies for capital gains treatment. If it is restricted stock, see this book's chapter on restricted stock for details. Employee gains on the stock are not deductible to the company.

If there is a non-lapse agreement, the employee pays capital gains taxes on the gain at sale. However, if the agreement is cancelled, most commonly for an anticipated sale of the company, then this can create taxable ordinary income for the difference unless the employee can show it is non-compensatory, such as the employer not taking a tax deduction for the amount.

5.6 Liquidity

Having an ownership stake may seem great, but unless it is liquid, it is more punishment (you bought the shares) than reward. Companies can provide liquidity in a variety of ways:

- The most common is the sale of the company. While this lifts all boats, it may seem (and be) both very hypothetical and far away.

Entrepreneurs may not be worried about this—they have the choice about if and when to sell. But employees who are not sure they will stay until this uncertain event will not find ownership appealing. If a company relies on this approach as its only liquidity vehicle, it should have a realistic plan to sell in the near- or mid-term.

- A second approach is redemption—the company repurchases the shares. One option is for shares to be purchased at a formula price by employees and then repurchased by the company at that price unless there is a sale. If sold at an appraised price, the company should repurchase the shares at an appraised price. Note this is done with after-tax dollars unless the company sets up an employee stock ownership plan (ESOP), which allows a company to buy back shares in pretax dollars.

- The least common approach is for employees to buy shares from one another. Companies should not become market makers—this can entail costly securities law compliance issues. They can informally let people know that shares are for sale. Employees can buy and sell shares at prices they negotiate.

5.7 Securities Laws

Securities laws exist at the state and federal level. Each state has its own rules, although there are broad similarities between states. Securities laws are a large and complex subject, but their two key elements are registration and disclosure. Registration means the filing of documents with the state and/or federal securities agencies concerning the employer whose stock is being sold. There are registration procedures for small annual offerings of stock to employees, but larger offerings require a lot of complex paperwork and fees often exceed $100,000. Registration requires the filing of audited financial statements and continuing reporting obligations to the federal Securities and Exchange Commission (SEC) and appropriate state agencies.

Generally, offers to sell securities (stocks, bonds, etc.) require registration of those securities unless there is a specific exemption. Individual stock purchases or choices about using existing benefit plan funds to buy company stock are covered by these registration requirements. In addition, companies with more than $10 million in assets and 2,000 or more shareholders (or 500 or more shareholders who are nonaccredited investors) are considered public firms under federal law and must comply with the reporting requirements of the Exchange Act of 1934 even if they do not have to register under the Securities Act of 1933. The nonaccredited number is more relevant to closely held companies because most employees will fall into this category. Accredited investors are, in general, people with a net worth exceeding $1 million, either alone or with a spouse (excluding the value of their primary residence), or income over $200,000 (or $300,000 including a spouse). Under the Jumpstart Our Business Startups (JOBS) Act of 2012, stock options granted under an "employee compensation plan" are not covered under the 2,000/500 shareholder threshold test until they are exercised. The JOBS Act also created a new category of company called an "emerging growth company." These are startups with assets under $1 billion. These companies are subject to less rigorous registration rules if they are deemed to be public.

Disclosure is normally required under any sale. Disclosure refers to providing information to buyers about what they are getting, similar to but frequently less detailed than what would be in a prospectus. At times, there are specific state and federal rules about what needs to go in these documents, including objective discussions of risks, the financial condition of the firm, officers' and directors' salaries, and other information. In the absence of requirements for the registration of the securities, disclosure is intended to satisfy the anti-fraud requirements of federal and state laws.

There are many exemptions under federal law to registration rules. States generally, but not always, track these rules. Offerings that are made only to residents of the state in which the offering is made are exempt from federal rules if the offeror has its principal office in that state, gets 80% of its gross revenue from business conducted in the state, and has 80% of its assets in the state.

Under a "private placement," an offering of to a small number of accredited, sophisticated investors who have access to the same information as provided in a public offering stock do not require registration. This may be useful for certain highly paid executive officers, but it will not work for broader offerings.

Under Rule 504, offerings up to $5 million in a 12-month period (less any offerings made to other investors under Section 3(b) of the 1933 Securities Act, which provides for easier registration rules for public offerings of stock) are exempt. Under Rule 506, offers to 35 of fewer investors who, on their own or with advice, can assess the investment, are also exempt.

The most commonly used exemption is Rule 701 of the Securities Act, covering offers to a company's employees, directors, general partners, trustees, officers, or certain consultants (those providing services to a company similar to what an employer might hire someone to do, but not consultants who help raise capital) that are made under a written compensation agreement. To qualify for Rule 701's exemption from registration requirements, total sales during a 12-month period of securities sold in reliance on Rule 701 must not exceed the greater of $1 million, 15% of the issuer's total assets, or 15% of all the outstanding securities of that class. The offerings must be discrete (not included in any other offer) and are still subject to disclosure requirements. For total sales under $10 million during a 12-month period to the specified class of people above, companies must comply with anti-fraud disclosure rules; for sales of over this amount, companies must disclose additional information, including risk factors, copies of the plans under which the offerings are made, and certain financial statements. These disclosures must be made to all shareholders.

5.8 Conclusion

Selling stock directly to employees may be very much what a company needs, but owners need to be aware that there are significant tax and securities law issues that must be addressed to put these plans in place. It is also important to understand that ownership will usually be more meaningful to entrepreneurs than employees, who may be more risk-averse and more focused on their day-to-day financial needs. Finally, it is critical to work with qualified legal and accounting advisors to make sure the plans are properly structured.

Accounting Issues

Daniel D. Coleman

Contents

The accounting treatment of a long-term incentive compensation program is a critical consideration (some would argue the *most* critical consideration) in determining what type of program is appropriate and how it should be structured. To determine the accounting treatment of a long-term incentive program under Accounting Standards Codification Topic 718 (ASC 718), the following three questions must be answered:

- How will the compensatory value of the award be measured?

- When will the compensatory value of the award be measured?

- Over what periods will the compensation expense be recorded?

The impact of each of these issues on the accounting treatment of a long-term incentive program is discussed below.

6.1 Fair Value (How Compensation Is Measured)

ASC 718 governs the accounting treatment of long-term incentives if (a) the award will be settled in shares of stock; (b) the award will be settled in cash, but the amount of the payment is based on the value of a share of stock; or (c) the vesting of the award is dependent upon attaining a target value or target level of appreciation in the value of a share of stock. The presence of any one of these three criteria will result in the award being subject to ASC 718. All three of the criteria do not have to be present for the award to be subject to ASC 718.

For all public and most privately held companies, compensation expense related to equity-based compensation under ASC 718 will be based on the fair value of the award, rather than the intrinsic value of the award. The fair value of time-vested and performance-vested stock options and stock appreciation rights (both cash-settled and stock-settled) will need to be estimated using an option-pricing model. The most common option-pricing model is the modified American Black-Scholes-Merton option-pricing model ("Black-Scholes"). However, ASC 718 does not specify a preference for a particular valuation technique or model for estimating the fair value of a stock option or stock appreciation right (SAR). Paragraph 718-10-55-21 requires the model used to estimate the fair value of a stock option or SAR to include, at a minimum, the following assumptions:

- The exercise price of the option or SAR,
- The current price of the underlying stock,
- The expected period of time until the option or SAR is exercised,
- The expected volatility of the price of the underlying stock over the period the option or SAR is expected to be outstanding,
- The expected dividends on the underlying stock over the period the option or SAR is expected to be outstanding, and

- The risk-free interest rate over the period the option or SAR is expected to be outstanding.

The development of the estimated fair value of a stock option or SAR is beyond the scope of this chapter. Additionally, a company may need to obtain advice from qualified valuation professionals with knowledge of the requirements of ASC 718 when developing the estimated fair value of a stock option or the assumptions used in the option-pricing model.

The fair value of time-vested and performance-vested restricted stock and phantom stock is based on the price of the underlying share. The fair value of a share of stock is generally defined in the plan document under which the award is granted. Fair value may be defined as the opening price, the closing price, or the average of the high and low price. All of these definitions are acceptable for purposes of ASC 718. For a publicly held company, the value of a share of stock is easily determinable based on trading activity. For a privately held company, the fair value of a share of stock will need to be estimated. If there are no recent stock transactions upon which the company can rely when estimating the fair value of its stock, the assistance of qualified valuation professionals may be required to develop the fair value estimate.

ASC 718 draws a distinction between vesting that is based on (1) a service condition, (2) a performance condition, and (3) a market condition. Plain-vanilla time vesting is a service condition. A performance condition is a goal that relates to the company's operation and/or performance but is not related to the value of the company's stock. A market condition is a goal that relates to the company's stock price, such as a target stock price, stock price appreciation, or shareholder return relative to the market or a group of industry peers. This chapter discusses the financial accounting treatment of long-term incentive awards that are subject to a service condition and/or a performance condition. A service condition and/or a performance condition are not reflected when estimating the fair value of an award. The effect of a market condition is included when developing the estimated fair value of the award. The fair value of an award that is subject to a market condition will need to be estimated using a path dependent valuation model, such as a Monte Carlo simulation.[1]

---

1. The valuation of awards that are subject to a market condition is highly complex and beyond the scope of this chapter.

A privately held company may be unable to estimate the fair value of a stock option because it is not practicable to estimate the expected volatility of the underlying stock. For a company in this situation, ASC 718 requires the historical volatility of an appropriate industry sector index to be used in the option-pricing model, instead of the expected volatility of the price of the company's stock, when estimating the fair value of the option or SAR. The resulting value is referred to as a calculated value rather than a fair value. Additionally, paragraph 718-10-55-52 provides that in certain situations, "it may not be possible for a nonpublic entity to reasonably estimate the fair value of its equity share options and similar instruments at the date they are granted because the complexity of the award's terms prevents it from doing so. In that case, paragraphs 718-10-30-21 through 30-22 require the nonpublic entity to account for its equity instruments at their intrinsic value, remeasured at each reporting date through the date of exercise or other settlement." These alternatives apply only to estimating the fair value of a stock option or SAR and do not apply to restricted stock or phantom shares. For purposes of ASC 718, a company must always develop a reasonable estimate of the fair value of its stock using an appropriate business valuation method.[2]

6.2 Equity Awards vs. Liability Awards (When Compensation Is Measured)

6.2.1 Awards Classified as Equity

Under ASC 718, the expense for an award of stock based compensation is estimated on the "measurement date." Before the issuance of Accounting Standards Update 2018-07 ("ASU 2018-07"), the financial accounting guidance drew a distinction between awards granted to employees and awards granted to nonemployees (e.g., independent contractors). Under the prior accounting regime the measurement date

---

2. At privately held companies with complex capital structures (common stock and one or more classes of preferred stock), the aggregate estimated fair value of equity will need to be allocated to each class of equity based on the class's respected rights and preferences. See the AICPA Practice Aid *Valuation of Privately-Held-Company Equity Securities Issued as Compensation* (AICPA, revised 2013) for additional detail on equity allocation methods.

for awards classified as equity granted to nonemployees was frequently the vest date. However, for fiscal years beginning after December 15, 2018, the measurement date for awards classified as equity granted to nonemployees will be the same as the measurement date as awards granted to employees. Additionally, to reflect the change in the financial accounting guidance, in the updated version of ASC 718 the term "employee" has been replaced with "grantee" and the term "employer" has been replaced with "grantor."

For an award that is classified as equity, the grant date is the measurement date. To be classified as an equity award, all of the following conditions must be satisfied:

- The grantor must intend to settle the award by issuing shares of the grantor's stock;

- The grantor must have the ability to settle the award by issuing shares of the grantor's stock; and

- The grantee cannot have the ability to require the grantor to repurchase the shares within six months of the date the restricted stock vested or the date the stock option was exercised.

For purposes of ASC 718, the grant date is the first date on which all of the following criteria are satisfied:

- The grantee and grantor reach a mutual understanding of the key terms and conditions of the award.

- The grantor becomes contingently obligated to issue the shares to grantees who provide the requisite service.

- The grantee begins to benefit from or be adversely affected by subsequent changes in the stock price.

- The award has been authorized.

For most companies, the day an award is issued will be the grant date. However, in certain circumstances an award may be considered to have been issued before the grant date. The issuance date will precede the grant date if all of the following criteria are met:

1. An award is authorized.

2. Service begins before a mutual understanding of the key terms and conditions of a share-based payment award is reached.

3. Either of the following conditions applies:

    a. The award's terms do not include a substantive future requisite service condition that exists at the grant date.

    b. The award contains a market or performance condition that if not satisfied during the service period preceding the grant date and following the inception of the arrangement results in forfeiture of the award.

If the criteria above are met, the day the award is issued is the "service inception date." The grant date will be the date on which the grantee and grantor reach a mutual understanding of the key terms and conditions of the award. During the period between the service inception date and the grant date, compensation expense will be marked-to-market. As a result, the estimated fair value of the awards will need to be updated at the end of each fiscal period between the service inception date and the grant date. The final measure of expense will equal the fair value of the award on the grant date. Following the grant date fair value of an equity award is not subsequently adjusted to reflect changes in the stock price.

6.2.2 Awards Classified as a Liability

Compensation expense for an award that is classified as a liability award is based on the award's fair value on the date the award is settled, rather than the award's fair value on the date of grant. The award will be considered to be a liability award if any of the following conditions are present:

*   The grantor intends to settle the award in cash;

*   The grantee can require the grantor to settle the award in cash; or

*   The grantee can require the grantor to repurchase the shares within six months of the date the restricted stock vested or the date the stock option was exercised.

ASC 718 requires the fair value of a liability award, and therefore the amount of expense produced by the award, to be remeasured at the end of each financial reporting period. As a result, the accounting treatment for a stock option or SAR that is classified as a liability award is sometimes referred to as "variable Black-Scholes." Of the types of equity-based long-term incentives discussed in this book, cash-settled SARs and phantom stock will always be classified as liability awards. Depending upon how the terms and provisions of a restricted stock or stock option award are structured, the award may be classified as either an equity award or a liability award. Plain-vanilla time-vested stock options and restricted stock awards generally will be classified as equity awards.

6.3 Expense Accrual Patterns

Compensation expense for an award of equity-based compensation is recorded over the award's service period. The service period is the period of time that the recipient needs to provide services to vest in the award. Depending upon its terms and conditions, an award of equity-based compensation may have an explicit service period, an implicit service period, a derived service period, or a combination of two or more types of service periods.

Time-vested awards have an explicit service period. For example, a restricted stock award that vests over four years, with 25% of the award vesting on each of the first four anniversaries of the date of grant, has a four-year explicit service period. Unless the award is modified after the date of grant, the explicit service period will not change.

The service period of a performance-vested award is implied by the award's vesting criteria (i.e., the award has an implicit service period). For example, if an award of restricted stock vests upon the completion of the development of a new product offering, and as of the date of grant management estimates the product development will take 30 months to complete, the award has a 30-month implicit service period. If one year after the date of grant, management estimates the product development will be completed in 12 months, the implicit service period would decrease from 30 months to 24 months. The impact of the change in the length of implicit service period on the expense accrual is recorded in the period of the change and is treated as a change in an estimate.

Compensation expense for awards that vest upon the attainment of a market condition is recorded over the award's derived service period. As noted in the discussion of fair value above, ASC 718 requires the fair value of an award that is subject to a market condition to be estimated using a path-dependent valuation model, such as a Monte Carlo simulation. The model used to estimate the fair value of the award will also calculate the award's derived service period.

Long-term incentive awards are sometimes subject to multiple vesting criteria. When vesting of an award is conditioned on satisfying one of two or more conditions, compensation expense is recorded over the shortest of the explicit, implicit, or derived service periods. For example, compensation expense for an award that vests upon the completion of four years of continuous employment *or* the development of a new product offering (which management estimates will be complete in 30 months) would initially be recorded over the 30-month implicit service period. If the award vests upon the satisfaction of two or more requirements, compensation expense is recorded over the longest of the explicit, implicit, or derived service periods. For example, compensation expense for an award that vests upon the completion of four years of continuous employment *and* the development of a new product offering (which management estimates will be complete in 30 months) would initially be recorded over the four-year explicit service period.

Once the length of the service period has been determined, a company will need to allocate the compensation expense to each accounting period within the service period. Paragraph 718-10-35-8 provides:

> [A company] shall make a policy decision about whether to recognize compensation cost for an award with only service conditions that has a graded vesting schedule in either of the following ways:
>
> (a) On a straight-line basis over the requisite service period for each separately vesting portion of the award as if the award was, in-substance, multiple awards
>
> (b) On a straight-line basis over the requisite service period for the entire award (that is, over the requisite service period of the last separately vesting portion of the award).
>
> However, the amount of compensation cost recognized at any date must at least equal the portion of the grant-date value of the award that is vested at that date.

This election applies only to time-vested awards. An award that is subject to either a performance condition and/or a market condition, even if the award is also subject to a time-vesting condition, must be expensed as if each separately vesting portion of the award was a separate award.

Under ASC 718, no compensation expense is recognized for awards that fail to vest because a recipient terminates the employment or vendor (in the case of independent contractors) relationship before satisfying a service condition, or if a performance condition is not achieved. Note, however, that if the award is subject to a market condition, compensation expense must be recorded if the requisite service is provided, regardless of whether the market condition is satisfied. For example, assume an employee receives a restricted stock award that vests only if the price of the company's stock appreciates by 15% during the one-year period following the date of grant. If the recipient is still employed at the end of the year (i.e., the grantee has provided the requisite service), the grantor must record compensation expense[3] for the award regardless of whether the target stock price has been attained.

Table 6-1 and table 6-2, respectively, summarize how compensation expense will be measured, when compensation expense will be measured, and when compensation expense will be recorded for long-term incentives that are classified as equity awards (most restricted stock and stock-settled SARs) and awards that are classified as liability awards (cash-settled SARs and phantom shares).

6.4 Illustrations

6.4.1 Stock-Settled Stock Appreciation Rights and Restricted Stock

Stock-settled appreciation rights and restricted stock awards will generally be considered equity awards for purposes of ASC 718. As noted in table 6-1, compensation expense for an equity award is based on the award's grant date fair value. Compensation expense is not subsequently

---

3. In this example, the per-share estimated fair value of the award would be less than the price of the underlying stock on the date of grant. The fair value estimate would need to be estimated using a path-dependent valuation model, such as a Monte Carlo simulation.

adjusted for changes in stock price. Additionally, compensation expense is not adjusted for vested SARs that expire without being exercised. The fair value of a SAR will be estimated using an option-pricing model as if the award were a stock option. The fair value of a share of restricted stock is based on the price of the underlying share.[4]

The aggregate grant date fair value of an equity award will be recorded as compensation expense over the award's service period. If the award is subject only to a service condition (i.e., plain-vanilla time vesting), compensation expense can be accrued on either a straight-line basis or separately for each tranche of the award as if each tranche were a separate award (i.e., tranche-specific vesting). Compensation expense for an award that is subject to any vesting conditions other than, or in addition to, time vesting must be recorded on a tranche-specific basis. The difference between accruing compensation expense on a straight-line basis or on a tranche-specific basis is illustrated in the following examples.

Assume that on January 1, 2019, a company granted 1,000 stock-settled SARs. The estimated grant date fair value equaled $8.43 per SAR.[5] The SARs vest ratably over five years, with 20% of the award vesting on December 31 of 2019, 2020, 2021, 2022, and 2023. If the company elected to accrue compensation expense for time-vested awards on a straight-line basis over the requisite service period for the entire award, rather than on a tranche-specific basis, each year the company would accrue compensation expense based on the percent of the total vesting period that had lapsed at the end of each year-end. Table 6-3 illustrates the accounting treatment.

---

4.   For purposes of ASC 718, the fair value of a share of restricted stock is established as if the share were vested on the date of grant. Restrictions that lapse once the share has vested, such as restrictions on transferability during the vesting period, may not be considered when determining the fair value of the award for purposes of ASC 718. Restrictions that remain after the share has vested, such as a requirement that vested shares be held for a minimum period of time before being sold, may be considered when determining the fair value of an award of equity-based compensation.

5   The fair value of the SAR was estimated using the Black-Scholes option-pricing model and the following assumptions: stock price = $20.00; exercise price = $20.00; expected life = 7.0 years; expected stock price volatility = 32.8%; expected dividend yield = 0.0%; and risk-free interest rate = 3.6%.

Table 6-1. Summary of the Accounting Treatment of Equity Awards Under ASC 718

	Time-vested stock-settled SARs	Performance-vested stock-settled SARs	Time-vested restricted stock	Performance-vested restricted stock
How is compensation expense measured?	Option-pricing model	Option-pricing model	Stock price	Stock price
When is compensation expense measured?	At grant	At grant	At grant	At grant
How is compensation expense recorded?	Straight-line or tranche-specific	Tranche-specific	Straight-line or tranche-specific	Tranche-specific

Table 6-2. Summary of the Accounting Treatment of Liability Awards Under ASC 718

	Time-vested cash-settled SARs	Performance-vested cash-settled SARs	Time-vested phantom stock	Performance-vested phantom stock
How is compensation expense measured?	Option-pricing model	Option-pricing model	Stock price	Stock price
When is compensation expense measured?	The fair value of the award is remeasured at the end of each accounting period until the award is exercised or expires unexercised. The final measure of expense will equal the gain realized by the participant at exercise.		The fair value award is remeasured at the end of each accounting period until the award vests. The final measure of expense will equal the amount of cash distributed to the participant.	
How is compensation expense recorded?	Straight-line or tranche-specific	Tranche-specific	Straight-line or tranche-specific	Tranche-specific

Table 6-3. Time-Vested Stock-Settled SARs

	Year				
	2019	2020	2021	2022	2023
Fair value (Black-Scholes value) per SAR on the date of grant	$8.43	$8.43	$8.43	$8.43	$8.43
Number of SARs outstanding	1,000	1,000	1,000	1,000	1,000
Total fair value of SARs	$8,430	$8,430	$8,430	$8,430	$8,430
Percentage of vesting period lapsed as of December 31	20%	40%	60%	80%	100%
Cumulative compensation expense	$1,686	$3,372	$5,058	$6,744	$8,430
Compensation expense recognized previously	0	1,686	3,372	5,058	6,744
Compensation expense recognized in the current year	$1,686	$1,686	$1,686	$1,686	$1,686

The accounting treatment is more complicated if the SARs are subject to performance-vesting conditions. In that case, each vesting tranche of the award is treated as a separate award, which results in front-loaded expense recognition. Assume in the example above that, instead of receiving 1,000 time-vested cash-settled SARs, the grantee received an award of 1,000 performance-vested SARs. Twenty percent of the award vests each year if certain annual EBITDA[6] goals are satisfied. Because the award is subject to performance-vesting conditions,[7] the award is treated as if the grantee received five separate grants. The accounting treatment at the end of 2019 would be as follows:

1. The first tranche of 200 shares was 100% vested. The fair value of the SAR on the date of grant was $8.43, so the company took a charge of 200 shares at $8.43 per share ($1,686).

2. The second tranche (200 shares vesting over a two-year period) was considered 50% earned, so a charge was taken for 100 shares at $8.43 per share ($843).

3. The third tranche (200 shares vesting over three years) was considered 33.3% earned, so a charge was taken for 66.7 shares at $8.43 per share ($562).

4. The fourth tranche (200 shares vesting over four years) was considered 25% earned, so a charge was taken for 50 shares at $8.43 per share ($422).

5. The fifth tranche (200 shares vesting over five years) was considered 20% earned, so a charge was taken for 40 shares at $8.43 per share ($337).

6. Overall, for 2019 the company took a charge of $3,850.

---

6. "EBITDA" means earnings before interest, taxes, depreciation, and amortization.

7. Care should be taken to ensure that all performance goals are established at the time the award is issued. ASC 718 requires that for a "grant date" to have occurred, the grantor and a grantee must reach a mutual understanding of the key terms and conditions of a share-based payment award. In the above example, if the grantor did not establish the 2020 EBITDA goal until January 1, 2020, the date of grant for this tranche of the award would be January 1, 2020, instead of January 1, 2019.

Table 6-4 illustrates this vesting percentage and the "front-loaded" accounting treatment.

The accounting treatment for each period between the date of grant and the exercise date is illustrated in table 6-5. This illustration is based on the same number of SARs and fair value assumptions included in table 6-3. However, this illustration assumes that 20% of the SARs vest upon the attainment of annual EBITDA goals. Assuming each of the performance goals are met, total compensation expense for the performance-vested SARs will be the same as the total compensation expense for the time-vested SARs—$8,430. However, 45.67% of the total compensation expense ($3,850 / $8,430) is recognized in the first year of the vesting period for performance-vested SARs, compared to 20% of total compensation expense ($1,686 / $8,430) for the time-vested SARs.

All of the above examples are based on stock-settled SARs. Because stock-settled SARs and restricted stock are both treated as equity awards for purposes of ASC 718, the accounting treatment for restricted stock awards would be similar to the accounting treatment of the SARs illustrated above. The only difference would be that compensation expense for restricted stock is based on the grant date stock price (or the estimated fair value if the stock is not publicly traded), while compensation expense for a SAR is estimated using an option-pricing model.

6.4.2 Cash-Settled Stock Appreciation Rights and Phantom Stock

For purposes of ASC 718, cash-settled SARs and phantom stock are each considered liability awards. The aggregate expense that results from a liability award will equal the amount of cash that is paid to grantees to settle the awards (i.e., total expense equals cash out the door). However, expense accruals for accounting periods between the date of grant and the date the award is settled will be based on the fair value of the award as of the end of each accounting period. The fair value of a phantom share will equal the fair value of the underlying stock. The fair value of a cash-settled SAR will be estimated using an option-pricing model, such as Black-Scholes. Compensation expense for time-vested awards can be accrued on either a straight-line basis or on a tranche-specific basis, while compensation expense for performance-vested awards must

Table 6-4. Illustration of Annual Expense Accruals Under Tranche-Specific Expense Attribution

Vesting tranche	Percentage of compensation expense recognized in:					Total
	2019	2020	2021	2022	2023	
Tranche one	20.00%					20.00%
Tranche two	10.00%	10.00%				20.00%
Tranche three	6.67%	6.67%	6.67%			20.00%
Tranche four	5.00%	5.00%	5.00%	5.00%		20.00%
Tranche five	4.00%	4.00%	4.00%	4.00%	4.00%	20.00%
Percentage of total expense recognized per year	45.67%	25.67%	15.67%	9.00%	4.00%	100.00%
Cumulative percentage of total expense recognized	45.67%	71.33%	87.00%	96.00%	100.00%	

Table 6-5. Performance-Vested Stock-Settled SARs

	Year				
	2019	2020	2021	2022	2023
Fair value (Black-Scholes value) per SAR on the date of grant	$8.43	$8.43	$8.43	$8.43	$8.43
Number of SARs outstanding	1,000	1,000	1,000	1,000	1,000
Total fair value of SARs	$8,430	$8,430	$8,430	$8,430	$8,430
Percentage of vesting period lapsed as of December 31	45.67%	71.33%	87.00%	96.00%	100.00%
Cumulative compensation expense	$3,850	$6,013	$7,334	$8,093	$8,430
Compensation expense recognized previously	0	3,850	6,013	7,334	8,093
Compensation expense recognized in the current year	$3,850	$2,164	$1,321	$759	$337

be accrued on a tranche-specific basis. The impact of changes in the fair value of an award before settlement and the expense accrual patterns are illustrated in the following examples.

Assume that on January 1, 2019, a company granted 1,000 cash-settled SARs with a strike price of $20.00. At the time of grant, the price of the company's stock equaled $20.00 per share, and the estimated fair value of the SAR (calculated using Black-Scholes) equaled $8.43. The SARs vest ratably over five years, with 20% of the award vesting on December 31 of 2019, 2020, 2021, 2022, and 2023, and may be exercised at any point after they vest. If the company elected to accrue expense for time-vested awards on a straight-line basis over the requisite service period for the entire award, rather than on a tranche-specific basis, the company would accrue compensation expense based on the percent of the total vesting period that had lapsed at the end of each year-end. Table 6-6 illustrates the accounting treatment.

In table 6-6, compensation expense for each year before the date the SARs are exercised is based on the fair value of the award at year-end and the amount of compensation expense accrued in prior years. For example, as of December 31, 2020, 40% of the vesting period would have lapsed. Based on an estimated fair value of $11.77 per SAR,[8] cumulative compensation expense to date would equal $4,708 ($11.77 * 1,000 * 40% = $4,708). Because compensation expense of $2,184 was accrued in 2019, compensation expense for 2020 equals $2,524 ($4,708 - $2,184).

Because compensation expense for a given year is based on the estimated fair value of the SARs at the end of the year less the amount of compensation expense recognized in prior years, it is possible for compensation expense for a given year to be negative if the estimated fair value of the SARs declines significantly (e.g., as a result of a significant drop in the stock price). Continuing with the example in table 6-6, as of December 31, 2021, the estimated fair value of declined to $3.70 per

---

8   The fair value of the SAR as of December 31, 2020, was estimated using the Black-Scholes option-pricing model and the following assumptions: stock price = $26.00; exercise price = $20.00; weighted average remaining expected life = 5.0 years; expected stock price volatility = 32.8%; expected dividend yield = 0.0%; and risk-free interest rate = 3.60%.

Table 6-6. Time-Vested Cash-Settled SARs

Compensation Expense for Unexercised Cash-Settled SARs							
	Year						
	2019	2020	2021	2022	2023	2024	2025
Fair value (Black-Scholes value) per SAR as of December 31	$10.92	$11.77	$3.70	$1.97	$12.39	$13.06	N/A
Number of SARs outstanding at year-end	1,000	1,000	1,000	1,000	1,000	1,000	0
Total fair value of outstanding SARs	$10,920.00	$11,770.00	$3,700.00	$1,970.00	$12,390.00	$13,060.00	N/A
Percentage of vesting period lapsed as of December 31	20.00%	40.00%	60.00%	80.00%	100.00%	100.00%	100.00%
Cumulative compensation expense for outstanding SARs	$2,184.00	$4,708.00	$2,220.00	$1,576.00	$12,390.00	$13,060.00	N/A
Compensation expense previously recognized for outstanding SARs	0.00	2,184.00	4,708.00	2,220.00	1,576.00	12,390.00	0.00
Expense (income) recognized in the current year for outstanding SARs	$2,184.00	$2,524.00	($2,488.00)	($644.00)	$10,814.00	$670.00	N/A

Compensation Expense for Cash-Settled SARs in the Year of Exercise							
	Year						
	2019	2020	2021	2022	2023	2024	2025
Stock price	$24.00	$26.00	$16.00	$14.00	$30.00	$32.00	$33.00
Exercise price	20.00	20.00	20.00	20.00	20.00	20.00	20.00
Intrinsic value per SAR	$4.00	$6.00	$0.00	$0.00	$10.00	$12.00	$13.00
Number of SARs exercised	0	0	0	0	0	0	1,000
Cumulative compensation expense for exercised SARs	$0.00	$0.00	$0.00	$0.00	$0.00	$0.00	$13,000.00
Compensation expense previously recognized for exercised SARs	0.00	0.00	0.00	0.00	0.00	0.00	13,060.00
Expense (income) recognized in the current year for exercised SARs	$0.00	$0.00	$0.00	$0.00	$0.00	$0.00	($60.00)
Total annual compensation expense	$2,184.00	$2,524.00	($2,488.00)	($644.00)	$10,814.00	$670.00	($60.00)

SAR,[9] resulting in cumulative compensation expense of $2,220. Because $4,708 of compensation expense had previously been recognized, the company would record $2,488 of compensation income in 2021 ($2,220 - $4,708). Note, however, that while compensation expense for a given period may be negative, cumulative compensation expense can never be less than $0.00.

Compensation expense for the year of exercise will equal the intrinsic value of the SARs at the time of exercise. If all 1,000 SARs are exercised on December 31, 2025, when the price of the company's stock equaled $33.00 per share, the final measure of compensation expense would equal $13.00 per SAR ($33.00 stock price - $20.00 exercise price), or $13,000 in aggregate. However, because the company had previously accrued $13,060 of compensation expense based on the fair value (Black-Scholes value) of the SARs on December 31, 2024, compensation expense for 2025 would equal negative $60.00 (i.e., $60.00 of compensation income). Compared to identical time-vested stock-settled SARs (table 6-3), which would result in $1,622 of expense for each year between 2019 and 2023 ($8.43 * 1,000 SARs / 5 years = $1,622), compensation expense for time-vested cash-settled SARs can be much more volatile.

The above example assumes that 20% of the SARs vest each year but that none of the SARs are exercised until December 31, 2025, at which point all of the SARs are exercised. However, employees frequently exercise SARs in pieces, rather than waiting to exercise the entire award at once. If the employee exercised part, but not all, of the award, future expense accruals would be based on the number of SARs that remain outstanding at the end of each year.

The example in table 6-7 assumes that 200 SARs are exercised on December 31, 2020, 400 SARs are exercised on December 31, 2023, and the final 400 SARs are exercised on December 31, 2025. As of December 31, 2020, the 200 SARs that were exercised had an intrinsic value of $6.00 per SAR, or $1,200.00 in aggregate. Because $2,184 of expense ($10.92 grant date Black-Scholes value * 200 stock options) had been recognized

---

9   The fair value of the SAR as of December 31, 2021, was estimated using the Black-Scholes option-pricing model and the following assumptions: stock price = $16.00; exercise price = $20.00; weighted average remaining expected life = 4.0 years; expected stock price volatility = 32.8%; expected dividend yield = 0.0%; and risk-free interest rate = 3.80%.

Table 6-7. Time-Vested Cash-Settled SARs with Exercises

	Compensation Expense for Unexercised Cash-Settled SARs						
				Year			
	2019	2020	2021	2022	2023	2024	2025
Fair value (Black-Scholes value) per SAR as of December 31	$10.92	$11.77	$3.70	$1.97	$12.39	$13.06	N/A
Number of SARs outstanding at year-end	1,000	800	800	800	400	400	0
Total fair value of outstanding SARs	$10,920.00	$9,416.00	$2,960.00	$1,576.00	$4,956.00	$5,224.00	N/A
Percentage of vesting period lapsed as of December 31	20.00%	25.00%	50.00%	75.00%	100.00%	100.00%	100.00%
Cumulative compensation expense for outstanding SARs	$2,184.00	$2,354.00	$1,480.00	$1,182.00	$4,956.00	$5,224.00	N/A
Compensation expense previously recognized for outstanding SARs	0.00	0.00	2,354.00	1,480.00	394.00	4,956.00	0.00
Expense (income) recognized in the current year for outstanding SARs	$2,184.00	$2,354.00	($874.00)	($298.00)	$4,562.00	$268.00	N/A

	Compensation Expense for Cash-Settled SARs In the Year of Exercise						
				Year			
	2019	2020	2021	2022	2023	2024	2025
Stock price	$24.00	$26.00	$16.00	$14.00	$30.00	$32.00	$33.00
Exercise price	20.00	20.00	20.00	20.00	20.00	20.00	20.00
Intrinsic value per SAR	$4.00	$6.00	$0.00	$0.00	$10.00	$12.00	$13.00
Number of SARs exercised	0	200	0	0	400	0	400
Cumulative compensation expense for exercised SARs	$0.00	$1,200.00	$0.00	$0.00	$4,000.00	$0.00	$5,200.00
Compensation expense previously recognized for exercised SARs	0.00	2,184.00	0.00	0.00	788.00	0.00	5,224.00
Expense (income) recognized in the current year for exercised SARs	$0.00	($984.00)	$0.00	$0.00	$3,212.00	$0.00	($24.00)
Total annual compensation expense	$2,184.00	$1,370.00	($874.00)	($298.00)	$7,774.00	$268.00	($24.00)

in 2019, $984 of compensation income ($1,200 issued upon exercise, less the $2,184 recognized in 2019) would be recognized for these 200 SARs in 2020. Note that the estimated fair value of a SAR is based on the SAR's remaining weighted average expected life as of the last day of the year (six years as of December 31, 2019, in this example). As a result, it is common for SARs that are exercised shortly after vesting to result in compensation income, because the SAR has not been outstanding long enough for the value of the underlying stock to appreciate to the levels included in the SAR's weighted average estimated fair value.

The 800 SARs that remain outstanding as of December 31, 2020, have a total fair value of $9,416.00, which results in cumulative compensation expense of $2,354.00. Because all of the compensation expense recognized in 2019 related to the 200 SARs that were exercised in 2020, net compensation expense for the 800 SARs that remain outstanding as of December 31, 2020, equals $2,354.00. Total compensation expense for 2020 equals $1,370.00 ($2,354.00 of compensation expense, less $984.00 of compensation income). The same process is used to calculate compensation expense for 2023 and 2025.

As with performance-vested stock-settled SARs and performance-vested restricted stock, compensation expense for cash-settled SARs and phantom stock that are subject to performance vesting conditions must be accrued on a tranche-specific basis. As a result, compensation expense for performance-vested awards will be front-loaded. The illustration in table 6-8 is based on the same number of SARs and fair value assumptions included in table 6-6. However, the illustration in table 6-8 assumes that 20% of the SARs vest upon the attainment of annual EBITDA goals, while the illustration in table 6-6 is based on time-vested awards. Assuming each of the performance goals are met, total compensation expense for the performance-vested cash-settled SARs will be the same as the total compensation expense for the cash-settled time-vested SARs—the intrinsic value at exercise of $13,000.00. However, 38.4% of the total compensation expense ($4,986.80 / $13,000.00) is recognized in the first year of the vesting period for performance-vested SARs (table 6-8), compared to 17% of total compensation expense ($2,184.00 / $13,000.00) for the time-vested SARs (table 6-6).

Once again, the above example assumes that 20% of the SARs vest each year but that none of the SARs are exercised until December 31,

Table 6-8. Performance-Vested Cash-Settled SARs with Exercises

| | Compensation Expense for Unexercised Cash-Settled SARs | | | | | | |
| | Year | | | | | | |
	2019	2020	2021	2022	2023	2024	2025
Fair value (Black-Scholes value) per SAR as of December 31	$10.92	$11.77	$3.70	$1.97	$12.39	$13.06	N/A
Number of SARs outstanding at year-end	1,000	1,000	1,000	1,000	1,000	1,000	0
Total fair value of outstanding SARs	$10,920.00	$11,770.00	$3,700.00	$1,970.00	$12,390.00	$13,060.00	N/A
Percentage of vesting period lapsed as of December 31	45.67%	71.33%	87.00%	96.00%	100.00%	100.00%	100.00%
Cumulative compensation expense for outstanding SARs	$4,986.80	$8,395.93	$3,219.00	$1,891.20	$12,390.00	$13,060.00	N/A
Compensation expense previously recognized for outstanding SARs	0.00	4,986.80	8,395.93	3,219.00	1,891.20	12,390.00	0.00
Expense (income) recognized in the current year for outstanding SARs	$4,986.80	$3,409.13	($5,176.93)	($1,327.80)	$10,498.80	$670.00	N/A

| | Compensation Expense for Cash-Settled SARs in the Year of Exercise | | | | | | |
| | Year | | | | | | |
	2019	2020	2021	2022	2023	2024	2025
Stock price	$24.00	$26.00	$16.00	$14.00	$30.00	$32.00	$33.00
Exercise price	20.00	20.00	20.00	20.00	20.00	20.00	20.00
Intrinsic value per SAR	$4.00	$6.00	$0.00	$0.00	$10.00	$12.00	$13.00
Number of SARs exercised	0	0	0	0	0	0	1,000
Cumulative compensation expense for exercised SARs	$0.00	$0.00	$0.00	$0.00	$0.00	$0.00	$13,000.00
Compensation expense previously recognized for exercised SARs	0.00	0.00	0.00	0.00	0.00	0.00	13,060.00
Expense (income) recognized in the current year for exercised SARs	$0.00	$0.00	$0.00	$0.00	$0.00	$0.00	($60.00)
Total annual compensation expense	$4,986.80	$3,409.13	($5,176.93)	($1,327.80)	$10,498.80	$670.00	($60.00)

2024, at which point all of the SARs are exercised. If the employee exercised part, but not all, of the award, future expense accruals need to be performed on a tranche-specific basis, based on the number of SARs from each tranche that remain outstanding at the end of each year. ASC 718 requires that awards be accounted for on a first-vested, first-exercised basis.

The example below assumes that vesting of the SARs is subject to annual EBITDA goals and that each of the goals is attained. Two hundred SARs are exercised on December 31, 2020, 400 SARs are exercised on December 31, 2023, and the final 400 SARs are exercised on December 31, 2024. As of December 31, 2020, the 200 SARs that were exercised had an intrinsic value of $6.00 per SAR, or $1,200.00 in aggregate. Because $2,184 of expense ($10.92 * 200) had been recognized in 2019, $984 of compensation income would be recognized for these SARs in 2020. The 800 SARs that remain outstanding would produce cumulative compensation expense of $6,041.93. Because $2,802.80 of compensation expense was recognized in 2019 for the 800 SARs that remain outstanding as of December 31, 2020, net compensation expense equals $3,239.13 for these SARs. Total compensation expense for 2020 equals $2,255.13 ($3,239.13 of compensation expense, less $984.00 of compensation income). The same process is used to calculate compensation expense for 2023 and 2025.

As previously noted, the ultimate measure of compensation expense for liability awards equals the amount of cash distributed to the grantee. This is the reason that aggregate compensation expense illustrated in table 6-7 of $10,400 is the same as of the aggregate compensation expense illustrated in table 6-9. However, 48% of the total compensation expense ($4,986.80 / $10,400.00) is recognized in the first year of the vesting period for performance-vested cash-settled SARs, compared to 21% of total compensation expense ($2,184.00 / $10,400.00) for the time-vested cash-settled SARs.

All of the above examples are based on cash-settled SARs. Because cash-settled SARs and phantom stock are both treated as liability awards for purposes of ASC 718, the accounting treatment for phantom stock awards would be similar to the accounting treatment of the SARs illustrated above. The only difference would be that compensation expense for phantom stock is based on the price of the underlying stock (or the estimated fair value if the stock is not publicly traded), while compen-

Table 6-9. Performance-Vested Cash-Settled SARs with Exercises

| | Compensation Expense for Unexercised Cash-Settled SARs | | | | | | |
| | Year | | | | | | |
	2019	2020	2021	2022	2023	2024	2025
Fair value (Black-Scholes value) per SAR as of December 31	$10.92	$11.77	$3.70	$1.97	$12.39	$13.06	N/A
Number of SARs outstanding at year-end	1,000	800	800	800	400	400	0
Number of SARs expensed and outstanding at year-end							
Tranche one	200						
Tranche two	100	200	200	200			
Tranche three	66.7	133.3	200	200			
Tranche four	50	100	150	200	200	200	
Tranche five	40	80	120	160	200	200	
Total SARs expensed and outstanding at year-end	456.7	513.3	670	760	400	400	0
Cumulative compensation expense for unexercised SARs	$4,986.80	$6,041.93	$2,479.00	$1,497.20	$4,956.00	$5,224.00	0
Compensation expense previously recognized for outstanding SARs	0.00	2,802.80	6,041.93	2,479.00	709.20	4,956.00	0.00
Expense (income) recognized in the current year for unexercised SARs	$4,986.80	$3,239.13	($3,562.93)	($981.80)	$4,246.80	$268.00	N/A

| | Compensation Expense for Cash-Settled SARs in the Year of Exercise | | | | | | |
| | Year | | | | | | |
	2019	2020	2021	2022	2023	2024	2025
Stock price	$24.00	$26.00	$16.00	$14.00	$30.00	$32.00	$33.00
Exercise price	20.00	20.00	20.00	20.00	20.00	20.00	20.00
Intrinsic value per SAR	$4.00	$6.00	$0.00	$0.00	$10.00	$12.00	$13.00
Number of SARs exercised	0	200	0	0	400	0	400
Cumulative compensation expense for exercised SARs	$0.00	$1,200.00	$0.00	$0.00	$4,000.00	$0.00	$5,200.00
Compensation expense previously recognized for exercised SARs	0.00	2,184.00	0.00	0.00	788.00	0.00	5,224.00
Expense (income) recognized in the current year for exercised SARs	$0.00	($984.00)	$0.00	$0.00	$3,212.00	$0.00	($24.00)
Total annual compensation expense	$4,986.80	$2,255.13	($3,562.93)	($981.80)	$7,458.80	$268.00	($24.00)

sation expense for a SAR is based on the estimated fair value before the SAR's exercise. For both cash-settled SARs and phantom stock, the final measure of expense is based on the intrinsic value of the award at the time of settlement.

6.4.3 Forfeitures

As a simplifying assumption, the above illustrations have ignored the impact of forfeitures. However, in the real world it is unlikely that at some point an award will not be forfeited because the participant terminated the employment or vendor (in the case of independent contractors) relationship before the vest date (i.e., the grantee will not provide the requisite service). In Accounting Standards Update 2016-09[10] the Financial Accounting Standards Board provided companies with a choice of either incorporating estimated forfeitures into the expense accruals or accounting for forfeitures as the occur. Because participants do not terminate the employment or vendor relationship at a uniform rate throughout the vesting period, incorporating estimated forfeiture into the expense accruals will reduce the potential variance in compensation expense but is more administratively burdensome. On the other hand, accounting for forfeitures as they occurs is administratively simpler, but can lead to much more volatility in the expense accruals.

6.5 Performance Award Plans

As noted previously, unless (a) the award will be settled in shares of stock; (b) the award will be settled in cash, but the amount of the payment is based on the value of a share of stock; or (c) the vesting of the award is dependent upon attaining a target value or target level of appreciation in the value of a share of stock, the accounting treatment of awards will not be covered by ASC 718. Instead, compensation expense is accrued as if the performance unit plan were a multi-year bonus plan. The guiding principle is that compensation expense (and income) should be recognized on a systematic and rational basis.

More specifically, under a performance award plan where compensation is earned based on attaining one or more particular goals over

---

10. Before Accounting Standards Update 2016-09, companies were required to incorporate estimated forfeitures into the expense accruals.

a period of time, compensation should be accrued over the period in relation to the results achieved to date. Also, to the extent results previously estimated or determined to have been achieved prove not to be sustainable, compensation expense is reversed.

The accounting is best explained in an example. Using table 6-10 and assuming that (1) 10 employees were each awarded 1,000 performance units for a total of 10,000 units (or a targeted payment of $1 million) and (2) performance was at target at the end of 2019, above target at the end of 2020 and 2021, but below target at the end of 2022 (2022 was a tough year and adversely affected aggregate performance), the annual expense (and income) would be as illustrated in table 6-11.

The above example also assumes that there are no forfeitures. To the extent any award recipient's employment or vendor relationship is terminated before the end of 2022, cumulative compensation expense with respect to that employee is reversed.

6.6   Impact of Equity-Based Compensation on Earnings per Share

Under ASC Topic 260, *Earnings per Share*, companies are required to disclose two computations of net income and income from continuing operations in their financial statements: basic earnings per share ("basic EPS") and diluted earnings per share ("diluted EPS"). Basic EPS is simply income available to shareholders of common stock divided by the weighted average number of common shares outstanding during the year. Diluted EPS represents the theoretical maximum dilution to earnings per share that would result if all dilutive instruments (stock options, convertible debt, convertible preferred stock, etc.) were converted into common stock.

The calculation of basic EPS is illustrated in table 6-12. Assume a company has net income of $2.5 million for fiscal 2019. The company has 50,000 shares of preferred stock outstanding that pay an aggregate annual dividend of $250,000, and the weighted average number of common stock outstanding during 2019 equaled 1,000,000.

The treasury stock method is the most commonly used method for calculating the dilutive impact of outstanding equity-based compensation, including stock-settled SARs and unvested restricted stock or RSUs. Note, however, that if an award is accounted for as a liability because

Table 6-10. Example of Performance Award Plan

			Unit value			
		<9%	6.0%	6.5%	7.0%	7.5%	8.0% or more
	7.20% or more	$0.00	$100.00	$112.50	$125.00	$137.50	$150.00
	7.10%	$0.00	$87.50	$100.00	$112.50	$125.00	$137.50
Average EBITDA growth 2019–2022	7.00%	$0.00	$75.00	$87.50	$100.00	$112.50	$125.00
	6.90%	$0.00	$62.50	$75.00	$87.50	$100.00	$112.50
	6.80%	$0.00	$50.00	$62.50	$75.00	$87.50	$100.00
	<6.80%	$0.00	$0.00	$0.00	$0.00	$0.00	$0.00

Return on Equity 2019–2022

Table 6-11. Performance Award Accounting

	Year			
	2019	2020	2021	2022
Margin and revenue results achieved to date (expressed in terms of unit values)	$100.00	$112.50	$112.50	$75.00
Number of units outstanding	10,000	10,000	10,000	10,000
Aggregate compensation expense	$1,000,000	$1,125,000	$1,125,000	$750,000
Cumulative percentage accrued	25%	50%	75%	100%
Cumulative compensation expense	$250,000	$562,500	$843,750	$750,000
Expense previously recognized	0	250,000	562,500	843,750
Expense (income) for current year	$250,000	$312,500	$281,250	($93,750)

Table 6-12. Basic EPS

Net income	$2,500,000
Less: preferred dividend	250,000
Net income available to common shareholders	$2,250,000
Weighted average number of common shares outstanding	1,000,000
Basic EPS	$2.25

there is a requirement to cash-settle that instrument, it would be excluded from the diluted EPS analysis. If there is an election to cash-settle the award, ASC 260 presumes the award to be settled in shares if it is more dilutive; however, that presumption can be overcome.

The treasury stock method assumes that all in-the-money stock options and stock-settled SARs are exercised, regardless of whether or not they are vested (restricted stock and RSUs are treated like an option with an exercise price of zero). The option proceeds are used to reacquire shares in the open market (i.e., to purchase treasury shares). The number of shares issued upon exercise of the stock options and stock-settled SARs, as well as the number of unvested full-value share awards, less the number of treasury shares assumed to be repurchased, is added to the weighted average shares outstanding. Awards that would increase EPS are considered antidilutive and are excluded from the calculation (e.g., underwater stock options and SARs).

When calculating the theoretical number of treasury shares reacquired, the proceeds available to repurchase the shares are assumed to include:

1. The aggregate exercise price of all dilutive options (i.e., in-the-money options)

2. The average unrecognized compensation expense for unvested awards

The impact of outstanding equity-based compensation on diluted EPS is illustrated in table 6-13. This illustration is based on the same assumptions included in table 6-12. Additionally, on December 31, 2019, the company has 50,000 stock options outstanding (the dilutive impact of stock-settled SARs is calculated in the same manner as stock options) with an exercise price of $30.00 per option. These options

Table 6-13. Diluted EPS

Shares issued upon option exercise	50,000
Proceeds	
Aggregate exercise price ($30 * 50,000)	$1,500,000
Unamortized compensation expense[a] (($750,000 + $500,000) / 2)	625,000
Total proceeds	$2,125,000
Average stock price	$75.00
Number of shares reacquired	28,333
Net number of shares issued	21,667
Weighted average number of common shares outstanding	1,000,000
Shares included in diluted EPS	1,021,667
Net income available to common shareholders	$2,250,000
Diluted EPS	$2.20

[a]Represents the average of the unamortized compensation expense at the beginning of the year ($15.00 * 50,000 = $750,000) and the unamortized compensation expense at the end of the year ($750,000 grant date fair value * two years remaining in vesting period at year-end/three-year vesting period = $500,000 of unamortized compensation expense at year-end) assuming compensation expense is accrued on a straight-line basis.

were granted on January 1, 2019, cliff vest on December 31, 2021, and had a grant date fair value of $15.00 per option. The company's average stock price during 2019 was $75.00. Based on these assumptions, diluted EPS would equal $2.20.

6.7 Dividend and Dividend Equivalents

6.7.1 Liability Awards vs. Equity Awards

Full-value share awards (i.e., restricted stock, restricted stock units, and phantom stock) frequently provide that participants will be entitled to receive dividends and dividend equivalents on unvested awards. Additionally, stock options and SARs are sometimes granted with dividend participation rights, which provide the grantee with dividend equivalents on the number of shares of stock underlying the stock option or SAR, but this is less common. Dividends and dividend equivalents may be paid at the same time that dividends are distributed to shareholders or may be escrowed and paid only at the time the full-value share vests or the stock option or SAR is exercised.

As with most things under ASC 718, the financial accounting treatment of dividends and dividend equivalents depends on whether the award is classified as a liability award or an equity award. Dividends that are paid on liability awards (i.e., SARs, phantom shares, and other cash-settled awards) are always treated as additional compensation. The financial accounting treatment of dividends paid on unvested restricted stock awards[11] depends on whether the underlying award vests. No compensation expense is recognized for dividends that are paid on equity awards that vest. However, if dividends are paid on an equity award that is subsequently forfeited and the grantee is not required to return the dividends to the grantor (or forfeit the dividends in the event the dividends are held in escrow during the vesting period), the grantor will recognize additional compensation expense for the value of the dividends paid on the forfeited award.

ASC 718 provides that accruals of compensation expense for equity-based compensation may include forfeiture estimates. If an equity award includes non-forfeitable dividends, the same forfeiture estimate would be used to accrue compensation expense for the non-forfeitable dividends. For example, assume that on January 1, 2019, a company granted 500 shares of restricted stock to each of 300 grantees. The awards include non-forfeitable dividends and the company pays an annual cash dividend of $0.20 per share. The restricted stock cliff vests on December 31, 2021, and the company estimates that 4.0% of the recipients will terminate the employment or vendor relationship each year before vesting. As a result, only 132,710 shares are expected to vest (500 * 300 * 96% * 96% * 96% = 132,710), and 17,290 are expected to be forfeited. The annual compensation accruals for the non-forfeitable dividends are shown in table 6-14.

---

11. The impact of dividend equivalents on stock options and stock-settled stock appreciation rights is reflected in the estimated grant date fair value of the award. Depending upon how the dividend equivalent rights are structured, the inclusion of the dividend equivalents may preclude the use of the Black-Scholes option pricing model and require the use of a lattice model to estimate fair value.

Table 6-14. Compensation Expense for Non-Forfeitable Dividends

	Year		
	2019	2020	2021
Number of restricted shares outstanding on January 1	150,000	144,000	138,240
Estimated annual forfeiture rate	4%	4%	4%
Number of shares estimated to be forfeited	6,000	5,760	5,530
Estimated annual dividend	$0.20	$0.20	$0.20
Aggregate compensation expense	$1,200	$1,152	$1,106

The expense accruals illustrated above would need to be trued up periodically, to the extent that actual forfeitures and dividend payments vary from expectations.

Alternatively, if the company elects to account for forfeitures as they occur, rather than including estimated forfeitures in the expense accruals, each time compensation expense is reduced to reflect the forfeiture of an award, the company would also need to record additional compensation expense equal to the value of the dividends or dividend equivalents that had previously been distributed on the forfeited shares.

6.7.2 EPS Considerations

As noted in section 6.6 of this chapter, ASC Topic 260, *Earnings per Share*, requires a company to calculate per-share net income and per-share income from continuing operations on a "basic" and "diluted" basis. The EPS calculations are typically done using the treasury stock method, as illustrated in table 6-12 and table 6-13. However, equity awards that include non-forfeitable dividends are considered "participating securities." When a company has participating securities outstanding, EPS is required to be calculated using the "two-class method"[12] rather than the treasury stock method. Under the two-class method, participating securities are required to be included in the denominator when calculating both basic EPS and diluted EPS, as opposed to only being included in diluted EPS under the treasury stock method. As a result, equity awards that include non-forfeitable dividends will be more dilutive to basic EPS than a similar award that includes forfeitable dividends.

---

12. The calculation of EPS using the two-class method is highly complex and beyond the scope of this chapter.

CHAPTER SEVEN

ESOPs, ESPPs, 401(k) Plans, and Stock Options: When the Old Standbys Still Make Sense

Corey Rosen

Contents

Clearly, there are many advantages to setting up a phantom stock, restricted stock, direct stock purchase, performance award, or stock appreciation rights (SAR) plan (for simplicity, I will call these plans "alternative equity plans" in this chapter). These plans are simple, they do not require any actual stock to be distributed, and they are supremely flexible in how they are designed. But there are some potentially serious disadvantages that need to be considered as well. In particular, these plans:

- Can raise regulatory issues unless properly designed;
- Have accounting disadvantages;
- Can leave employees skeptical that actual benefits will be distributed;
- Have less favorable tax consequences than other kinds of employee ownership plans;
- May, if they require employees to buy stock, make ownership riskier and available mostly to higher-paid people with sufficient discretionary income; and
- Fail to create a way for people who own stock to provide for business continuity.

But even if a company decides it wants one of these plans, that does not preclude it from using one or more of the plans that have been the mainstays of broad-based employee ownership for years: employee stock ownership plans (ESOPs), stock options, employee stock purchase plans (ESPPs), and, in some cases, 401(k) plans.

This chapter looks at each of the potential disadvantages to the plans discussed in this book. These disadvantages may mean that these plans might not be appropriate at all or might need to be used in combination with the more standard kinds of plans mentioned in the paragraph above. This is followed by a very brief discussion of some of the other kinds of plans that may deserve consideration. First, though, we need to discuss a key reason people set up these plans in the first place: to avoid losing control.

7.1 The Specter of Losing Control: Why It Is Not a Key Issue

First, it's useful to consider one of the principal reasons why employers often think they specifically need a phantom stock plan or stock appreciation rights plan instead of a more traditional equity plan (discussed below): they don't want to risk losing control. This is rarely as important an issue as it seems. The issue comes up almost entirely in closely held companies; actual share ownership by employees in public companies is almost never substantial enough to provide any meaningful control. In almost any variation on the plans described in this book, it would be rare for there to be more than a small minority of shares held by any one employee or even a group of employees at any one time. If companies are concerned that employees might sell their shares to outsiders, companies can require the shares be sold back to the company or retain a right of first refusal. If state securities law allow, they could also provide that awards are for non-voting shares, although this should lower the per-share value of shares acquired.

If ownership is through an employee benefit plan qualified under ERISA (the Employee Retirement Income Security Act of 1974), such as an ESOP (described below), the risk of losing control is similarly small. In an ESOP, the trustee is considered the legal owner of record. The trustee actually votes the shares. While many closely held ESOP companies allow employees to direct the trustee as to the voting of the shares, most do not. Instead, the trustee either uses independent judgment or is instructed by a third party, often the board of directors. Employees must be able to direct the trustee, however, on a few "mandatory" issues, the most important of which are sale of all or substantially all the assets (but not on sale of the stock), liquidation, reclassification (such as going public), and mergers. These issues rarely, if ever, come up. More important, we do not know of a single case where employees have been able to prevent management from doing something it wanted to do based solely on their ability to vote on these required issues. Where management does not want employees to have effective control, the board appoints the trustee, and the trustee votes for the board, an entirely circular arrangement. While many, and perhaps now even most, ESOPs voluntarily allow at least some employee input (if not actual voting control) into corporate-level decisions, it is not legally required.

A more serious issue with ESOPs is that the fiduciary responsibilities of the trustee are to operate the plan for the benefit of plan participants. This can place some, if not many, limits on management behavior. For instance, a trustee of the Delta Star Company successfully sued the company's CEO when he paid himself a salary of $3 million, which was what the company earned that year. Because the trustee can be an appointee of management, however, trustees very rarely sue management. Instead, what normally happens is that employees sue the trustee for failing to follow fiduciary standards. The most frequent causes of action are the ESOP paying too much for the shares and the plan's failing to make distributions according to its own rules or the law. All but a few of these cases involve what most observes would agree is egregious behavior by management. Plans that are run in conventional ways with sound legal advice almost never are sued. In the years between 1990 and 2016, there were only 328 ESOP cases of any kind that reached court (out of probably 20,000 ESOPs over this time). So while owners give up some control with an ESOP, they don't have to give up much, and if the ESOP owns a minority of the shares, they give up virtually no control.

This is even truer in profit sharing or 401(k) arrangements in which the plan invests in company stock. There are no voting requirements in these plans. Only fiduciary rules impose any constraints on management control. Because both qualified ERISA plans and stock option plans have much better tax treatment than phantom stock and similar plans, if losing control is the only reason for avoiding these more favored plans, then the decision should probably be reconsidered.

7.2 Risks and Disadvantages of Alternative Equity Plans

As discussed earlier, one of the issues in setting up a broad-based phantom stock plan or stock appreciation rights plan is that their terms may make them a *de facto* retirement plan subject to regulation under the Employee Retirement Income Security Act (ERISA). It is, of course, possible to avoid this by limiting the design of the plan so that it covers only key people or, if broad-based, it makes periodic payouts, or paying only a liquidity event (normally the sale of the company), rather than waiting solely until termination of employment or retirement. But some companies want to structure their plans as both broad-based and with long-deferred payouts. Deferring the payouts conserves cash, at least in the short run, and gives employees more of an incentive to stick around. Giving up these features may not be worth the advantages of a phantom stock or stock appreciation rights plan. Restricted stock and direct purchase plans should not run the regulatory risks of being covered under ERISA, and some kinds of equity plans can be structured to allow deferrals past the vesting date. However, deferring compensation under some of these plans can subject the participant to punitive taxes under Section 409A of the Internal Revenue Code (the "Code"). See the relevant chapters in this book for details on whether and how Section 409A affects individual plans such as phantom stock.

A second issue is accounting treatment. Until 2006 (2005 for public companies), companies did not have to record a current compensation charge for the value of options granted to employees, but did for all other kinds of equity plans. As the chapter on accounting in this book notes, individual equity compensation plans (such as stock options, phantom stock, restricted stock, and SAR plans) now all require that companies determine their cost at the time the awards are granted, based on their current fair value, and recognize that cost over the service period for the award. For public companies, the changed rules for stock options at first appeared to be an important issue. Many of these companies had gone to some lengths to minimize the costs of stock awards as current charges to income because they feared the public would view their earnings more negatively. That turned out to be a greatly exaggerated concern. The leveling of the playing field for equity accounting, in the end, simply allowed companies to choose the plans that fit their compensation philosophies most closely rather than choose plans for their accounting features.

For closely held companies, the issue is even less important. Pre-IPO companies generally care a great deal about what their income statements look like. So do many companies seeking an acquirer. But investors, buyers, and investment bankers marketing an IPO are sophisticated enough to look through the accounting treatment of various award structures to evaluate their actual economic impact on company earnings. For companies not looking to be sold or go public, income statements are of most concern to their bankers and other creditors. If they have a good relationship with these entities, the accounting issues can usually be explained. Companies can honestly point out that they could have set up a plan with more favorable accounting rules, but that the real effect on cash and on shareholder equity would be much the same. Because of all these considerations, there is no good argument to be made for choosing equity plans other than options simply because of accounting treatment. With an ESOP, the value of shares allocated to employee accounts already incurs a compensation charge on the income statement. When an ESOP borrows money to buy shares, the shares are held in a suspense account and allocated as the loan is repaid. If the share value goes up, the accounting charge does as well, even though the actual cost to the company is always the original purchase price of the shares. This rule, adopted in 1992, caused many public companies to replace leveraged ESOPs with annual stock contributions to a 401(k) plan. The accounting charge in this case would be the value of each year's contribution. While the accounting charge for a leveraged ESOP may seem less favorable than for a 401(k) or the grant of some form of broad-based individual equity, this needs to be balanced against the far greater tax benefits ESPOs provide compared to these other plans. Accounting conventions do not change how much a company actually spends (or saves via tax incentives) on sharing ownership by one dollar more or less. The experience with stock options showed that investors understand this and do not make choices based on varying accounting treatments.

A third issue is taxes. Phantom stock, restricted stock, RSUs, and SARs really have no significant tax benefits for companies, and, for restricted stock, only a very limited tax benefit for employees. Like any other kind of compensation, employees must pay tax when they acquire a non-forfeitable right to a benefit, even if they do not actually receive it. For restricted stock (but not restricted stock units), employees can choose Section 83(b) treatment, but this means the employee may risk paying taxes on a benefit the employee may never receive (and the taxes will not be credited back). Once paid, the employee cannot avoid paying ordinary income tax. The employer, meanwhile, takes no deduction for the award until paid, even though the expected future cost of an award will show up on the company's income statement when the award is granted. Direct stock purchase plans require employees to buy stock with after-tax money.

In contrast, incentive stock options allow employees to take capital gains treatment on their awards. Moreover, no tax is due until sale of the stock (employers cannot take a tax deduction, however, if employees who have these kinds of options keep them for the full tax holding period). In an ESOP or other qualified ERISA plan, employers get a deduction *at the time the contribution is made*, but employees do not pay any tax until they actually receive the stock or its cash value years later. Qualified ERISA plans such as ESOPs are the only kind of compensation where the normal tax rule that companies can only take a deduction at the time the employee incurs a tax obligation does not apply. Qualified ERISA plans, unlike all other kinds of equity compensation, also allow the employee to further defer taxation by rolling over amounts into other defined contribution plans or into IRAs. Employers and sellers get additional tax benefits as well, as described below. Moreover, companies with an ESOP can deduct dividends paid on ESOP shares that are used to repay an ESOP loan (a loan to the ESOP to acquire company shares, repaid with company contributions and/or dividends), are passed through to employees, or are voluntarily reinvested by employees in company stock.

A fourth issue is that phantom plans and SARs cannot create a market for an owner's shares. Many owners of closely held companies want to use employee ownership as a means for providing business continuity. Phantom plans and SARs simply give away bonuses based on equity value; they do nothing to provide a market for owners' shares.

With direct stock purchase plans, two significant problems can arise. First, because employees are using their own money to buy stock, they are taking considerably more risk than in other plans. That means they will probably expect more (often including some say in how the company is run), be more discouraged if the company does not do well, and be more likely to sue if things go very badly. Second, ownership will be available only to those with the means to buy it. For companies wanting to get a broad distribution of ownership to employees, this will be a significant problem.

Finally, and often most importantly, employees may not respond as positively to phantom plans or SARs as other kinds of plans. In part, this may just be familiarity. Many employees know about stock options, ESOPs, 401(k) plans, and profit sharing plans. Restricted stock lies somewhere in between; it is real stock, with specific rules about its use, but it is less familiar (so far) to employees than other plans. That familiarity may breed greater confidence that the plans really will pay off. Moreover, these plans have various rules they must follow; the plans described in this book have rules the company determines entirely on its own. Moreover, where employees get something based on what the company says is its equity value, employees may be skeptical about how this is measured, at least in closely held companies. Employees may also be skeptical about whether the plan really will make payouts or the stock will be liquid, although that concern can be lessened over time as the company builds a history on this. One result of these concerns is that companies with the kinds of plans described here, ironically, may need to be *more* open about their books, their strategies, and their appraisal methods than companies with other plans if they are to make the plans believable. However, these same concerns would apply to ESOPs, stock options, 401(k) plans, and profit sharing plans used to acquire stock in private companies as well.

This recital of problems does not mean these plans do not have substantial advantages, as the rest of this book describes. It does mean that companies should at least consider other alternatives.

7.3   Plan Types

There are a number of other kinds of employee ownership plans com-panies should at least consider. In this section, we will look at four of the principal vehicles: ESOPs (employee stock ownership plans), 401(k) plans, stock options, and qualified stock purchase plans.

7.3.1 ESOPs

An ESOP is a kind of employee benefit plan. Governed by ERISA, ESOPs were given a specific statutory framework in 1974. In the ensu-ing years, they were given a number of other tax benefits. Like other qualified deferred compensation plans governed by ERISA, they must not discriminate in their operations in favor of highly compensated employees, officers, and owners. To assure that these rules are met, ESOPs must appoint a trustee to act as the plan fiduciary. This can be anyone, although larger companies tend to appoint an outside trust institution, while smaller companies typically appoint a manager or create an ESOP trust committee.

The most sophisticated use of an ESOP is to borrow money. In this approach, the company sets up a trust. The trust then borrows money from a lender. The company repays the loan by making tax-deductible contributions to the trust, which the trust gives to the lender. The loan must be to acquire stock in the company. Proceeds from the loan can be used for any legitimate business purpose. The stock is put into a "suspense account," where it is released to employee accounts as the loan is repaid. After employees leave the company or retire, the company buys back the stock purchased on their behalf. In practice, banks often require a second step in the loan transaction of making the loan to the company instead of the trust, with the company reloaning the proceeds to the ESOP.

In return for agreeing to funnel the loan through the ESOP, the company gets a number of tax benefits, provided it follows the rules to assure employees are treated fairly. First, the company can deduct the entire loan contribution it makes to the ESOP, within certain payroll-based limits described below. That means the company, in effect, can deduct interest and principal on the loan, not just interest. Second, the company can deduct dividends paid on the shares acquired with the proceeds of the loan that are used to repay the loan itself (in other words, the earnings of the stock being acquired help pay for stock itself). Reasonable dividends passed through to employees or voluntarily reinvested in the company's stock (including through putting the dividends into a 401(k) plan offering company shares). Again, there are limits, as described below in sections on the rules of the loan and contribution limits. Finally, if the company is an S corporation, then the share of corporate earnings attributable to the ESOP are not subject to corporate income tax. Note, however, that rules designed to prevent abuses of this extraordinary tax benefit generally make it impractical for an S corporation ESOP to have fewer than 10 participants or be limited primarily to management.

The ESOP can also be funded directly by discretionary corporate contributions of cash to buy existing shares or simply by the contribution of shares. These contributions are tax-deductible up to 25% of the covered payroll of ESOP participants.

7.3.1.1 *ESOP Applications*

The ESOP can buy both new and existing shares, for a variety of purposes.

- The most common application for an ESOP is *to buy the shares of a departing owner of a closely held company.* Owners in closely held C corporations (but not S) who have owned the stock for at least three years can defer tax on the gain they have made from the sale to an ESOP if the ESOP holds 30% or more of the company's stock once the purchase is completed. Any subsequent sales also qualify for the tax deferral. To qualify for the deferral, owners must reinvest the sale proceeds in stocks and bonds of U.S. corporations not receiving more than 25% of their income from passive investment. Sellers have 12 months after the sale to select the replacement property. The tax break is a deferral; when the replacement investments are sold, capital gains taxes are due going back to the original basis on the closely held company's stock. Moreover, the purchase can be made in pretax corporate dollars.

- ESOPs can *buy newly issued shares in the company, with the borrowed funds being used to buy new capital.* The company can, in effect, finance growth or acquisitions in pretax dollars while these same dollars create an employee benefit plan. ESOPs can also be used this way to fund a match to a 401(k) plan.

- The above uses generally involve borrowing money through the ESOP, but a company can simply contribute new shares of stock to an ESOP, or cash to buy existing shares, *as a means to create an employee benefit plan.* As more and more companies want to find ways to tie employee and corporate interests, this is becoming a more popular application. In public companies especially, an ESOP contribution is often used as part or all of a match to employee deferrals to a 401(k) plan.

7.3.1.2 *Basic ESOP Rules*

Shares in the ESOP trust are allocated to individual employee accounts. Although there are some exceptions, generally all full-time employees over 21 participate in the plan. Allocations are made either on the basis of relative pay or some more equal formula. As employees accumulate seniority with the company, they acquire an increasing right to the shares in their account, a process known as vesting. Employees must be 100% vested within three to six years.

When employees leave the company, they receive their stock, which the company must buy back from them at its fair market value (unless there is a public market for the shares). Private companies must have an annual outside valuation to determine the price of their shares. In private companies, employees must be able to direct the trustee as to the voting of their allocated shares on a very limited number of major issues, such as closing or relocating, but the company can choose whether to pass through voting rights (such as for the board of directors) on other issues. In public companies, employees must be able to vote all issues.

There are a number of other rules and benefits of ESOPs that are beyond the scope of this brief summary. The NCEO publishes a number of detailed books on this subject. For most companies considering an equity-equivalent plan, the decision on whether to do an ESOP instead usually comes down to a few key points:

1. ESOPs are more complicated and require extensive and expensive legal, appraisal, and administrative costs; a leveraged ESOP generally costs at least $75,000 to set up and $15,000 per year to operate.

2. ESOPs must follow specific rules about how stock is allocated and distributed, rules that do not allow for individual discretion as to who gets what when.

3. ESOPs provide substantial tax benefits, particularly for business continuity.

4. ESOPs can only buy shares at an appraised value or less; if sellers are convinced their stock is worth more, an ESOP may not work.

7.3.2 Section 401(k) Plans

Section 401(k) plans allow employees to defer part of their pay on a pretax basis into an investment fund set up by the company. The company usually offers at least four alternative investment vehicles. Because the law requires that participation in the plans not be too heavily skewed toward more highly paid people, companies generally offer a partial match to encourage broad participation in these voluntary plans. This match can be in any investment vehicle the company chooses, including company stock. There is a limit of 25% of taxable pay that the company can contribute to the plan. This limit is reduced by other company contributions to other defined contribution plans, such as ESOPs or profit sharing plans. Employees can annually defer up to $19,000 on a pretax basis into the plan (as of 2019; this amount is indexed annually for inflation). However, the sum of employee deferrals and employer contributions to all defined contribution plans cannot exceed the lesser of $56,000 or 100% of pay (as of 2019). The $56,000 figure is also indexed for inflation.

There are several factors that favor the use of a 401(k) plan as a vehicle for employee ownership. In public companies, company stock may be one of the most cost-effective means of matching employee contributions. If there are existing treasury shares or the company prints new shares, contributing them to the 401(k) plan may impose no immediate cash cost on the company; in fact, it would provide a tax deduction. Other shareholders would suffer a dilution, of course. If the company has to buy shares to fund the match, at least the dollars being used are used to invest in itself rather than other investments. From the employee standpoint, company stock is the investment the employee knows best and so may be attractive to people who either do not want to spend the time to learn about alternatives or have a strong belief in their own company.

Public companies also often use an ESOP to provide the match to the employees' deferrals into 401(k) plans. This technique allows the company to deduct dividends paid to the ESOP that are used to repay an ESOP loan, that are passed though to employees, or that employees voluntarily reinvest in company stock. Balanced against these advantages, of course, must be an appreciation on both the part of the employee and the company that a failure to diversify a retirement portfolio is very risky. This gained considerable attention in 2001 and 2002 with the Enron bankruptcy, as well as similar debacles for employee retirement accounts at Global Crossing, Lucent, Rite-Aid, and other large companies. In 2006, Congress passed the Pension Protection Act, which requires that 401(k) plans in public companies (including plans integrated with an ESOP) allow employees to choose to diversify any investments in company stock at any time; shares contributed by the company must be diversifiable after three years in the plan. These rules do not apply to stand-alone ESOPs, or to 401(k) plans or ESOPs in closely held companies.

In 2014, the Supreme Court ruled in *Fifth Third Bank v. Dudenhoeffer* that trustees of ESOPs, 401(k) plans, or other plans with employer stock in them cannot be presumed to be prudent for buying, holding, and/or offering company stock in the plans. Appellate courts in the past have generally granted this presumption. The Court set out a series of new requirements for plaintiffs to meet to prevail in a lawsuit against plan trustees that seeks compensation for losses from company stock in employee accounts. Private companies with ESOPs will be little affected by this ruling, if at all, but public companies should be more cautious in their management of stock in the plan.

For closely held companies, 401(k) plans are less appealing as an employee ownership vehicle, although very appropriate in some cases. If employees are given an option to buy company stock, this can often trigger securities law issues most private firms want to avoid. Employer matches make more sense, but require the company to either dilute ownership or reacquire shares from selling shareholders. In many closely held businesses, the first may not be desirable for control reasons and the second because there may not be sellers. Moreover, the 401(k) approach does not provide the "rollover" tax benefit that selling to an ESOP does, and the maximum amount that can be contributed is a function of how much employees put into savings. That will limit how much an employer can actually buy from a seller through a 401(k) plan to a fraction of what the ESOP can buy.

Despite these limitations, 401(k) plans may be attractive as ownership vehicles where a company wants employees to become owners, but has no need to buy out existing owners or use the borrowing features of an ESOP. A company can match employee deferrals with company stock or make a straight percentage of pay contribution to all employees eligible to be in the plan in the form of company stock. Companies do need to be cautious, however, to assure that employees have enough diversified investments in their accounts so that if the company fails, their retirement is not at risk.

As noted above, 401(k) plans and ESOPs can be combined, with the ESOP contribution being used as the 401(k) match. This can work on either a nonleveraged or leveraged basis. In the nonleveraged case, the company simply characterizes its match as an ESOP. That adds some set-up and administrative costs, but allows the company to reap the additional tax benefits of an ESOP. In a leveraged case, the company estimates how much it will need to match employee contributions each year, then borrows an amount of money such that the loan repayment will be close to that amount. If it is not as much as the promised matching amount, the company can either just define that as its match anyway, make up the difference with additional shares or cash (if the loan payment is lower), or pay the loan faster. If the amount is larger, the employees get a windfall. Combination plans must meet complex rules for testing to determine if they discriminate too heavily in favor of more highly paid people.

7.3.3 Stock Options

As noted above, ESOPs are qualified under ERISA, meaning they must meet federal rules to assure that participation in them does not excessively favor more highly compensated people. Not every company wants to abide by these rules, nor does every company want the additional tax benefits they can offer. Moreover, some companies believe ownership means more if employees have to put something up to get it. Some growing companies find that contributing or purchasing existing stock is too much of a strain on either their capital structure or their finances, or both. They would prefer to give employees a right to future ownership. Even if they do have the means to contribute stock or pay cash awards through a SAR or phantom plan, companies may prefer stock options because they do not impose an unpredictable future cash expense. Options, in effect, impose a shareholder expense rather than a cash expense, unless the company chooses to settle the option by buying back shares. Many growing private companies do not pay taxes, so the tax benefits of an ESOP may not be attractive, making the greater flexibility of options more appealing.

For companies persuaded by one or more of these arguments, stock options may make an attractive choice. In the past, options were granted primarily to highly paid executives. In recent years, however, more and more companies have decided to grant options well beyond managerial and supervisory ranks. We at the NCEO estimate that 9%

of public companies do this, and that a majority of these companies are outside the technology sector. A 2006 survey from VentureOne found that 87% of pre-IPO technology companies granted options to most or all employees as well. Of course, many companies, including companies with other employee ownership plans, also grant options just to a limited number of people.

7.3.3.1 *What Is a Stock Option?*

A stock option gives an employee the right to buy shares at a price fixed today (usually the market price, but sometimes lower) for a defined number of years into the future. The options might be granted on a percentage of pay basis, a merit formula, an equal basis, or any other formula the company chooses. Most plans provide grants regularly (every one to three years), either on the basis of the passage of time (every year, for instance) or an event (a promotion, meeting certain corporate or group targets, or a performance appraisal, for instance). The options are typically subject to three- to five-year vesting, meaning that if someone is 20% vested, he or she can exercise only 20% of the options. An employee can usually exercise vested options at any time. Most options have a 10-year life, meaning the employee can choose to buy the shares at the grant price at any time they are vested for up to 10 years. The option life, however, can be any amount (except in the case of incentive stock options, as described below). The difference between the grant price and the exercise price is called the "spread."

Most public companies offer a "cashless exercise" alternative in which the employee exercises the option, and the company gives the employee an amount of cash equal to the difference between the grant price and the exercise price, minus any taxes that are due. Options also can be exercised with cash, although employees must have enough to pay for the shares and taxes (if any), by exchanging existing shares employee own, or by selling just enough of the shares acquired through the options to pay the costs and taxes, then keeping the remaining shares.

In closely held firms, employees usually have to wait until the company is sold or goes public to sell their shares, although some companies have arrangements to purchase the shares themselves or help facilitate buying and selling between employees. When an employee exercises an option, however, this constitutes an investment decision subject to securities laws. Companies rarely have to register the underlying securities, but they must comply with antifraud financial disclosure statements. For this reason, stock options are used most frequently in closely held firms when the intention is to sell or go public.

7.3.3.2 *Nonqualified Options*

Nonqualified stock options are options that do not qualify for any special tax consideration. Anyone, employees or nonemployees, can be given a nonqualified option on any basis the company chooses. When a nonqualified option is exercised, the employee must pay ordinary income tax on the "spread" between the grant and exercise price; the company can deduct that amount.

For example, say that an employee makes $40,000 per year and gets options worth 10% of pay each year, which vest at 20% per year over five years. In year one, the employee then gets the right to buy $4,000 worth of stock at the current market price. Let us assume that is $20 per share, so the employee can buy 200 shares. In five years, the options will be fully vested and can all be exercised at that $20 price. Typically, the plan will have a provision allowing the employee to delay exercise for an additional number of years, usually five more. Say that in year seven, the employee chooses to exercise. The company's stock price is now $32 per share. So $6,400 in stock (200 x $32) can be bought for $4,000. The employee can pay the money up front or, in most companies, have the company arrange a form of cashless exercise in which the employee will, in effect, end up immediately selling the shares and having the exercise price plus ordinary income taxes on the spread taken out, with either the remaining cash or shares given to the employee.

Nonqualified options can be issued at fair market value or a discount, but if they are issued at a discount, they are subject to the deferred compensation tax rules under Section 409A of the Code, meaning that unless recipients choose well in advance when to exercise the award, the award would be subject to heavy current taxation to the company and employee. Discounted options, therefore, are likely to disappear as a plan choice.

7.3.3.3 *Incentive Stock Options*

With an incentive stock option (ISO), a company grants the employee an option to purchase stock at some time in the future at a specified price. With an ISO, there are restrictions on how the option is to be structured and when the option stock can be transferred. The employee does not recognize ordinary income at option grant or exercise (although the spread between the option price and the option stock's fair market value may be taxed under something called the alternative minimum tax, or AMT), and the company cannot deduct the related compensation expense. The employee is taxed only upon the *disposition* of the option stock. The gain is all capital gain for a qualifying disposition. For a disqualifying disposition (i.e., one not meeting the rules specified below for a qualifying disposition), the employee will recognize ordinary income as well as capital gain based on the lower of (1) the difference between the exercise price and grant price at exercise ("the spread") or (2) the difference between the grant price and the sale price. However, the spread is a "preference item" for AMT purposes, meaning people who exercise must add back the spread as a taxable item to calculate their AMT obligation and see whether they must pay this tax. ISOs are not subject to the deferred compensation rules under Section 409A of the Code.

For a stock option to qualify as an ISO and thus receive special tax treatment under Section 421(a) of the Code, it must meet the requirements of Section 422 of the Code when granted and at all times beginning from the grant until its exercise. The requirements include:

- The option may be granted only to an employee (grants to nonemployee directors or independent contractors are not permitted), who must exercise the option while an employee or no later than three months after termination of employment (unless the optionee is disabled, in which case this three-month period is extended to one year).

- The option must be granted under a written plan document specifying the total number of shares that may be issued and the employees who are eligible to receive the options. The plan must be approved by the stockholders within 12 months before or after plan adoption.

- Each option must be granted under an ISO agreement, which must be written and must list the restrictions placed on exercising the ISO. Each option must set forth an offer to sell the stock at the option price and the period of time during which the option will remain open.

- The option must be granted within 10 years of the earlier of adoption or shareholder approval, and the option must be exercisable only within 10 years of grant.

- The option exercise price must equal or exceed the fair market value of the underlying stock at the time of grant.

- The employee must not, at the time of the grant, own stock representing more than 10% of the voting power of all stock outstanding, unless the option exercise price is at least 110% of the fair market value and the option is not exercisable more than five years from the time of the grant.

- The ISO agreement must specifically state that the ISO cannot be transferred by the option holder other than by will or by the laws of descent and that the option cannot be exercised by anyone other than the option holder.

- The aggregate fair market value (determined as of the grant date) of stock bought by exercising ISOs that are exercisable for the first time cannot exceed $100,000 in a calendar year. To the extent it does, Code Section 422(d) provides that such options are treated as nonqualified options.

Closely held companies must have an acceptable way to determine fair market value at grant, such as an appraisal or a formula acceptable to the IRS.

Stock options require a charge to income based on a present value calculation for grants. To calculate this, companies must use a formula such as Black-Scholes or a binomial model. Such formulas factor in stock volatility, dividends, the term of the option, and other factors to determine what an option would be worth if sold before exercise.

7.3.4 Employee Stock Purchase Plans

Finally, millions of employees become owners in their companies through employee stock purchase plans (ESPPs). Many of these plans are organized under Section 423 of the Code and thus are often called "Section 423" plans. Other ESPPs are "nonqualified" plans, meaning they do not have to meet the special rules of Section 423 and do not get any of the special tax treatment. Most of these plans, however, are very similar in structure. In addition to these broad-based stock purchase plans, companies can simply sell stock to selected employees on terms determined by the company.

Because of the need to comply with securities laws, broad-based stock purchase plans are almost exclusively found in public companies or, to a lesser extent, closely held companies planning on an IPO in the next year. The most tax-favored plan is a Section 423 plan. In these plans, companies must allow all employees to participate (except for 5%-or-more shareholders, who must be excluded), but they can exclude those with less than two years' tenure, part-time employees, and highly compensated employees. All employees must have the same rights and privileges under the plan, although companies can allow purchase limits to vary with relative compensation (most do not do this, however). Plans can limit how much employees can buy, and the law limits it to $25,000 per year.

Section 423 plans, like all ESPPs, operate by allowing employees to have deductions taken out of their pay on an after-tax basis. These deductions accumulate over an "offering period." At a specified time or times, employees can choose to use these accumulated deductions to purchase shares or they can get the money back. Plans can offer discounts of up to 15% on the price of the stock. Most plans allow this discount to be taken based on *either* the price at the beginning or end of the offering period (this is called a "look-back" feature). The offering period can last up to five years if the price employees pay for their stock is based on the share price at the end of the period, or 27 months if it can be determined at an earlier point.

Plan design can vary in a number of ways. For instance, a company might allow employees a 15% discount on the price at the end of the offering period but no discount if they buy shares based on the price at the beginning of the period. Some companies offer employees interim opportunities to buy shares during the offering period. Others provide smaller discounts. Offering periods also vary in length. NCEO studies, however, show that the majority of plans have a look-back feature and provide 15% discounts off the share price at the beginning or end of the offering period. Most of the plans have a 6-month or 12-month offering period, with three months the next most common.

In a typical plan, then, an employee might start participating in an ESPP plan when the shares are worth $40. She puts aside $20 per week for 52 pay periods, accumulating $1,040. The offering period ends in the 52nd week, and the employee decides to buy shares. The current price is $45. The employee will obviously choose to buy shares at 15% off the price at the beginning of the offering period, meaning he can purchase shares at $34. For her $34, she gets shares now worth $45. If the share price had dropped to $38 at the end of the offering period, she could buy shares instead at 15% off $38.

The tax treatment of a 423 plan is somewhat similar to that of an incentive stock option. If the employee holds the shares for at least two years after grant and one year after purchase, she pays ordinary income tax on the lesser of (1) the discount as of the time of grant (i.e., the fair market value at the date of grant minus the discount percentage), and (2) the actual gain (the difference between the purchase price and the sale price). She pays capital gains taxes on all additional gain, i.e., the amount of the difference between the purchase price and the sale price that has not been taxed as ordinary income (or, if the sale price is less than the purchase price, there is no ordinary income and she recognizes a capital loss). The company gets no tax deduction, even on the 15% discount.

In our example, suppose that the employee, having bought the shares for $34 (a 15% discount from the $40 value at the date of grant), holds them for at least two years after grant and one year after purchase and sells them for $48 per share. In that case, she will pay ordinary income tax on $6 per share (the lesser of the 15% discount at the date of grant, i.e., $6, and her actual gain of $14). She will pay capital gains tax on the remaining gain, $8 per share ($48 sale price - $34 purchase price - $6 taxed as ordinary income). If the employee does not meet the holding period rules because she sells earlier, then she will pay ordinary income tax on $11 per share, the entire difference between the purchase price

($34) and the market value at purchase ($45). Any increase or decrease in value between the market value at purchase and the sale price is a capital gain or loss. The company gets a tax deduction for the amount recognized as ordinary income ($11 per share in this case).

Nonqualified ESPPs usually work much the same way, but there are no rules for how they must be structured and no special tax benefits; in fact, nonqualified ESPPs that offer discounts are subject to the deferred compensation rules of Code Section 409A, which effectively means the employee would have to choose a payout date in advance or pay steep penalty taxes.

ESPPs are found almost exclusively in public companies because the offering of stock to employees requires compliance with costly and complex securities laws. Closely held companies can, and sometimes do, have these plans, however. Offerings of stock only to employees can qualify for an exemption from securities registration requirements at the federal level, although they will have to comply with antifraud disclosure rules and, possibly, state securities laws as well. If they do offer stock in a stock purchase plan, it is highly advisable they obtain at least an annual appraisal.

As with options, companies must show the cost of an ESPP as a charge to income, based on a present value calculation of the value of the discount plus any look-back feature. Discounts of 5% or less with no look-back feature, however, are not covered by this requirement.

7.4 Making the Choice

Deciding on what kind of equity award plan to have requires careful consideration of several factors, most prominently:

- Is there a substantive reason for not giving out shares to employees, such as a legitimate concern about losing control or a corporate structure that does not provide for shares (such as an LLC or partnership, or the company is an operating unit of a foreign corporation that cannot or does not want to make its share available)?

- Is the company willing to forego the tax benefits of other kinds of ownership plans in return for the greater flexibility of a phantom stock, restricted stock, or SAR plan?

- Does the owner of a closely held company either not want to sell or not need or care about the tax benefits offered by an ESOP?

- Is there a strong philosophical commitment to employees actually buying shares, but qualified plan approaches to this look too cumbersome or restricted?

- Is the company too small to make the legal costs of a more formal plan practical?

- Is the employer-employee relationship strong enough so that employees will believe that stock appreciation rights or phantom shares are "real?"

- Does the employer have other plans already in place (such as a 100% ESOP or an S corporation with close to 100 shareholders) that may preclude providing options or other share plans to a selected group of employees it wants to reward?

If the company does not fall into one of these categories, then the four plans described in this section (ESOPs, stock options, 401(k) plans, and ESPPs) at least deserve a careful look.

CHAPTER EIGHT

A Tiered Approach to Equity Design with Multiple Equity Compensation Vehicles

Martin Staubus
Blair Jones
Daniel Janich
Scott Rodrick

Contents

There was a time, not so very long ago, when equity compensation was simple. With technology companies leading the way, employers who wanted to give their people a stake in the growth of the company turned to a single, "no-brainer" solution: stock options. And who could argue with that strategy? After all, stock options are unrivalled in the linkage they create between employee compensation and growth in a company's stock price. Even better for the employers of that era, those options were free—free in terms of cash costs, free in terms of financial reporting, and free of taxation to the employees (at least until exercise).

My, how things have changed. In the years since the technology-led "bubble economy" burst, changing economic conditions have brought the limitations of stock options sharply into focus. Companies have learned that while stock options perform admirably when equity prices are rising, they lose their luster when growth slows, and blow up in your face when stock prices fall. And options are no longer free. Today's accounting standards now require that stock options be expensed on corporate financial statements, thereby taking an uncomfortable bite out of the reported bottom line.

As the significant limitations of stock options have become apparent, many companies have turned to other equity compensation vehicles, with restricted stock having received the most acclaim as the "true successor" to stock options for twenty-first century equity compensation design. While that vehicle—and variations on the theme such as restricted stock units—has been implemented by a good number of companies, there is a notable absence of consensus that it is indeed the "chosen one," the worthy successor to stock options as "the" answer to every company's equity compensation needs.

Indeed, an undeniable truth is that there simply is no "true successor" to stock options in equity compensation—no single, universally embraced approach of the "one size fits all" variety. Instead, the picture that is emerging as the business cycle moves through a new round of growth has two notable features. First, companies are no longer acting in lockstep, all using essentially the same approach, as they did during the dot-com era. Instead, companies have come to recognize that each must evaluate for itself its own unique needs and circumstances to fashion an equity program that works well for it, and that the program that is right for one company may be quite different from the one being implemented by competitors down the street. Second, few companies are finding the perfect and complete answer in a single equity compensation vehicle. As outlined in table 8-1, there is a range of vehicles that companies can draw on in fashioning their equity plans that extends well beyond options and restricted stock. Instead of relying upon just one equity compensation vehicle, effective equity compensation programs are increasingly composed of a combination of vehicles, uniquely blended at each company to achieve a range of business objectives, and with each element offsetting the potential vulnerabilities of the others.

There is nothing new per se in having multiple equity compensation plans. Public companies especially have frequently employed a mix of equity vehicles, typically including stock options, ESPPs, 401(k) matches, and more. However, companies both public and private often lack a well-developed strategy for coordinating their multiple equity plans and integrating those diverse vehicles into a comprehensive employee ownership program.

We present here just such a strategy, which we call a "tiered" approach to equity program design. This approach can help a company harness the advantages of multiple equity vehicles with an eye toward the big picture to achieve coordinated, comprehensive results. For companies that have only a single equity plan, this chapter will show the benefit of using multiple equity plans. For companies that already have multiple equity plans, this chapter will discuss how they may be organized to work more effectively together. Also included are examples of how individual companies are applying the tiered approach to equity compensation design. Finally, we illustrate how a private company can use an ESOP to make a market for shares that employees acquire through the other equity vehicles in the company's tiered program—an important consideration where there is no existing market for the shares.

8.1 Preliminary Considerations

When companies restructure their equity compensation programs, whether to attract and retain talent, motivate individuals to achieve key goals, build a team-oriented culture, or achieve something else, they will be required to address a host of critical issues that relate to the continuing appropriateness of their equity compensation designs. The following four considerations will serve as guideposts when going through this process.

Table 8-1. Tax and Accounting Impacts of Different Equity Vehicles

Vehicle	Tax		Accounting
	Company[a]	Employee	
Stock options	Spread deductible at exercise	Spread taxable at exercise	Fair value of options expensed
Performance-based stock options/shares	Spread deductible at exercise/full value deductible when earned	Spread deductible at exercise/full value deductible when earned	Full value of option shares earned expensed over performance period
Cash-settled SARs	Spread deductible at exercise	Spread taxable at exercise	Treated as a liability
Stock-settled SARs	Spread deductible at exercise	Spread taxable at exercise	Treated like a stock option
Stock grants	Full value deductible at grant	Full value taxed at grant	Full value expensed
Restricted stock/ restricted stock units	Full value deductible at vesting/issuance	Full shares taxable at vesting/issuance	Full value expensed over vesting period
ESOPs	Contributions and dividends deductible when made	Taxed when benefits are received	Interest and cost of allocated shares expensed
Qualified (423) stock purchase plans	No deduction	Taxed at sale (ordinary income/ capital gain)	Fair value expensed if discount is greater than 5%
Nonqualified stock purchase plans	Spread and discount deductible at exercise	Spread and discount taxable at exercise	Fair value is expensed
401(k)	Pretax contributions deductible when made	Taxed when benefits are received	Contributions expensed
Qualified and nonqualified deferred compensation	Deductible when benefits paid	Taxed when benefits are received	Expensed and carried as a liability

[a] Subject to Section 162(m) or applicable tax qualification rules, as the case may be.

8.1.1 Think Deeply About Why You Want to Share Company Equity and How It Will Lead to Improved Business Performance

As wise heads have long pointed out, "If you don't know where you're going, any road will get you there." And indeed, in their rush to "benchmark" and keep up with what everyone else was doing, many companies in the past plunged into equity compensation without a carefully developed idea of how (i.e., by what mechanisms) such a program would improve the performance of the company. During the technology boom, many companies certainly didn't need a profound analysis. The reality they encountered, very simply, was that they couldn't hire the people they needed unless they offered stock options. Understandably, that was all the reason they needed to implement an equity plan.

With labor markets less overheated today, there is room for deeper reflection on the question of whether and how a company might improve corporate results by giving employees an equity stake in the business. In general, approaches to employee stock ownership tend to fall into two camps:

- The "compensation" camp cleaves to a traditional model of the business organization, seeing employees as people who are hired to work in an enterprise that is ultimately operated for the benefit of others (outside shareholders). With little inherent interest in their employer's success, these individuals need incentives—incentives to come to work for the employer and, once there, incentives to perform diligently. For adherents to the compensation camp, equity serves as a useful addition to the array of incentives that are available to organizations to foster effective performance by employees.

- The "ownership" camp seeks to redefine traditional employee roles and relationships, using shared equity as the foundation for a new approach in which the people at all levels of the organization see themselves as partners in a team united by, and focused on, a common financial stake in the success of the business. While traditional companies typically feature an "us" and "them" culture that divides management from the rest, companies in the ownership camp seek to create an organization in which there is only "us"—co-owners with a shared commitment to company success.

Fundamental to a company's reexamination of equity compensation strategies and programs, then, is an assessment of where it wants to be along the spectrum of organizational models—whether it wants to "incent" employees who are otherwise seen as lacking an intrinsic reason to perform, to build an organizational culture in which employees are "co-owners" and central stakeholders in their own right, or whether it wants to design equity programs to achieve both of these goals.

8.1.2 Look More Broadly Than Stock Options

There is a diverse range of equity compensation vehicles from which companies can choose in fashioning programs to share ownership and create long-term incentives. These include grants of stock (usually "restricted" by a vesting requirement), stock purchase programs, qualified retirement programs such as 401(k) plans and ESOPs, deferred compensation, synthetic equity (SARs and phantom stock) and a host of variations on these basic themes.

Determining which of these many choices may be right for a given company will involve an assessment of that company's business situation. Selecting the right equity vehicle(s) for a given company will be influenced by:

- The current growth stage of the business (i.e., startup, growth, or maturing).

- The long-term strategic goals (i.e., is the goal to push for maximum short-term growth and then sell the company, or is the goal to create a company that is "built to last"?).

- The specific purposes that the plan is intended to achieve (e.g., attraction and retention of good employees, motivating employees to improve performance, building a nest egg for retirement, or repositioning employees as central stakeholders).

- The accounting impact (see table 8-1) and economic impact—i.e., what is affordable for the company in terms of impact on cash flow, dilution, and unwanted turnover.

8.1.3 Do Not Assume a Single Vehicle Will Emerge as the Clear Choice for Every Company

It was, and remains, too much to expect any single equity vehicle to be "all things to all companies." Bottom line, the vehicles that work for one company may not be appropriate for another company or even for the same company at a later stage in its development. For example, many commentators have suggested that Microsoft chose to move from stock options to restricted stock units in recognition of its transition from a company experiencing rapid growth to one that is more mature and focused upon longer-range goals. The creation of an effective equity compensation program, therefore, requires that it be designed to fit the company's present situation with an understanding that its elements will likely change with the company's circumstances.

8.1.4 Employ a Combination of Vehicles for Maximum Impact

Each equity vehicle has both strong points and weak points. When a company attempts to rely on just one vehicle, the danger is that the weaknesses inherent in that particular vehicle may cripple the program and result in its falling short of ideal effectiveness. As an alternative, companies may find that if they assemble an equity-sharing program that employs more than one equity vehicle, the weaknesses inherent in any one vehicle may be offset to some degree by strengths in one or more other vehicles. Like investors who diversify their investments among several different stocks so that weak performance by one can be offset by strengths in others, companies are likely to find that they will create the most effective equity compensation program by combining several equity compensation vehicles into a multi-tiered program.

8.2 Building Effective Equity Programs by Combining Vehicles: A Tiered Approach to Equity Design

As discussed above, the choices on the equity compensation menu are many: stock options, restricted stock, ESPPs, ESOPs, 401(k) plans, synthetic equity, stock-settled SARs and more. How does one go about selecting from these diverse choices to produce an effective employee ownership program? Do you just throw them at the wall to see what sticks? Or can there be a method to this madness?

To get a handle on the effective design of equity programs, it may be effective to think about a company's program as having three tiers, as illustrated in table 8-2.

Table 8-2. A Tiered Approach to Multiple Equity Vehicle Programs

Tier	Purpose	Example equity vehicles
Investment tier	• Encourages employees who are committed to the company to invest their own money in the business • At a private company especially, this can be a special privilege that outsiders do not have	• ESPP • Nonqualified compensation deferral • 401(k) employee investment
Performance tier	• Awards more ownership to individuals who contribute more to the growth of the company	• Stock options • Restricted stock
Base tier	• Assures that every employee will have at least a basic financial stake in the future success of the company	• ESOP • 401(k) employer match

Each tier is focused on achieving different objectives for the business:

- A *base tier* is used to create broadly shared, long-term employee ownership, ensuring that every employee has a stake in the company's success. It sends the message that "we're all in this together, we all have a stake in the fortunes of this company." In most large organizations, this would likely be in the form of a highly tax-efficient vehicle such as an employee stock ownership plan (ESOP) or 401(k) employer-matching contributions.

- The *performance tier* is designed to offer additional ownership to incent and reward those employees who make special contributions to the growth of the company. This will typically be done through such vehicles as stock options or restricted stock awards. In this tier, awards are tied to individual performance, and payouts should be clearly linked to the creation of shareholder value.

- The *investment tier* allows employees who are committed to the company to invest their own money in the business. Public companies can take advantage of the ESPP vehicle for this purpose, while private companies can offer direct share purchase opportunities.

This tiered approach to equity compensation design allows a company to use equity in various ways to motivate and reward behaviors of different groups of employees that are required to drive the company's success. While most companies will have elements relevant to each tier, different emphasis may be placed on different tiers, and different designs may be used to accomplish objectives in the three tiers. These differences might depend upon whether the company is public or private.

8.3 Six Benefits of Using Multiple Equity Vehicles in a Tiered Approach

Companies may find a number of appealing advantages to using multiple equity vehicles in a tiered approach to equity design, including:

1. *Achieves multiple objectives:* Using more than one equity vehicle can allow a company to achieve multiple objectives. For example, a company may wish to build an organizational culture that focuses company-wide attention on business performance and encourages conscientious job performance through a base tier that is built on a longer-term focused vehicle (such as an ESOP or equity grants at hire). At the same time, the company may want to focus top management and other key contributors on building intermediate and longer-term shareholder wealth through a tier of performance-based restricted stock, stock options, or annual incentives that pay out in stock or restricted stock. Selected individuals could also have the opportunity to invest further in the company through a nonqualified deferred compensation plan with company stock as an investment alternative. In this way, the company uses multiple equity vehicles to achieve multiple objectives, where one vehicle standing alone may end up "just missing" on all objectives.

2. *Maximizes tax efficiency while retaining flexibility:* While ESOPs and 401(k) plans offer tremendous tax benefits—giving the company a

deduction for the full value of any equity contributed to the plan while imposing no current tax liability on the employees who receive that equity—these tax-qualified vehicles come with rules that significantly limit the company's ability to determine which employees will get how much of the total equity pie. By using a tax-qualified plan as the base tier while "topping off" as needed with a second vehicle that is not restricted by federal income tax nondiscrimination rules (but at the cost of the favorable tax treatment), a company can capture most of the tax benefits that could be obtained by relying exclusively on a qualified plan while gaining the flexibility to create incentives and rewards for those who earn them.

3. *Protects against unintended consequences within a tier:* Multiple equity vehicles within a tier can be structured to complement each other to achieve the right objectives in the right way. For example, stock options alone allow holders to realize gains based on absolute stock price appreciation. However, complementing stock options with restricted stock that vests based on relative total shareholder return can create a powerful combination that sends the message that the real focus is sustained above-average wealth creation for shareholders.

4. *Provides a balance between long-term and short-term equity interests:* Another advantage of combining vehicles is that it enables a company to provide part of its equity awards in a form that gives the employee-shareholder the freedom to control when he or she will liquidate the equity while providing other equity that must be held for the long term. If employees cannot cash in their equity except at retirement, many will see a very limited value in that equity. At the same time, if employees can, and do, sell off their equity within a short time after receiving it, the linkage between company performance and the employee's financial well-being will come to an end. ESOPs and 401(k) plans, for example, are retirement programs that pay out only after the employee leaves the company (except for certain exceptions such as dividends on ESOP-held stock paid directly to employees), while gains on vested stock options and the value of restricted stock (once vested) may be realized whenever the employee chooses. Providing a balance of long-term and short-term equity interests will likely produce the optimal outcome.

5. *Manages dilution:* Companies also need to be cognizant of the fact that different vehicles tend to lead to different levels of dilution. By using vehicles with different dilutive impacts, companies can manage dilution. For example, a company that has in the past relied solely on stock options (a highly dilutive vehicle) could reduce dilution by substituting another, less dilutive, vehicle (such as performance-restricted stock) in place of at least some of the erstwhile option awards.

6. *Manages predictability of payout:* Different equity vehicles also provide distinct future gain opportunities. While future stock option gains may be difficult to predict, restricted stock values operate within a more certain range. Therefore, companies can gauge the level of predictability required for their equity compensation program by adjusting grant patterns of different vehicles to balance near-term pay delivery needs with longer-term opportunities.

8.4 ESPPs After the Accounting Changes

Statement of Financial Accounting Standards No. 123 (revised 2004), Share-Based Payment ("FAS 123R"), became effective for reporting periods beginning after June 15, 2005, for large public companies and December 15, 2005, for small public companies and private companies. As of September 2009, FAS 123(R) has now been codified as ASC Topic 718 for grants to employees and ASC Subtopic 505-50 for grants to nonemployees. The rules themselves, however (referred to below simply as the "accounting rules"), remain the same.[1]

The accounting rules require companies to recognize the fair value of stock options as an expense on their financial statements. The accounting rules also affect the recognition of expense relating to ESPP awards by requiring such awards to be treated for accounting purposes as the grant of a stock option when the offering period commences,

---

1. The Financial Accounting Standards Board (FASB) reclassified FAS 123(R) as Accounting Standards Codification (ASC) Topic 718, "Stock Compensation" (for grants to employees) and ASC Subtopic 505-50, "Equity-Based Payments to Non-Employees" (for grants to nonemployees) as part of the codification of all generally accepted accounting principles (GAAP), effective for reporting periods ending after September 15, 2009.

unless three conditions are satisfied that would allow such awards to receive "noncompensatory" treatment. These three conditions require the plan to (1) offer a discount that does not exceed the cost of offering shares through an underwriter; (2) be broad-based; and (3) have no option-like features such as look-backs, which allow the purchase price to be set using the lower of the stock price on the first or last day of the offering period.

Although the accounting rules allow companies to assume that their underwriting costs are at least 5%, thus allowing for a 5% discount without triggering compensatory accounting treatment, the failure of the conditions for "noncompensatory" treatment to allow either a look-back period or a greater discount akin to the 15% discount allowed for a tax-qualified Section 423 ESPP initially caused some companies to conclude that perhaps the days of ESPPs were over. Early survey data, however, showed that although some companies eliminated their plans, on the whole ESPPs were here to stay as companies recognized that ESPPs promote an ownership culture and that the accounting expense is manageable.[2] Subsequent surveys have confirmed that ESPPs remain a viable option for companies, although accounting rules have influenced plan design.[3]

The earnings charge—and thus the "on-the-books-cost" of maintaining an ESPP—that the accounting rules require to be recognized may be reduced in one or more of the following ways: by reducing the maximum amount employees can invest; by reducing the employee purchase discount; by shortening the offering period; or by eliminating or reducing the look-back. Many companies responded to FAS 123(R) by eliminating the look-back feature, and as of 2009, one survey found that most respondents did not have one.[4] Likewise, some companies

2. See, e.g., Pam Chernoff, "NCEO Survey Shows Most Companies Keeping Their ESPPs, with Few Changes," *Journal of Employee Ownership Law and Finance* 18, no. 3 (summer 2006): 41–47.

3. See, e.g., National Center for Employee Ownership, "2009 ESPP Survey: Comprehensive Report of Survey Results" (Oakland, CA: NCEO, 2009); PriceWaterhouseCoopers, "Trends in the International ESPP Landscape," presentation made at the New York/New Jersey NASPP chapter meeting, July 24, 2009.

4. Chernoff, "NCEO Survey Shows Most Companies Keeping Their ESPPs," 44 (in 2005 and 2006, many companies were eliminating the look-back or planned

have shortened the offering period or currently plan to do so. However, most companies still offer a full 15% discount or something close to it.[5] More and more companies are modifying their plans to qualify for "noncompensatory" treatment (and thus no accounting expense), with features such as no look-back and a discount of 5% or less, but these plans are still in the minority.[6] The most effective plan design changes attempt to balance their affect on the earnings charge against any adverse impact the changes will have upon the plan's continuing employee participation levels.

Although the accounting rules have caused companies to reexamine the role of ESPPs in overall equity compensation strategy, newer ESPP plan designs that effectively control the accounting expense have a secure place in the mix of equity compensation programs from which employers may choose in designing their multi-tiered programs.

8.5 Risks to Be Managed When Combining Multiple Vehicles

Despite the advantages that companies might realize by combining equity vehicles, a number of risks exist that also need to be managed when designing a multi-vehicle equity compensation program. These risks include:

1. *Too many vehicles can become too complex:* From a practical design perspective, the idea is not to use multiple vehicles for multiple vehicles' sake but to use multiple vehicles in pursuit of a stronger program than would exist using one vehicle. This means every vehicle needs to have a specific role to play, and to the extent the

---

to do so). For 2009 data, contrast National Center for Employee Ownership, "2009 ESPP Survey," 2 (38% of respondents had no look-back) with Price-WaterhouseCoopers, "Trends in the International ESPP Landscape," 5 (56% of respondents had no look-back).

5. PriceWaterhouseCoopers, "Trends in the International ESPP Landscape," 5; National Center for Employee Ownership, "2009 ESPP Survey," 2, 23; Chernoff, "NCEO Survey Shows Most Companies Keeping Their ESPPs," 44–45.

6. PriceWaterhouseCoopers, "Trends in the International ESPP Landscape," 12 (14% in 2006, 22% in 2007, and 27% in 2009).

design of the vehicle can make its purpose transparent, all the better. Well-designed communications can also ease concerns about complexity and greatly enhance the effectiveness of a given design.

2. *The performance tier may have inadequate leverage:* Many companies have responded to the reduced appeal of stock options by replacing some, or all, of their performance tier stock option opportunity with another equity vehicle. These companies must be mindful that replacing stock options with a vehicle that has less potential upside for employees could dampen the entrepreneurial drive that this tier of the equity program is intended to foster.

3. *The equity design may become all about pay delivery:* A multi-tiered design would be misused if it were seen solely as a way of delivering immediate pay to employees. Companies must make sure that the overarching focus of its equity program is not so much on what the equity is worth at grant but on what the employees, through their performance, can make it worth in the future. If a grant of $10,000 of equity is seen simply as $10,000 of pay, it loses its power to incent employees to build shareholder value or to promote a culture in which employees are seen, and behave, as owners themselves.

8.6 Public Companies: Emerging Practices

Most activity among public companies appears to be in the performance tier, where companies are diversifying the vehicles they are using to address the current environment and stock options' shortfalls. A few companies are sticking steadfastly with stock options as their vehicle of choice in the performance tier, they are likely to be in the minority. These tend to be companies that have historically exceeded peer group performance levels and have strong communication to help employees understand how their jobs impact stock price performance.

Initially, diversification focused primarily on the replacement of options with service-vested restricted stock. To drive greater performance in the performance tier, this trend has evolved to include a high prevalence of performance restrictions, which ultimately might prove to be a powerful adjunct to stock options, linking vesting to achievement of strategic business results. Another interesting variation in the restricted stock arena is to allow executives to voluntarily defer bonus payments to buy discounted restricted stock, typically with cliff vesting provisions (e.g., at HCA).

Common to all of these practices, the desire on the part of investors that senior executives in particular have some "skin in the game" is as strong as ever, given the continuing corporate scandals that have fueled regulatory and legislative changes. This has raised interest at some companies in new investment tier alternatives. In many cases, the vehicles now fulfilling the objectives of the investment tier are simpler than their earlier counterparts but no less powerful in the messages that they send. One of the more popular methods currently in practice is to mandate executives to defer a portion of their bonuses into company stock, often with ownership requirements attached. First coming to prominence in the early 1990s, ownership guidelines, which require executives to hold a certain level of stock (often expressed as multiples of salary) are making a return in aligning executive and shareholder interests.

Tables 8-3 and 8-4 (see next page) illustrate what two public companies are doing at this time with multi-tier equity programs.

8.7 Private Companies: Emerging Practices

Private companies may have more latitude, especially in the investment tier, because their stock will generally be unavailable for purchase unless specially offered by the company. Our first example is one of the growing legends in the world of employee stock ownership, Springfield ReManufacturing Corporation (SRC) and its remarkable CEO, Jack Stack (author of "The Great Game of Business" and "A Stake in the Outcome"). From its beginnings in the mid-1980s as a management buyout of a grimy little diesel engine rebuilding plant from an old and dying International Harvester, SRC has used its employee stock ownership programs as the foundation for an operation philosophy that has seen its stock price climb from $1 a share at the time of the buyout to more than $390 a share currently.

SRC's employee stock ownership system consists of three tiers. At its base is an ESOP, which assures a solid, long-term ownership stake for all employees on highly tax-advantaged terms (for both the company and the employees). The ESOP holds about one-third of the equity in the

Table 8-3. Public Company Example A:
Multi-Billion Dollar Pharmaceutical Company

Investment tier	A nonqualified bonus deferral program allows a select group of senior management to defer portions of their salaries and bonuses, with company stock as one investment option.
Performance tier	Stock options combined with performance shares earned based on financial performance focus executives on intermediate drivers of business value in addition to longer-term stock price appreciation.
Base tier	Company-wide stock option grants every two years provide lots of opportunity for all employees to build ownership in their company and a 401(k) investment option in company stock.

Table 8-4. Public Company Example B:
Multi-Billion Dollar Hospital Management Company

Investment tier	A nonqualified stock purchase plan allows members of the executive team to defer their bonuses to purchase restricted stock at a 25% discount to fair market value. The restricted stock cliff-vests after three years and is coupled with stringent ownership expectations to ensure significant long-term ownership levels.
Performance tier	Stock options, combined with earned annual equity, reinforce short- and longer-term performance achievement. Earned annual equity is restricted stock that is earned based on achievement of annual performance objectives within individuals' control. Once earned, the restricted stock vests over two years. This approach reinforces employee ownership and complements stock options by providing a vehicle with higher "line-of-sight" because the basis for earning awards is within employees' control.
Base tier	An ESOP ensures all employees have some stake in the company.

SRC employee stock ownership system. To combat any tendency toward complacency, the company also issues stock options to anyone in the organization who is in a position to be a key driver of growth for the organization. The outstanding stock options represent another one-third of the equity in the program. The final third of the employee-owned stock is represented by shares of stock that employees have purchased for their own investment.

Tables 8-5 and 8-6 illustrate how two other private firms—an engineering firm and a management consulting firm respectively—have structured their multi-tier equity programs.

Table 8-5. Private Company Example B:
150-Employee Engineering Firm

Investment tier	Annual cash profit-sharing bonuses may be invested in company stock, with employee-investors receiving a "free" stock option for every two shares purchased.
Performance tier	Stock options granted to reward actions that are anticipated to produce revenue in the future. Restricted stock granted to reward current revenue production.
Base tier	Employee stock ownership plan (ESOP) that purchases shares from founding shareholders to hold for all permanent, full-time employees.

Table 8-6. Private Company Example C:
100-Employee Management Consulting Firm

Investment tier	Purchase opportunities granted to newly hired consultants to give them the ability to increase their ownership stake early on.
Performance tier	Restricted stock granted to reward current revenue production.
Base tier	Employee stock ownership plan (ESOP) that purchases shares from founding partners and from employees who want to sell shares they acquired through the other tiers of the equity program.

8.7.1 The ESOP as a Market for Shares Owned by Employees in Private Companies

Note that in example C (table 8-6), the company is using the ESOP not only as the base tier of its equity ownership program *but also as a market for stock that employees acquire through the other tiers.* This creative method of gaining multiple benefits from diverse equity vehicles offers tremendous power to private companies, who otherwise inevitably struggle with the difficulty of providing liquidity to shareholders, including employees who acquire company equity.

Generally, money that a company spends on redeeming stock from a shareholder is not deductible; it is an after-tax expenditure. A company with an ESOP, however, can channel the money that it has earmarked for stock redemptions through the ESOP, making every penny of that money deductible for corporate income tax purposes. With companies in most states paying a combined federal and state tax bill in excess of 40%, a company that provides liquidity to employee-shareholders via its ESOP is in effect getting the IRS and the state to provide 40% of the funding for such redemptions. These redemptions by the ESOP in turn provide a continuing source of shares to feed into the "base tier" so that new employees can participate and all employees can build their equity interests over time as they remain with the company. The result is a dynamic system of employee stock ownership in which equity can be acquired by employees through multiple, flexible vehicles while providing a financially efficient mechanism for shareholder liquidity and a continuous renewal of the program.

8.8 Conclusion

Many companies are reconsidering their use of stock options. That does not mean that they will abandon employee stock ownership. A truly effective equity plan starts with a soul-searching evaluation of what the company wants to get out of it. By fashioning a set of complementary equity vehicles into a multi-tiered program, a company can tailor its equity program to fit its individual needs. Don't be disheartened by the end of the glory days for stock options. There are plenty of other equity vehicles out there, and more than one is likely to be suitable as an adjunct to, or substitute for, stock options.

Using the Model Plan Documents

The CD attached to the inside back cover of this book provides model plan documents for most of the various forms of individual equity compensation plans discussed in this book: phantom stock, SARs, restricted stock and units, and performance units. At various points in these documents, optional provisions and comments to the book's readers have been inserted in square brackets. In some documents, footnotes comment on various provisions.

Please note that these model documents contain common features found in these types of plans but are drafted to provide general terms only. The terms of any actual plan, however, should be tailored to the needs and situation of a particular company. For example, state securities laws vary and may affect the drafting of a plan.[1]

The model plans and agreements have been prepared for use by stock corporations. For information on using equivalent plans in a limited liability company (LLC), see the NCEO's book *Equity Compensation for Limited Liability Companies*.

Although the authors have attempted to identify certain legal or accounting issues relating to common provisions in these types of plans, by publishing these documents, neither the NCEO nor the authors and their firms shall be deemed to be providing legal advice. Before using any of the model documents, a company must consult with its own legal and accounting advisors.

---

1. See Joseph Phelps, "State Securities Law Considerations for Equity Compensation Plans," chapter 3 in *Selected Issues in Equity Compensation*, 15th ed. (Oakland, CA: NCEO, 2019).

The Omnibus Incentive Plan

All of the model plan documents here (the phantom stock award, restricted stock award, etc.) are organized under the omnibus incentive plan provided in the folder *Omnibus 1*, pursuant to which the company may grant several types of incentive awards. The omnibus approach (i.e., adopting an overall incentive plan under which various types of awards can be granted) is very common.

Hard-Copy and Electronic Versions of Awards

For each award under the omnibus plan (in folders *Omnibus 2* through *Omnibus 7*), there is a version providing for hard-copy administration and an alternative version providing for electronic administration. The electronic versions include the word "electronic" in their filenames for ease of reference.

Annotations in Footnotes

As you read through the plan documents, you will see that many of them include annotations in footnotes. Needless to say, if you prepare such a document for your own use, you will need to strip out these annotations as you customize it.

Document Format

Each document on the CD is provided in Microsoft Word format (not the current .docx format but rather the older .doc format that is universally recognized not only by Word but also by a variety of other programs).

Contents of the CD

The table on the next page displays the folder and file structure of the CD.

Contents of the CD Included with This Book		
Folder name	**Description**	**Filenames in that folder**
Omnibus 1	Omnibus incentive plan	Omnibus incentive plan.doc
Omnibus 2	Phantom stock grant	Phantom stock grant.doc
		Phantom stock grant (electronic).doc
Omnibus 3	Cash-settled SAR award	SAR award, cash-settled.doc
		SAR award, cash-settled (electronic). doc
Omnibus 4	Stock-settled SAR award	SAR award, stock-settled.doc
		SAR award, stock-settled (electronic). doc
Omnibus 5	Restricted stock award	Restricted stock award.doc
		Restricted stock award (electronic). doc
Omnibus 6	Restricted stock unit award	RSU award.doc
		RSU award (electronic).doc
Omnibus 7	Performance unit award	Performance unit award.doc
		Performance unit award (electronic). doc

Index

About the Authors

Joseph S. Adams is a partner in the Chicago office of the law firm Winston & Strawn LLP, where he advises companies, service providers, and individuals regarding executive compensation and employee benefits programs. His areas of expertise include the design, drafting, and ongoing operation of 401(k) and profit sharing plans, ESOPs, cash balance, and other defined benefit pension plans; complying with ERISA requirements and resolving Department of Labor and IRS audits as well as complex participant claims for benefits; drafting incentive compensation arrangements such as bonus plans, "omnibus" long-term incentive plans, stock option and stock appreciation rights agreements, restricted stock and restricted stock unit agreements, and other phantom and actual equity arrangements; designing nonqualified retirement plans and ensuring compliance with the Section 409A deferred compensation rules; representing employers, executives, and compensation committees regarding employment agreements and separation agreements; advising on the impact of mergers, acquisitions, divestitures, and spinoffs on employee benefit plans, executive compensation arrangements, and individual executive employment agreements; and analyzing the need for executive compensation programs and employee benefit plans to comply with SEC requirements, IRS rules, corporate governance standards such as Sarbanes-Oxley and Dodd-Frank, and stock exchange requirements. Joe received his BA in economics, with honors, from the University of Chicago, and he received his JD, cum laude, from Cornell Law School, where he served as an editor for the Cornell Law Review. He has written for many publications and has received several honors and awards.

Barbara Baksa is the executive director of the National Association of Stock Plan Professionals (NASPP). She is a frequent speaker on equity compensation-related topics and has spoken at NCEO, NASPP, and other industry events. In addition to her speaking engagements, she has authored several white papers and contributed chapters to four books on stock compensation and is the author of the book *Accounting for Equity Compensation*, also published by the NCEO. Barbara also serves as the editor of the *NASPP Advisor* and co-editor of the *Corporate Executive*. She is a Certified Equity Professional (CEP) and serves on the Certified Equity Professional Institute's advisory board.

Daniel Coleman is a partner with Aon Equity Services in Chicago, were he serves as the Midwest and Canadian market leader for the firm's equity-based compensation valuation practice. Dan has more than 20 years of experience in plan design, valuation, tax, financial accounting, and disclosure issues related to all types of executive and broad-based compensation programs for public and privately held companies. Dan specializes in the valuation of employee options and performance shares under ASC 718 using Black-Scholes, lattice-based models, and Monte Carlo simulations; valuation of contingent consideration, common and preferred stock, debt, stock warrants, and derivatives embedded in convertible debt and convertible preferred stock; and tax and financial accounting issues related to equity-based compensation. He is a certified public accountant (CPA) and a certified equity professional (CEP). Dan graduated from the University of Pennsylvania's Wharton School of Finance, where he obtained a Bachelor of Science degree in Economics.

Daniel N. Janich is the resident partner in the Chicago office of the law firm Holifield Janich Rachal Ferrera, PLLC. He has extensive experience counseling businesses and executives on all aspects of their employee benefits and executive compensation plans and arrangements, including the tax, securities, corporate, and ERISA law issues. He also litigates employee benefits and executive compensation claims in state and federal court. Mr. Janich is a fellow of the American College of Employee Benefits Counsel, and has served as senior editor of the legal treatise *Employee Benefits Law*. Mr. Janich has served previously as a board member of the National Center for Employee Ownership, and as chair of the Employee Benefits Committee of the Chicago Bar Association. He is a frequent speaker and author of publications in the field. Mr. Janich has a BA degree cum laude in history from Marian University, Indianapolis; a JD degree from the John Marshall Law School, Chicago; and an LLM degree in taxation from DePaul University, Chicago.

Blair Jones is a managing director at Semler Brossy Consulting Group, a compensation consulting firm. She has been an executive compensation consultant since 1991 and has worked extensively across industries, including healthcare, automotive, retail, professional services, heavy equipment manufacturing, and consumer products. She has particularly deep expertise working with companies in transition. Blair started her consulting career at Bain & Company, and before joining Semler Brossy, she was the practice leader in Leadership Performance and Rewards at Sibson Consulting.

Scott Rodrick is the director of publishing and information technology at the National Center for Employee Ownership (NCEO). He designed and created the NCEO's present line of publications and is the author or coauthor of several books himself, including the best-selling *An Introduction to ESOPs* (18th ed. 2018). Since 1994, he has been involved with the NCEO's presence on the Internet. He is an attorney and served at the U.S. Department of Labor as an attorney-advisor before coming to the NCEO.

Corey Rosen is the cofounder and former executive director of the NCEO. He is the coauthor, along with John Case and Martin Staubus, of *Equity: Why Employee Ownership Is Good for Business* (Harvard Business School Press, 2005). Over the years, he has written, edited, or contributed to dozens of books, articles, and research papers on employee ownership. He is generally regarded as the leading expert on employee ownership in the world. Rosen received his PhD in political science from Cornell University in 1973, after which he taught politics at Ripon College in Wisconsin before being named an American Political Science Association Congressional Fellow in 1975. In 1981, he formed the NCEO. He stepped down as the NCEO's executive director in April 2011 and now serves as its senior staff member.

Martin Staubus is the executive director of the Beyster Institute at the Rady School of Management, University of California, San Diego, where he teaches in the MBA program and consults to a wide range of companies. He has more than 25 years of experience in employee ownership, human resources, law, and organizational development.

Trained as an attorney, Mr. Staubus has served as a practicing lawyer, a consultant, and a corporate vice president of human resources. His career includes service as a policy analyst for Labor Secretary Robert Reich, legal advisor to the California State Labor Relations Board, and deputy director of the ESOP Association. He is a past member of the NCEO's board of directors. Martin holds a BA in economics from the University of California, Berkeley; an MBA in organizational development from George Washington University, Washington D.C.; and a law degree from Golden Gate University, San Francisco.

Robin L. Struve is a partner at Latham & Watkins LLP. She advises U.S. and multinational companies regarding the application of U.S. tax, ERISA, securities, and other laws to employee benefit plans and executive compensation matters. A substantial portion of Ms. Struve's practice includes the structuring, drafting, amendment, termination, and legal compliance of benefit plans, with a focus on nonqualified deferred compensation plans, equity-based compensation plans (including plans for non-corporate entities such as LLCs and partnerships), and bonus plans for both public and private companies. Ms. Struve holds a JD from Harvard University and a BA from the University of Colorado, with distinction. She is the author of several articles on ESOPs as well as a frequent speaker on a variety of executive compensation and employee benefit plan topics.

Dan Walter, CECP, CEP, became a managing consultant at FutureSense, a holistic human capital consulting firm, in 2018. He has worked in the field of compensation since 1994. Dan was previously the founder and CEO of Performensation. His expertise includes equity compensation, performance-based pay, executive compensation, and talent management issues. Dan is an industry thought leader for all forms of equity, including stock options, restricted shares and units, stock purchase plans, and performance-based programs. In addition to his focus on plan design, he has been the architect of software solutions and administrative and technological best practices used by many companies. Dan has coauthored several books on compensation and is a popular blogger on the topic. He is also a popular speaker and does dozens of presentations every year.

About the NCEO

The National Center for Employee Ownership (NCEO) is widely considered to be the leading authority in employee ownership in the U.S. and the world. Established in 1981 as a nonprofit information and membership organization, it now has over 3,000 members, including companies, professionals, unions, government officials, academics, and interested individuals. It is funded entirely through the work it does.

The NCEO's mission is to provide the most objective, reliable information possible about employee ownership at the most affordable price possible. As part of the NCEO's commitment to providing objective information, it does not lobby or provide ongoing consulting services. The NCEO publishes a variety of materials on employee ownership and participation; holds dozens of seminars, webinars, and conferences on employee ownership annually; and offers online courses. The NCEO's work also includes extensive contacts with the media, both through articles written for trade and professional publications and through interviews with reporters.

Membership Benefits

NCEO members receive the following benefits:

- The members-only newsletter *Employee Ownership Report.*
- Access to the members-only resources of the NCEO's website, including the Document Library.
- Free access to live and replay webinars.
- Discounts on books and other NCEO products and services.
- The right to contact the NCEO for answers to questions.

To join or order publications, visit our website at www.nceo.org or telephone us at 510-208-1300.